ORIGINAL SIN

Origins, Developments, Contemporary Meanings

Tatha Wiley

Cf also
Celia Deane-Drummond, "In Adam
All Die" in William Cavanaugh and
James Smith, eds. Grand Rapids:
Eerdmans, 2017, 23-47

Gabriel Daly.

PAULIST PRESS
New York/Mahwah, N.J. *2002*

Cover image: James Jacques Joseph Tissot (1836–1902), *God's Curse*. Copyright © The Jewish Museum of New York / Art Resource, NY.

Book design by Theresa M. Sparacio

Cover design by Lynn Else

Library of Congress Cataloging-in-Publication Data

Wiley, Tatha.
    Original sin : origins, developments, and contemporary meanings / Tatha Wiley.
        p.   cm.
    Includes bibliographical references and index.
    ISBN 0-8091-4128-0
    1. Sin, Original. I. Title.
BT720 .W54 2002
233'.14—dc21

2002012509

Published by Paulist Press
997 Macarthur Boulevard
Mahwah, New Jersey 07430

www.paulistpress.com

Printed and bound in the
United States of America

ORIGINAL SIN

CONTENTS

For
Michael

PREFACE

CONTEMPORARY CHRISTIANS are uneasy with the doctrine of original sin. Something about the doctrine doesn't fit. If we were Christians in the early church, we would speak easily of Adam and Eve's sin in the garden. If we were medieval Christians, we would debate confidently the difference in human nature before and after the fall. Reformation-era believers, separated as Protestant and Catholic opponents, pummeled one another over conflicting nuances in their interpretations of a doctrine that both sides heartily endorsed.

For us, though, modern persons that we are, this talk about what Adam and Eve did, a time before the fall and after, and a sin transmitted from the first of our kind down to each of us today elicits a feeling of disconnect between the world known through the natural sciences, history, and other modern disciplines and the world known through religious doctrines. The plethora of questions raised about the doctrine—exegetical, historical, philosophical, theological—signals the rough fit the traditional doctrine has in the modern world. We no longer *can* take the doctrine for granted in the same way as our predecessors did. That its meaning is opaque and not transparent, as it was for Christians of earlier ages, points to a vastly changed social and intellectual context.

Because we have so many questions about the doctrine, one temptation is summarily to dismiss the doctrine as a holdover from a premodern world and be done with it. Another temptation, possibly born of fear that the whole edifice is imperiled, may be to stifle all doubts and questions. I think a third way is much more beneficial. Question boldly—and then set out to do the work of discovering the answers to the questions raised. If the doctrine of original sin lies at the heart of Christian belief, as Christian theology has long asserted, it has to be coherent and speak to our experience and situation as human beings.

1

Blind faith renders religious beliefs incoherent. Faith, in its journey toward authenticity, embraces the search for the intelligibility of the religious truths we affirm.

The book ahead traces a path of discovery—what the idea of original sin meant for those who first introduced it, how the idea of original sin has functioned as an explanatory principle in the theological tradition, why the doctrine has been under such assault in the modern era, and how Christian theologians from different traditions and starting points have sought to recover the doctrine's meaning in language and concepts that belong to our age, not someone else's. This path over two millennia takes us into the nitty-gritty of the doctrinal and theological development. We are part of that development. Thinking about sin and redemption continues in our desire to understand who we are, what we are up to, and why we seem at times to fail so miserably at the one task that belongs uniquely to us—the task of being fully human.

I hope the discussion that follows answers some of the questions you already have, elicits ones that had not yet occurred to you, and surprises you with others you might not have thought connected to this staid old doctrine. Our engagement with this one doctrine may become, if we let it, an engagement with the whole of Christian faith.

INTRODUCTION

THE HUMAN SEARCH for meaning encounters its most difficult hurdle in the fact of evil. Why is human living marred by hatred, brutality, and tragedy? Why is evil universal? Responding to this mystery, each religious tradition submits its own explanation. In the Christian worldview, human evil is contrasted to the goodness of divine creation and the hope of divine redemption. Yet why is the created order, brought into being through divine decision and love, warped by evil? Christians believe that because God desires the good, human evil is sin against God. But what will overcome the estrangement from God caused by evil?

In early Christianity, theologians brought divine creation, human sin, and redemption by Jesus Christ into a unified framework through a theology of original sin. The doctrine became a compelling explanation of why human beings are as they are and what they need.

For Christians today, however, the idea of original sin itself prompts questions. How are human beings born with someone else's sin? How is a newborn baby sinful? Would an unbaptized infant be kept from union with God? Is human nature evil? Why have women been blamed for the origin of sin? What about religious believers who do not undergo a Christian baptism? If the Genesis story is symbolic, how does sin come from Adam and Eve?

Some Christians are surprised to discover that original sin is still part of Christian teaching. Roman Catholics are apt to think it went out with Latin masses in the 1960s after Vatican II. Preachers rarely choose original sin as their topic. It is even infrequent, outside of baptism and Holy Week, to hear original sin mentioned explicitly. If there is a black hole for church doctrines, original sin is in one.

Yet the doctrine of original sin remains the pivot of Christian beliefs. The assumption of an inherited sin shaped the starting point and

3

contours of other primary Christian doctrines. One example of a doctrine in which original sin is central is redemption. What does Christ do for humankind? He takes away original sin. This catechetical question and answer lies at the heart of the tradition's theology of redemption. It starts with original sin. What happens to our understanding of redemption when original sin is cast into a theological black hole?

The idea of original sin first arose as an answer to this very question of redemption. For early church theologians, the burning question was not about the character of evil but of the need for Christ. What, they asked, makes Christ's redemption universal? Why do all persons need Christ's grace of forgiveness? The emergence and development of a theology of original sin are one response. Because of Adam and Eve's sin, humankind is sinful. All, then, are in need of Christ's redemption.

The modern era challenged the basic historical premise of the classical doctrine of original sin. Modern empirical sciences and history produced an alternative to the Christian story of human origins. Some Christians reacted to modern developments with biblical literalism. They insisted that the Genesis stories of creation and expulsion from the garden be accepted as divine revelation of human origins and the beginning of sin. If Genesis 3 was to be regarded as divine revelation, its historicity had to be maintained, too. This approach became increasingly difficult and was in fact a kind of reductionism. It made the meaning of the doctrine of original sin equivalent simply to the story of Adam and Eve.

Questions about the doctrine of original sin are not going away. They arise because the doctrine comes from a premodern way of thinking, while our thinking is shaped by the modern world. The questions are ours. We raise them spontaneously. They have to be met in an intellectually satisfying and coherent way. This process of meeting questions is an intrinsic dimension of an engaged life of faith.

In searching for the meaning of this doctrine, believers carry forward the understanding of theology given prominence by the twelfth-century theologian Anselm of Canterbury. Anselm understood theology as *fides quaerens intellectum.* Theology is faith seeking understanding. By *faith,* however, Anselm did not mean a proposition but a *person.* Persons seek to understand. Anselm presumed we already believe. We want to understand that which we already affirm as true. But just what is it we affirm as true in the doctrine of original sin?

Contemporary theologians, both Protestant and Catholic, have addressed modern questions about the doctrine of original sin at great length. They have found that giving new expression to the meaning of original sin is not a simple task. The chapters following explore why this is the case.

Development

What exactly is the teaching called "original sin"? While the theology of original sin developed only gradually in early Christian reflection, Augustine of Hippo is credited with casting its classical expression as a theological doctrine in the fifth century C.E.

Augustine differentiated two meanings of original sin. He used the Latin term *peccatum originale originans,* "original sin as originating," to refer to the historical event of Adam and Eve's sin. A second Latin term, *peccatum originale originatum,* "original sin as originated," referred to the condition of sin in humankind caused by the transmission of Adam and Eve's sin to all. This distinction between the event and condition of original sin remains in the doctrinal teaching of original sin today.

Medieval theologians further developed the anthropology of original sin. Their interest was in human nature. They conceived of the condition of original sin, *peccatum originale originatum,* by what was lost to nature through sin. They called original sin a "sin of nature." The event of the first sin had caused a defect in the human nature now inherited from Adam. What is inherited is not nature as created but nature as distorted by sin.

Like their patristic predecessors, medieval theologians located the remedy for human sin in divine redemption. They saw the incarnation of Jesus as God's solution to the problem of original sin. Through Christ, God's forgiveness of original sin is mediated historically and universally in the church's sacrament of baptism. They understood the baptismal infusion of sanctifying grace as the healing and repairing of a nature wounded by the inheritance of Adam's sin. Even after baptism and the removal of original sin, however, disordered desire, *concupiscence,* the punishment for original sin, remains permanently in human nature.

The concept of original sin answered a range of questions for Christian theologians. By locating the origin of evil in human beings rather than divine agency, the idea of original sin partly resolved the dilemma of how to balance God's goodness and the fact of evil—what in an intellectual argument is called a *theodicy*. Christians specifically rejected other religious options offered by the ancient world. They refused to ground evil in a divine principle or to see the material world as the source of evil. Original sin provided the fundamental component of a Christian theodicy.

The idea of original sin also illuminated the purpose of the incarnation. Early Christian theologians drew on the images of restoration and divinization to describe the effect of redemption on human nature. Christ restored to human nature its original capacity for union with divine mystery by taking away original sin as the basic impediment between human beings and God. Original sin also provided the reason for the church. The church mediated the forgiveness of original sin necessary for eternal salvation through its sacramental life.

For Roman Catholics, the Council of Trent in 1563 confirmed the theology of original sin shaped by the patristic and medieval theologians as a dogma of the church. While differing somewhat from Catholics in their understanding of the doctrine, Martin Luther and other Reformers also affirmed original sin as a central truth of Christian faith.

Hesitations

Acceptance of a doctrine of original sin did not occur in the church's theological tradition without resistance and challenge. One patristic disagreement was about infant baptism.

From the beginning of the Christian movement in the first century C.E., baptism was the central initiation ritual. It confirmed an individual's conversion and response to the proclamation of the risen Christ. By the third century, however, the practice of infant baptism was firmly in place, as the writings of Tertullian (d. 228) show.[1] Tertullian objected to the baptism of infants. He posed a basic question: How could an infant be guilty and in need of baptism, when an infant has not yet committed personal sins? That Tertullian posed his question offers evidence that the notion of an *inherited* sin—distinct from personal or actual sin—was not yet embedded in the theological horizon of the early church writers. In an age of high infant mortality, the matter of infant death was of great moment to the Christian faithful. Would a loving God deny divine union to their unbaptized infant? This life issue posed a personal and pastoral difficulty, not merely an intellectual dilemma.

Pelagius, a contemporary of Augustine of Hippo (d. 430), is the most noted theological opponent of original sin. He thought Augustine's view that human beings inherit the actual sin of Adam was unwarranted theological speculation. Pelagius maintained that infants are born without sin. The miseries of the human situation are not due to the consequences and punishment for an original fault, as Augustine believed. Pelagius feared that belief in original sin would act as a disincentive to a Christian's attempt to live a moral life.[2] If human nature has a predisposition toward evil, why try to do the good?

The medieval theologian Peter Abelard (d. 1142) also opposed original sin. His contemporary, Anselm of Canterbury (d. 1109), had argued that Adam's sin created a debt owed to God. Given the transcendent status of the one insulted by the sin, no mere human being could repay the debt. Only a God-man could satisfy it for humanity. This, Anselm argued, was the reason for the incarnation. Christ paid back the debt through his death on the cross. To Anselm, however, Abelard offered a simple but profound rejoinder:

> Why could not God, like any good lord, simply pardon, on whatever condition seemed appropriate, those who repented? Why resort to the cruelty of subjecting his Son to a pitiless death? What, after all, was so terrible about the ordinary sins of ordinary people, who themselves were bidden to forgive sins, that made them incapable of receiving free forgiveness in return for love?[3]

The basic premise of the classical doctrine of original sin—that Adam's sin is inherited—also invited many questions. *Righteousness* and *sin* are religious terms. They denote right and wrong ways of being in relation to the divine. Every religious tradition posits a norm by which right and wrong relation may be judged. In ancient Israel, for example, obedience to Torah commands was the priestly criterion. As moral wrongdoing, the idea of sin assumes human freedom and the human capacity to choose the good—what would conform with the divine desire—or to choose something that is contrary to what would be truly good. How can another's bad decision—his or her wrongdoing or moral failure—be *inherited?*

Inheritance is a biological term, not a religious one. What is biologically given does not lie on the level of human choice and decision.

The fusion of religious and biological categories in theological speculation about original sin raised questions about the basic claim of the doctrine: the sin of Adam and Eve is transmitted biologically through
physical procreation.

The difficulties raised in the tradition by Tertullian, Pelagius, and
Abelard remain concerns today. Their questions are joined by new ones
reflecting distinctively modern issues: Must a Christian understanding
of human nature start from original sin rather than original goodness?
Are human beings alienated from God at their birth? Are the doctrine's
foundational biblical texts interpreted appropriately? By placing salvation exclusively in Christ, does the doctrine preclude a salvific role for
non-Christian religions? Does the idea of the transmission of an individual sin to individuals privatize sin, making the complexity of systemic evil difficult to grasp? If sin comes through sexual intercourse,
does this mean marital sexual relations are evil? Has the doctrine contributed to sexism and the victimization of women by blaming Eve for
the fall and insisting that female subordination is divinely willed?

Meaning

The *concept* of original sin and the *reality* to which the concept
refers are different. The reality is the way in which human beings
alienate themselves from the divine source of their being. What is this
way, this root sin? The consequence of turning away from divine
goodness—and the good that God desires—is human evil, the distortion of the personal and social dimensions of human living. Concepts
of alienation and evil change. They reflect their time and place. The
writer of the Genesis expulsion story thinks symbolically, expressing
his understanding in a story of crime and punishment. For him, the
root sin is disobedience. The medieval theologian Anselm worked out
his understanding through a metaphysical anthropology and theory of
original sin. He conceived of alienation and evil as the loss of something God had bestowed on Adam's nature. The condition of original
sin was the "privation of original justice," the absence of a supernatural gift. Theologians today may seek to understand the roots of alienation and evil existentially through self-reflection and theoretically
through the help of ethics, philosophy, and sociology. They describe
our "root sin" in categories such as unauthenticity.

The foundational biblical text for the classical doctrine is Genesis 3, the Hebrew story of the first sin. The story's historicity has been challenged since the rise of modern science and historical disciplines in the eighteenth century. Many have thought the doctrine would disappear along with the historicity of its primary text. But the doctrine answered basic questions for the early Christians. These questions remain, with or without the traditional appeal to Genesis. Human alienation from God is a fact. Evil is a fact. What we are understanding through the idea of "original sin," Dutch theologian Piet Schoonenberg suggests, is human solidarity in sin: "Even if we prescind from any original sin and its influence on each of us, this solidarity exists."[4]

The commonplace reduction of the meaning of the doctrine to the Adam and Eve story has overshadowed the fundamental reality to which Christian teaching points. Evil is a feature of our existence prior to our personal choices and decisions. We are born into a world shaped—distorted—by such evils as violence and abuse in families, apartheid, genocide, and discrimination. The doctrine of original sin was one means by which the early Christians named this dimension of human existence and its threat to human well-being.

The Work Ahead

The chapters following accomplish a twofold task. Chapters 1 through 4 concentrate on Christian origins, patristic developments, and medieval interpretations of original sin. We trace the emergence of the idea of original sin, the questions the idea answered, and the development of original sin as a Christian doctrine in the early centuries of Christianity. Chapters 5 through 9 treat the modern scientific, historical, and philosophical challenges posed to the doctrine and contemporary reinterpretations of the meaning of original sin.

As a personal appropriation of *fides quaerens intellectum,* I invite you to take up with me the question of our root sin. Naming what distorts our personal relations and social structures is a necessary and ongoing task. It is also our entry into understanding the nature of divine redemption. What is it that redemption transforms?

PART I

ORIGINS AND DEVELOPMENTS OF THE DOCTRINE

1. CHRISTIAN ORIGINS

THE CHRISTIAN CONCEPT of original sin grew incrementally during the first four centuries of the church's tradition. When fully developed, this idea attributed the universality of human sinfulness to the inheritance of sin and its beginning to the disobedience of Adam and Eve. To provide a context for this theological development, we start with Christian origins in a first-century C.E. Jewish messianic movement. Our specific interest lies with the thinking about sin found in the Hebrew and Christian scriptures, the preaching of Jesus, and in the movement initiated in Jesus' name. Even without a doctrine of original sin, thinking about sin abounds.

Jewish Beginnings

In its origin and first decades, the messianic movement initiated by followers of Jesus was distinct within Jewish social and religious life but not separate from it. As a Jewish sect, the Jesus movement constituted one of Israel's many religious expressions.

The Jewish world as Jesus knew it came to a tragic end in 70 C.E. The Jewish-Roman War of 67–70 C.E. culminated with the Roman destruction of Jerusalem and the Temple. The form of Judaism familiar in subsequent centuries, Rabbinic Judaism, was a second-century development.[1] The movement of rabbis to the center of Jewish life responded to the catastrophe of war. Rabbinic Judaism secured a Jewish future without the land of Palestine, the city of Jerusalem, and the heart of Jewish worship, the Temple. After the Jewish-Roman War, relations between the messianic Jews and other Jews grew ever more tense. Bitter denunciations were hurled back and forth. The polemical language against the Jews in the Christian Gospels of Matthew and John reflect this intra-Jewish conflict.

13

By the second century, the movement proclaiming Jesus as the Jewish Messiah, Christ in Greek, was predominantly Gentile or non-Jewish. Gradually two religions were differentiated, Judaism and Christianity.[2] But in their initial decades, the Jesus followers did not conceive of themselves as beginning a new religion. They understood themselves as the true Israel. Their disagreements were Jewish. One of their first major conflicts, for example, was over the membership requirements demanded of Gentiles. This problem remains opaque to us until the Jewish context is recovered. The issue was how Gentiles become members of Israel.

With this historical context in mind, then, it is not surprising to find that the beliefs and practices of this messianic movement reflect distinctive aspects of Jewish religious life.[3] In appropriating the themes of their heritage, however, the Jesus followers also transformed them. One central belief was that the divine remedy to the problem of human evil works through a community in which hearts and minds are reoriented to God in a relationship of intimacy and fidelity. These themes of religious conversion and covenant so deeply embedded in the theology of Israel became central in Christian theology, too.

Conversion and Covenant

First-century Jews shared the view that Israel was formed as a people by God's election of them. Their scriptures are permeated with descriptions of Israel as the object of God's choosing, adopting, embracing, and desiring. God initiates a covenant relation with them. The expression of their covenant relation is poignant: "I will take you as my people, and I will be your God."[4] God is known by the liberating act done for Israel: "I am the LORD your God who brought you up out of Egypt."[5] Pledged to one another, God and Israel each have obligations. God promises faithfulness. Israel has a bit more to do: "Today you have obtained the LORD's agreement: to be your God; and for you to walk in his ways, to keep his statutes, his commandments, and his ordinances, and to obey him."[6]

While Jews shared the idea of Israel as a covenant community, they differed greatly in their interpretations of what was central to their covenant identity. Intense debate revolved about four basic symbols— land, Torah, Temple, and ethnic distinctiveness. Even the biblical writers do not speak with uniformity about covenant identity. Two competing voices, for example, are those of priest and prophet.

The priestly voice dominates the Torah, the first five books of the Hebrew scriptures.[7] Here Israel's covenant identity is framed in terms of its obligation to observe the distinctive way of living set out in the Torah. What is asked of Israel is an orientation, a direction, an inclination of the life of their community toward God:

> So now, O Israel, what does the LORD your God require of you? Only to fear the LORD your God, to walk in all his ways, to love him, to serve the LORD your God with all your heart and with all your soul, and to keep the commands of the LORD your God and his decrees that I am commanding you today, for your own well-being.[8]

Most important, Israel was to be *holy*.[9] To be holy is to be like God, in whose image humankind was made. Both Israel's obligation as well as the means for becoming holy were given by God. The Torah was perceived as a divine gift to Israel. It provided the means for meeting God's demand for holiness. Holiness would meet the problem of sin. Living the way of the Torah would reorient the community back to God and away from evil.

Embedded in the priestly story of Israel and the giving of the law is a theology of sin and redemption. Genesis 3, the story of Adam and Eve, symbolically presents the human problem. Sin is the failure to remain in a relation of faithfulness with God. It is expressed in the disobedience of God's will. Redemption begins with the shaping of a community in Genesis 12. Abraham is the answer to Adam. He is the origin of a community whose life is lived in the light of God's self-disclosure. The divine solution to sin is deepened in Exodus 19 by the giving of the law to Moses. The law places the whole of human living in the presence of God. It meets the problem evil creates: evil destroys life. The divine remedy transforms evil through a redemptive community in which human hearts are turned in love to God and to neighbor. Loving God offers life, as God declares: "You will love the LORD your God with all your heart and with all your soul, in order that you may live."[10] The prophet Amos echoes the divine solution with his straightforward ethical principle: "Seek good and not evil, that you may live."[11]

Living the way of Torah created a "fence" around Israel. Doing the works of the law separated Jews from non-Jews. In the priestly perspective that placed Torah at the center of Israel's identity, Gentiles were sinners by default because they did not follow the way of living mandated by Torah. If

Gentiles desired to become part of Israel and worship Israel's God, they must do so by becoming Jewish and doing the works of the law.

Every religion articulates a norm by which to judge righteousness and sin. The standard often takes the form of law, as it did in ancient Israel. In Israel's tradition, God gave the law directly to Moses: "The LORD said to Moses, 'Come up to me on the mountain, and wait there; and I will give you the tablets of stone, with the law and commandment, which I have written for their instruction.'"[12] In the development of human cultures, law formalizes the community's apprehension of right and wrong. The moral and cultic commands of the Torah reflect developments over a long period of time. As with any tradition, they reflect both genuine insights and the blind spots created by privilege and power.[13]

For the priestly writer, Torah was the norm of righteousness and sin. Fidelity to its way put persons in right relation to God. This is the meaning of righteousness. Infidelity to Torah commands put persons in wrong relation to God. This is the meaning of sin. The relations of righteousness and sin, however, were not static. They could be reversed. Righteousness was broken by unfaithfulness to the Torah. The status of sinner could be reversed.[14] The sinner could be justified—set right again—by renewed fidelity to Torah and by acts of atonement such as prayer and the offering of ritual animal sacrifice. The reconciliation of sinner with God was a primary function of the Temple sacrifice.[15]

In the prophetic writings, the priestly perspective gives way to the portrayal of covenant life in terms of justice and compassion. The prophet Amos can be a little mean about the priestly emphasis on ritual. Amos's God says, "I hate, I despise your festivals, and I take no delight in your solemn assemblies....I will not listen to the melody of your harps, but let justice roll down like waters, and righteousness like an ever-flowing stream."[16] The prophet Micah echoes this conception of covenant obligation, saying to the people, "And what does the LORD require of you but to do justice, and to love kindness, and to walk humbly with your God?"[17] The prophets see sin through a social lens. They correlate righteousness with justice and sin with injustice. Sinners are the unjust who exploit the vulnerable for gain. Micah describes their actions graphically. They "covet fields, and seize them; houses, and take them away; they oppress the householder and house, people and their inheritance."[18]

Both the priestly and the prophetic perspectives—as well as others—were present in the thinking of Jews at the time of Jesus. Groups were shaped by their distinctive interpretation of covenant identity. Four groups whose memory survives in writings are the Sadducees, Pharisees, Essenes, and Zealots. Each emphasized a different symbol of covenant identity.[19] Some made Temple worship and the sacrificial system central. Others focused on purity and separation from Gentiles. Some emphasized everyday fidelity to the way of the Torah. Others fastened on God's promise of the land and political independence to Israel. First-century Jewish thought and life was a complex amalgam of these themes. The early Christian interpretation of Jesus' death as a means of reconciliation of humankind with God comes out of the symbol of the Temple and the function of sacrifice.

Sacrificial Reconciliation

The Christian interpretation of Jesus' death as sacrifice illustrates the way in which a minority religious movement draws on existing symbols and transforms them.[20]

As the early Jewish followers sought meaning in the violent end put to Jesus' life by the Romans, it is not surprising that they appropriated the language of sacrifice so familiar to them. It was not a great leap for Jesus followers to conceive of Jesus' death as sacrificial and as a means of their reconciliation with God. The apostle Paul did. "We were reconciled to God through the death of his Son," he writes.[21] While the sacrificial interpretation of Jesus' death did not originate with Paul, Gerard Sloyan points out, he built upon it as a foundation. Sloyan writes that Paul developed the idea that "Christ gave himself for human sins to deliver the entire race from 'the present evil age' as he conceived it. In this he went beyond viewing Jesus' death as expiatory for past sins, teaching that Jesus identified believers with himself as Lord of the new age over which he presides."[22]

The Letter to the Hebrews offers a primary New Testament source for this sacrificial understanding of Jesus' death. Jesus is the sacrifice "offered once to bear the sins of many."[23] The sacrifice of Jesus is contrasted with that offered by Israel: "For if the blood of goats and bulls, with the sprinkling of the ashes of a heifer, sanctifies those who have been defiled, how much more will the blood of Christ, who through the eternal Spirit offered himself without blemish to God, purify our conscience

from dead works to worship the living God!"[24] While the offering of sacrifices in the Temple facilitated an ongoing mediation of divine reconciliation, Christians asserted that Jesus' sacrificial death achieved this for
humankind as a once-and-for-all event. Jesus' death established a new
covenant. In this covenant, the Holy Spirit has written the law in the hearts
of believers.[25] This Christian proclamation recalls the prophet Jeremiah:
"I will put my law within them, and I will write it on their hearts; and I will
be their God, and they shall be my people."[26]

The interpretation of Jesus' sacrificial death did not stand alone
from the proclamation that God had raised Jesus from the dead. Resurrection, too, was an idea deeply embedded in the thinking of ancient Jews.[27]

Resurrection Faith

The Jesus followers' proclamation that "this Jesus God raised up"
was a theological rather than christological claim.[28] The claim refers
first to God rather than to the messianic or divine status of Jesus. God is
the actor. Raising Jesus is a meaningful divine action. It reflects divine
choice and decision. Jesus is the recipient of God's act. He is raised up
by God. Expectation that God would raise up a person killed unjustly
was familiar in ancient Israel. It expresses a deep-rooted conviction of
an oppressed people that the lives of persons whose deaths resulted
from the violent whim of dominant powers would be validated. It
expresses the hope that their lives and deaths are not without meaning.
This proclamation about Jesus, Stephen Patterson writes, "connects
Christian faith to Jewish reflection on resurrection in a martyrological
context that extends back centuries."[29] The announcement that God had
raised Jesus reflects the Jesus followers' conviction that Jesus was right
about God and the vision of God's reign he proclaimed.[30] God's resurrection of Jesus signals God's response to evil.

Thinking about resurrection also appears in what E. P. Sanders calls
"Jewish restoration eschatology."[31] Expectation of resurrection was part of
a complex set of ideas about history, the future, and evil. In Jewish thinking, the end-time, *eschaton,* was not the end of history but the renewal of
creation. In the eschatological age, God would act decisively against evil.[32]
The present reign of evil would be replaced by God's reign of justice and
compassion. Israel would be liberated from her occupiers and the divine
promise of the land fulfilled. A new stage would begin in God's covenant

relation with Israel. The event of resurrection was thought to be one signal by which God would announce the beginning of the *eschaton.*

Jesus' preaching of the reign of God was eschatological. The core of his message is summarized in the Gospel of Mark at the opening of his ministry: "Now after John was arrested, Jesus came to Galilee, proclaiming the good news of God, and saying, 'The time is fulfilled, and the kingdom of God has come near; repent, and believe in the good news.'"[33] The Gospel of Luke fills out the content of the good news from Jesus' reading the prophet Isaiah in the synagogue:

> The Spirit of the Lord is upon me, because he has anointed me to
> bring good news to the poor. He has sent me to proclaim release to
> the captives and recovery of sight to the blind, to let the oppressed
> go free, to proclaim the year of the Lord's favor.[34]

The resurrection preaching of the Jesus followers was also eschatological. They conceived of God's raising Jesus up as a validation of Jesus' message and as a signal that in fact the reign Jesus announced was beginning.[35] God would end the present evil age and begin a new age.[36] The continuity between Jesus' preaching and the praxis of the Jesus communities lies in these eschatological ideas and hopes.

The missionary preaching of Jewish Jesus followers to Gentiles was rooted in these eschatological expectations as well. Deeply embedded in Jewish thinking about the future was that God had given Israel "as a light to the nations, that my salvation may reach the end of the earth," as the prophet Isaiah says of God's purposes.[37] Underlying this language of commission is a distinctive perception of how God intends to meet the problem of human evil. Israel is to bring everyone to God by its example. The divine remedy—expressed in story, poetry, song, law—is the transformation religious conversion effects in human beings. Redemption is being known by God, as the prophet Isaiah writes: "But now thus says the Lord....Do not fear, for I have redeemed you; I have called you by name, you are mine."[38]

Religious conversion meets the core problem of sin. For the biblical writers, in its deepest sense, sin is failing to seek and love God. The psalmist draws a correlation between not seeking God and evildoers, saying, "Why do the wicked renounce God, and say in their hearts, 'You will not call us to account.'"[39] The Torah is a way of living that orients all of ordinary life toward God. It was first the means for Israel to

become good in the sight of God and then for Israel to be a catalyst for
the reorientation of "the nations" to God and away from evil. A
covenant-making text in Genesis 17 places this expectation of the eventual inclusion of the Gentiles at the beginning of Israel's history with
God confirming Abraham as ancestor of many nations.[40]

In fact, many Gentiles in the ancient world were attracted to the
moral and religious life of Jews. Some became full members of Israel
by becoming Jewish. Others observed some of the law but did not
undergo full conversion. In the eschatological age, Jews thought, Gentiles would enter into the covenant community of Israel the same way
as in the present time.[41] Female Gentile converts entered Israel through
the ritual of baptism.[42] For male converts, the means of initiation was
slightly more painful. The sign of full covenant membership for an
Israelite male was circumcision.[43] So, too, for male Gentile converts.
The requirement was based on an unambiguous text. In Genesis 17,
God says to Abraham, "This is my covenant, which you shall keep,
between me and you and your offspring after you: Every male among
you shall be circumcised....Any uncircumcised male who is not circumcised in the flesh of his foreskin shall be cut off from his people; he
has broken my covenant."[44]

Upon their circumcision, Gentile males became Jewish males.
Because of the demands of living as a fully Torah-observant Jew for
both females and males, not to say circumcision for males, many Gentile women and men attracted to Israel chose to remain at a midpoint in
their affiliation with Israel. Known as "God-fearers," these Gentiles
observed some but not all Jewish practices.

Full conversion required that Gentile men and women observe the
Torah commands specific to their gender. The obligation to live as a
Jew, to do the works of the law, is clear in the covenant-making cere-
mony portrayed by the Deuteronomist writer:

> Today you have obtained the LORD's agreement: to be your God,
> and for you to walk in his ways, to keep his statutes, his command-
> ments, and his ordinances, and to obey him. Today the LORD has
> obtained your agreement: to be his treasured people, as he prom-
> ised you, and to keep his commandments; for him to set you high
> above all nations that he has made, in praise and in fame and in
> honor; and for you to be a people holy to the LORD your God, as he
> promised. (Deut 26:16–19)

The Redemptive Community

Messianic Jesus followers conceived of themselves as the true Israel. The Acts of the Apostles presents baptism as the response to acceptance of Jesus' resurrection: "Now when [the Israelites] heard this, they were cut to the heart and said to Peter and to the other apostles, 'Brothers, what should we do?' Peter said to them, 'Repent, and be baptized every one of you in the name of Jesus Christ so that your sins may be forgiven; and you will receive the gift of the Holy Spirit.'"[45] The shorthand phrase, "faith in Jesus," became a compact way of signaling an interrelated set of religious convictions—that God had validated Jesus through raising him from the dead, that God's reign was beginning, as Jesus announced, that God's Spirit was given to each who believed, and that God's covenant was now open to all—Jews and Gentiles, women and men—as equals.

To signal his conception of Israel's new openness, the apostle Paul contrasts *faith in Christ* with *works of the law*.[46] By "works of the law," James D. G. Dunn says, Paul means "living as a Jew."[47] Paul's contrast occurs in the context of an intense conflict between missionary groups within the Jesus movement in the mid-50s of the first century. Paul's Letter to the Galatians reflects his side of the disagreement. The argument was over the condition by which Gentiles entered into the Jesus communities. Given the Jewish setting for the movement at this time, the issue is clearer if put this way: What was the requirement for Gentiles to enter into—and stay in—the eschatological Israel? Were Gentile women and men required to become Jewish women and Jewish men, as they were presently required? Were they to be Torah-observant, performing the obligations prescribed for women and those for men?[48] At least some Jesus evangelists thought that doing the works of the law was necessary for Gentile inclusion. Paul argued that the Gentiles' faith in Christ was sufficient. Their point of difference on the Gentiles was this: Were things different in the new Israel than before? To this question, Paul's opponents apparently thought No. Paul's answer was Yes.

While Paul's view appears to be radically opposed to his tradition, he continues its fundamental themes. With the tradition, he roots the redemption of Gentiles in the covenant community of Israel. Here their lives will be reoriented to God's will. Their religious conversion—prompted by the resurrection preaching—is the means by which God meets the problem of sin. But instead of conceiving of the Torah as the means by which God reorients human minds and hearts away from sin, as the priestly writer does, Paul conceives of the Spirit—the self-giving of God—as the means by which human sinfulness will be transformed.

Paul's opponents demanded that Gentiles come into the new Israel in the normal way. Their appeal to circumcision was shorthand for the requirement that Gentiles become fully Torah-observant. Upon full conversion, Gentile men and women would be obligated to live as Jewish men and women. Paul countered that the Gentiles had already received God's Spirit.[49] In this self-giving, God had affirmed their faith in Jesus as sufficient for inclusion in the redemptive community. Their inclusion was thus not contingent on their living as ethnic Jews but on religious conversion and response to resurrection proclamation. The gift of God's Spirit validated a different way for Gentile inclusion into Israel.

Paul's rejection of the necessity to do the works of the law applied only to Gentile Jesus followers. The polemical and harsh tone of his argument against the law served the purpose of protecting the gospel Paul had preached to them about their inclusion in Israel. His gospel was connected to Paul's interpretation of Jesus' death. Jesus' death by crucifixion marked him as a sinner, one outside the law. Gentiles were also outside the law. God's raising a crucified man from the dead validated him as righteous. Now, in light of the resurrection, the covenant was opened to those who are outside as non-Jews, the Gentiles.[50] But for the Gentile Jesus followers, ethnic identity and a distinctively Jewish way of living would not be the norm of covenant membership or righteousness before God. Gentile inclusion in Israel would rest on their confession of Jesus as Lord and on a moral life empowered in them by the indwelling of God's Spirit.[51] By "living in the Spirit," their lives would be oriented toward good and away from evil. The Spirit would provide for Gentiles what the Torah had long supplied for Jews—a moral way of living oriented toward doing God's will.[52]

The male obligation to observe the whole Torah and the female exemption from many commands created the hierarchical and unequal status of men and women within Israel.[53] *Faith in Christ* denotes a gender-neutral condition for membership and participation in the covenant community. Just as God's gift of the Spirit dissolved differences in covenant status between Jew and Gentile, so, too, it dissolved status differences between women and men. A fragment from a baptismal ceremony included by Paul in his Letter to the Galatians points to the apprehension of a radically new communal reality in which privilege had been abolished: "There is no longer Jew or Greek, there is no longer slave or free, there is no longer male and female; for all of you are one in Christ Jesus."[54] The closing section of Paul's Letter to the Romans signals the leadership of women with whom he was associated.[55]

The short baptismal fragment points to a distinctive apprehension of both sin and redemption. The implied human sinfulness is social and systemic. Three forms of domination or privilege are denounced as sin: the religious privilege of covenant insider over outsider, class privilege of owner over owned, and gender privilege of male over female. The "No more" of the formula implies the evil intended. Evil is the unjust subjugation of some to the rule of others. Redemption is experienced in the transformation of hierarchical relations into those of equality. This transformation creates a different kind of community. Now, in the redemptive community, relations of mutuality mirror the divine desire for humankind. The baptismal fragment recalls Jesus' vision of the inclusive reign of God and the prophetic tradition that had shaped his preaching.

With regard to gender, egalitarian features in the first-century Jesus communities may reflect the participation and leadership of women in diaspora synagogues. The *diaspora* refers to Jewish communities outside Palestine.[56] It may have been that the closer to Jerusalem and the Temple, the more the priestly conception of covenant identity dominated and the unequal spheres for women and men mandated by Torah held sway. Geography may have had something to do with the Galatian conflict, too. Paul's Gentile communities were diaspora assemblies. The Jesus preachers who insisted that Gentile men be circumcised are thought to have been from Jerusalem.[57]

The relation between the Torah as written and history as lived, however, is complex. Both Jewish and Christian scholars caution against taking biblical or later rabbinic writings as straightforward historical description. The texts portray male restriction of females from social and religious participation. The actual lives of Jewish women may not have corresponded to the portrait painted of their lives.[58]

Archaeological evidence reveals the diversity of Judaism as actually practiced. That the activities of Jewish women did not conform to the view found, for example, in the Mishnah, Shaye Cohen writes, "demonstrates the pluralistic nature of ancient Judaism."[59] Titles accorded to Jewish women suggest a prominence in the synagogue community independent of their husbands. Identified by inscriptions as donors, women built and maintained synagogues. In some synagogues, women were *archisynagogues,* heads of synagogues. Their responsibility, Cohen notes, was "supervising the services, specifically deciding who should read the Bible, lead the prayers, and give the sermon."[60]

The Jesus movement was part of this pluralism of ancient Judaism. Its egalitarian features are one expression of its diversity and evaluation of sin. As Bernadette Brooten points out, "The inscriptural evidence for Jewish women leaders means that one cannot declare it to be a departure from Judaism that early Christian women held leadership positions."[61] Elisabeth Schüssler Fiorenza argues in a similar vein: "The reconstruction of the Jesus movement as the discipleship of equals is historically plausible only insofar as such critical elements are thinkable within the context of Jewish life and faith."[62]

Meeting Evil

Many Jews did not accept the Jesus followers' claim that God had raised Jesus from the dead. Their hesitation was not due to the strangeness of resurrection. The symbol of resurrection was deeply embedded in Israel's eschatological hopes for liberation from foreign occupation, the exploitation of elites, and the reign of evil. Among identifiable groups, the Sadducees were alone in their rejection of the belief in a future resurrection.[63]

The problem posed by Jesus' resurrection was the manner of his death. Paul calls the proclamation of the crucified Christ "a stumbling block" to other Jews.[64] One reason is the correlation made in the scripture between crucifixion and sin:

> When someone is convicted of a crime punishable by death and is executed, and you hang him on a tree, his corpse must not remain all night upon the tree; you shall bury him that same day, *for anyone hung on a tree is under God's curse.*[65]

One cursed by God is a sinner. A sinner is exactly the one who is not right before God. That a crucified man could be God's anointed one would have appeared deeply incongruous to first-century Jews.[66] The emphasis that New Testament writers place on Jesus' obedience, faith, and sinlessness may reflect a deliberate counter to this resistance. Paul contrasted Christ's obedience with Adam's disobedience to show the former as the divine means of salvation. His text became a foundational one in subsequent centuries for a doctrine of original sin: "For just as by the one man's disobedience the many were made sinners, so by the one man's obedience the many will be made righteous."[67]

For the Jesus followers, God's raising Jesus validated his words, his actions, and his life. They expressed the import of this validation by honorific titles: Messiah, Lord, Savior. Even for believers, however, these claims invited questions. What is the relation of the transcendent God to the risen Christ? What is the relation in the divine being of the Son to the Father? Holding two basic premises of faith in balance—that God is one and that Christ is the self-disclosure of God—was not easy. In Christian reflection, these questions generated the shift from the metaphorical language of scripture to technical terms and distinctions. Christological arguments and controversies persisted until definitions were formulated at the fourth- and fifth-century councils of Nicaea (325 C.E.) and Chalcedon (451 C.E.).[68]

In addition to these christological questions, there were also soteriological questions: Why did Christ come? What is the purpose of the Christ-event? What is accomplished for humankind by the life, death, and resurrection of Jesus?[69] It was in answering these questions that a doctrine of original sin developed in the work of early church writers. The New Testament writers present a range of answers. In Romans, for example, Paul offers several: Through Christ, believers are redeemed from the power of sin (3:9); Christ's obedience is the means of salvation (5:19); believers are given new life and the hope of eternal life (5:21); creation has been set free from its bondage to sin (8:21).

Paul's conception of sin and redemption often draws on the images of bondage and freedom. Human beings are in slavery to the powers of evil. Sin is bondage to works of the flesh. The whole of creation is in bondage to sin. Paul's characterization of creation in bondage to sin points to the unrestricted character of evil. Evil is pervasive not only in individual acts but permeates historical reality through oppressive social structures and systems. Such acts and structures expose the human failure to seek and love God. They reflect the absence of an orientation toward the good inculcated and sustained by genuine religious conversion. For Paul, Christ breaks the powers of evil and frees persons from their bondage to sin. The fruit of living in Christ, in the Spirit, is love, joy, kindness, and gentleness. The new Israel is the Body of Christ. In the redemptive community, loving God generates love of the other as fully human.[70]

The baptismal fragment in Galatians 3:28 manifests the Jesus followers' experience of redemption as freedom from ideologies of superiority. It also pinpoints the continuity between the reign of God that Jesus preached and the praxis of the Jesus communities. Against the injustice, oppression, and violence of the social order in which he lived, Jesus envisioned God's reign, Walter Wink writes, "as a domination-free order characterized by partnership, interdependence, equality of opportunity, and mutual respect between men and women that cuts across all distinctions between people."[71] The Pauline letters are glimpses into the first-century efforts of Jesus followers to live this vision in their relations with one another.

The early Jesus followers referred to themselves in a number of ways, including the "Way" or "people of the Way."[72] They designated their religious groups as *ekklesia*, church. The secular Greek term *ekklesia* carried a political meaning. It referred to those with full rights of citizenship assembled for legislative purposes. Jews had already appropriated the term in religious discourse. By the first century, historian W. H. C. Frend notes, *ekklesia* referred to Israel assembled as "the people of God."[73]

For the Jesus followers, *ekklesia* referred to the assembly of the new Israel.[74] Against the sinfulness of unjust hierarchical relations and structures—such as slavery—they created a discipleship community of faith and friendship. In this community, disciples of Jesus were full and equal citizens.[75] Paul appealed to a Christian slave owner, for example, to take back his runaway slave who had become Paul's convert. He asks the owner, Philemon, to take the slave, Onesimus, "no longer as a slave but more than a slave, a beloved brother....Welcome him as you would welcome me."[76] Philemon would welcome Paul as an equal, as a *person,* not as a possession. Paul encourages Philemon to bring this redemptive reality into being at Onesimus's return. Whether Philemon's religious conversion bore fruit in a new relation of equality between himself and Onesimus is lost to historical memory.

The Jesus followers also conceived of themselves as a new family. In the ancient world, family referred to the kinship group constituted by the biologically related and dependent members (servants, slaves) of the patriarchal household.[77] All members of the household were subordinate to the head of the household, the *paterfamilias,* the father. The structure of the patriarchal family extended from individual kinship groups to the emperor. The whole empire was the emperor's household. Its land and people were the emperor's property to rule and dispose of as he wished. This principle of authority residing in the head of the household applied to each *paterfamilias.*

Patriarchy is often equated with male domination. It is true that the most basic and pervasive form of domination in patriarchal cultures is the subjugation of females to male rule. But patriarchy is much more. It is a domination system. Such systems, then and now, are characterized, Wink writes, by "unjust economic relations, oppressive political relations, biased race relations, patriarchal gender relations, hierarchical power relations, and the use of violence to maintain them all."[78] Jesus announced God's reign as a domination-free order. His preaching and activity offered a vision of an alternative to patriarchy.[79]

Jesus' thinking about the social world was not theoretical. But using the symbol of *basileia* to model an alternative kind of social order reflects a profound grasp of the arbitrary character of the world of privilege, power, poverty, and powerlessness. Contrary to what the powerful would argue, it is not natural. Patriarchy is socially constructed, to use modern terms. Like all constructions, a domination system can be evaluated. Jesus' critique of his world points to an apprehension of the social and structural dimensions of sin. His interest lay in its transformation.

The conception of the Jesus community as an *ekklesia* and as a non-kinship family is significant. It reflects the experience of evil. The *ekklesia* counters evil by creating in the *ekklesia* itself the transformed order desired by God. The new family is not a patriarchal family. It is constituted by relations of mutuality, not domination and subordination.[80] The *ekklesia* modeled Jesus' rejection of the patriarchal family and his advocacy of a discipleship group that does God's will.[81]

Like the stories of Israel and God's gift of the Torah in the Hebrew Bible, a theology of sin and redemption is embedded in the New Testa-

ment stories of Jesus and the early Jesus communities. The rejection of
the patriarchal family as normative points to a grasp of the systemic
dimensions of sin. Domination systems are intrinsically sinful. They
create injustice. To some, the status of person is given. To others, the
status is denied. Slaves and women are often explicitly deemed less than
fully human.[82] Jesus' portrayal of God's reign as an inclusive banquet
counters this basic feature of the reign of evil. He discloses redemption
as the transformation of privilege, power, and violence.[83] It works
through religious conversion, through hearts and minds reoriented by
God's love. Conversion promotes the value of the other. It generates the
transformation of relations that undergird social oppressions and sustains relations of equality. Each member of the new family is a person.
No longer are some possessions of others. The redemptive community
acknowledges each member as fully human and made in the image of
God. As Paul's letters suggest, however, even for the first charismatic
communities, living this redemptive reality was not easy. He appeals to
the Galatian Jesus followers not to "devour one another" through their
disagreements with one another.[84]

At least for some early Jesus followers, the eschatological *ekklesia*
stood in opposition to the patriarchal structures and values of the ancient
world. The egalitarianism of the movement was countercultural.[85] Some
believers took Jesus' teaching and the model of his life as the basis for
their lives, setting aside the Mosaic Torah as a way of life. The Gospel of
Matthew presents Jesus as the new Moses and his teaching as the new
law.[86] Others unified the life of Torah observance and life in Christ.[87]

Thinking about Sin

Early Christians retained the Hebrew scriptures as their own. They
read them backward, so to speak, in light of the resurrection event. God's
salvific plan had worked through the election of Israel and culminated in
the incarnation. Christians also produced their own writings. Over time,
some became revered as part of divine revelation, as sacred scripture. By
the fourth century, a selected group of writings formed the collection of
the New Testament.[88]

The Christian reading and interpretation of scripture will occupy
us throughout this book. Our primary focus will be on the foundational
texts from which early Christian writers derived the doctrine of original

sin. In this final section we highlight the centrality of sin in the scriptures, the expulsion from the garden story, and the concept of a fall.

The Centrality of Sin

For the biblical writers, *the* problem undermining human well-being is the alienation of humankind from God and the evil that human beings inflict on one another as a result. It is a rare story that does not deal with sin in some fashion. The Hebrew writers locate the origin of evil in the ambiguity of human desire. The desires and passions of human nature reflect an inner struggle between two impulses, the inclination to do good, *yetser ha-tov,* and the inclination to do evil, *yetser ha-ra.*[89]

In Genesis, *yetser ha-ra* is depicted in a portrayal of what God sees in humankind: "The Lord saw that the wickedness of humankind was great in the earth, and that every inclination of the thoughts of their hearts was only evil continually." The pull of *yetser ha-ra* is a permanent problem: "The inclination of the human heart is evil from youth."[90] The psalmist shows God looking down from heaven, "to see if there are any who are wise, who seek after God. They have all gone astray, they are all alike perverse; there is no one who does good, no, not one." Humankind is entangled in a solidarity of sin generation after generation, reaching back even into the womb: "Indeed, I was born guilty, a sinner when my mother conceived me."[91] In Christian writings, Hermas, author of the second-century C.E. Christian work, *The Shepherd,* is the only writer to refer to *yetser ha-ra* as the origin of evil.[92]

Israel's prophets attribute human wickedness to an evil heart. For Jeremiah, even God is perplexed: "The heart is devious above all else; it is perverse—who can understand it?" Ezekiel conceives of God transforming evil hearts through the gift of a new heart and a new spirit. The remedy God will provide for evil will be God's self-presence. The indwelling of divine presence empowers Israel to do what is right:

> A new heart I will give you, and a new spirit I will put within you;
> and I will remove from your body the heart of stone and give you a
> heart of flesh. I will put my spirit within you, and make you follow
> my statutes and be careful to observe my ordinances.[93]

The Hebrew *yetser ha-ra* is translated by the Greek term *epithumia* in the New Testament. The Greek word carries a slightly more negative meaning. Rather than the inclination or tendency toward evil of *yetser ha-ra, epithumia* is evil desire. The author of the Letter to James writes that "one is tempted by one's own desire, being lured and enticed by it; then, when that desire has conceived, it gives birth to sin, and that sin, when it is fully grown, gives birth to death."[94] The negative meaning of *epithumia* was intensified in its translation by the Latin *concupiscentia*.[95] In the writings of early Christian theologians, *concupiscence* meant "disordered desire."

James Gaffney points to a subtle shift in meaning from the Hebrew to the Latin term. For the Hebrew writer, *yetser ha-ra* is why Adam *could have* sinned. For the fifth-century Christian Augustine, concupiscence *came from* Adam's sin as its penalty.[96] Theologically, *yetser ha-ra* and concupiscence have quite different connotations. The Hebrew terms *yetser ha-tov* and *yetser ha-ra* name psychological experience. In human deliberating and choosing is experienced the desire to be responsible (*yetser ha-tov,* the inclination toward the good) as well as the desire to do what in fact is irresponsible (*yetser ha-ra,* the inclination toward evil). The Latin term *concupiscence* describes psychological experience, too. But for Augustine, the experience of disordered desire was not natural. He did not consider it an intrinsic dimension of created nature, as did the Hebrews in their understanding of *yetser ha-ra*. For Augustine, concupiscence reflects a change in created nature due to *peccatum originale originans,* original sin.

Reflection on psychological experience is part of thinking about sin. Why do persons sin? Why is evil universal? Both the Hebrew Bible and the New Testament assume the universality of sin. The question of its origin is not primary. In the New Testament, John the Baptizer preaches a "baptism of repentance for the forgiveness of sins."[97] The apostle Peter appealed for repentance. He, too, called for a baptism for the forgiveness of sins.[98] Paul talks of "both Jews and Greeks" as under the power of sin.[99] "All have sinned and fallen short of the glory of God."[100] John's Gospel names the universality of human sinfulness "the sin of the world."[101] The author of 1 John takes the acknowledgment of sin as a first principle of self-knowledge: "If we say that we have no sin, we deceive ourselves, and the truth is not in us."[102]

The New Testament writers portray Jesus' mission in relation to sin. Jesus takes away the sin of the world.[103] He comes for sinners and not for the righteous.[104] He has the authority to forgive sins.[105] The human sickness is sin. Christ is the physician and healer.[106]

For the Jesus followers, God answers the problem of sin through Jesus and the gift of the Spirit. Israel's covenant was now open to all. God's salvation is offered to both Jew and Gentile. The means of righteousness and salvation are now predicated on religious conversion and personal decision: "If you confess with your lips that Jesus is Lord and believe in your heart that God raised him from the dead, you will be saved."[107] The power of the Spirit now engenders a moral way of life for all, Jew and Gentile.[108]

With the biblical writers, Paul linked sin with death as cause and effect. Human beings are subject to death because of sin. Without sin, there would have been no death: "Sin came into the world through one man, and death came through sin."[109] This text will later be foundational in the doctrine of original sin. Paul asserted that believers will be freed from death, too. "For the law of the Spirit of life in Christ Jesus has set you free from the law of sin and death."[110] Faith in Christ and the experience of the Spirit denote religious experience—the experience of conversion, reorientation, turning toward God. Being oriented toward God, and living out of God's love, is exactly the opposite of sin: not seeking God and not living according to God's desire for the human good.

Expulsion from the Garden

Early Christian theologians focused on the story of Adam and Eve's expulsion from the garden as the story of sin. For the Hebrew writers, however, Genesis 3 was not so central. It was the first of many stories of sin. The paradigmatic story of sin is Exodus 32. Idolatry is the root of sin. While Moses is on Mt. Sinai receiving the commandments from God, the people below build a golden calf to worship as a god. In the priestly perspective, idolatry is manifest in infidelity to God's covenant demands.

In a book on original sin, such as this one, the text of Genesis 3 will come up more than once. Here we bring three features into perspective: its composition history and setting in the Pentateuch, its appearance in other Jewish and Christian writings, and the notion of a fall.

Biblical scholars concur that the narrative unity of the Pentateuch reflects a long process of composition. The designations *Pentateuch* and *Torah* refer to the same five books: Genesis, Exodus, Leviticus, Numbers, and Deuteronomy. These writings are also called the Books of Moses. The literary evolution of the Pentateuch includes the creativity of different writers, older oral traditions freely drawn upon, and the integration of narrative traditions by editors or redactors who introduced further nuances and themes.

In its completed form, the Pentateuch blends four major narrative traditions together. Each tradition is differentiated by time, place, and perspective from the others.[111] Scholars designate these four narrative traditions, writers in a broad sense, by the letters *J* (Yahwist writer), *P* (Priestly writer), *E* (Elohist writer), and *D* (Deuteronomistic writer).[112]

The *J* narrative includes the second creation story (Gen 2:4–24) and the story of the expulsion from the garden (Gen 3). The first creation story (Gen 1:1–2:3) belongs to the *P* writer. It originates in the sixth century B.C.E., during the time of the Babylonian Exile. The *P* writer integrated the narrative traditions together into the present form of the Pentateuch. The setting of the *J* writer is the royal court of Solomon, around 950 B.C.E. It incorporates earlier oral and possibly written materials. The expulsion story shows a combining of more than one garden story, for example.[113] In the early Christian era, the story of expulsion from the garden became the primary revelatory text for why the forgiveness of Christ is universally necessary.

J's creation and expulsion stories form a unity. Humankind is incomplete until two human beings exist in relation to one another. But the solidarity they share will be the source of tragedy as well as fulfillment. Created together, the two humans sin together. By refusing to live in response to God's desire for them, they bring about a world of suffering, conflict, and death.[114]

In the extended narrative shaped by the *P* writer, *J*'s stories set the stage for the real focus of the Pentateuch, God's election and covenant with Israel. The ancient biblical writers would not have considered the events of creation and expulsion "in history" in the same way that the stories of Abraham and Moses are events in Israel's history. The origins of the world, human beings, and sin are "before time," primeval history. God's call to Abraham in Genesis 12 begins the covenant history of Israel.[115]

The literary genre of the Genesis 1–3 stories is myth. As symbolic narrative, myth often utilizes the literary device of describing the past, "what happened," to disclose the meaning of the present, "what is always happening." The past event is causal. It explains why things are the way they are. *J*'s myth of expulsion functions in this way. Underlying the story are questions about the created order: Why are things the way they are? Why is a world created by divine choice and goodness permeated by evil? Why do human beings not seek and obey God's desires for them? The myth creates a narrative world in which the answers to these questions are performed rather than explained.

For *J*, as for us, human existence is ambiguous. Good is disrupted by evil, joy paralyzed by sorrow, achievement thwarted by failure, and life haunted by death. Ordinary experience—the pain of childbirth, gender subordination, the hardship of survival, the tragedy of death—prompt questions of meaning and purpose.[116] How is creation good? Clearly, human existence is not paradise.[117] But the expulsion story avoids what seems an unavoidable conclusion—that the created order is not good. The reason for human suffering is placed in a distant event. *J* depicts a human act as the primordial cause for why divine creation is afflicted by evil.

Yet *J* does not locate the origin of evil entirely in an event. The *possibility* of choosing the wrong course of action is an intrinsic dimension of human freedom. The figure of the tempter externalizes this psychological reality. Temptation is the awareness of an alternative to what is perceived as responsible. Obedience and disobedience are created potentialities of human freedom. They correspond to the internal norm of conscience and external norm of ethical precept and law. The narrative world of the garden is an exploration of a perplexing fact of humanness. We can know the good and yet succumb to the temptation of the alternative. We orchestrate our expulsion from the garden time and time again.

The Expulsion Story in Jewish and Christian Writings

The story of Adam and Eve is not mentioned again in the writings included by Jews in the Hebrew canon. It appears only in a few apocryphal—noncanonical—writings. In the Apocalypse of Moses (first century C.E.), Eve says to God, "I have sinned, I have sinned, God of the universe, I have sinned against you...against the angel elect...against the cherubim; and through me all sin entered creation."[118] In Baruch 54:19 (early second century C.E.), Adam is the focus: "But each of us has been the Adam of his own soul."[119]

Genesis 3 is mentioned in writings included by Christians, but not Jews, in the Hebrew Bible. Protestants call these "apocryphal writings." Roman Catholics call them "deuterocanonical." In Sirach 25:24 (c. 200 B.C.E.), woman is the cause of death: "From a woman sin had its beginning, and because of her we all die." In the Wisdom of Solomon 2:23–24 (late 100s B.C.E.), an allusion to Genesis 3 again makes the link between sin and death. "For God created us for incorruption, and made us in the image of his own eternity, but through the devil's envy death entered the world and those who belong to his company experience it."

The primary question in these texts regards the origin of *death,* not the origin of sin. Why do we die? Both Sirach and the Wisdom of Solomon give the same answer. Sin brought death. If human beings had loved God and lived according to God's will, there would be no death. Death is the divine punishment for not seeking God. Now, because of sin, all face death. Sirach locates the cause of death in the woman's sin. The Wisdom of Solomon locates the cause of death in the figure of the devil, not in either the man or woman.

The story of Genesis 3 does not figure prominently in the New Testament. Only brief allusions to the figures of Adam and Eve occur. Paul's reference to Adam in Romans 5:12 links death with sin: "Sin came into the world through one man, and death came through sin." Similarly, in 1 Corinthians 15:21–22, Paul locates the cause of death in Adam's sin, drawing a parallel between the cause of death (Adam) and the cause of life (Christ): "For since death came through a human being, the resurrection of the dead has also come through a human being; for as all die in Adam, so all will be made alive in Christ."

Paul refers to Eve in 2 Corinthians 11:3: "But I am afraid that as the serpent deceived Eve by its cunning, your thoughts will be led astray from a sincere and pure devotion to Christ." The author of 1 Timothy refers directly to Adam and Eve. His concern lies with church order and proper gender roles in the *ekklesia* rather than with the origin of sin itself. He links the legitimacy of male domination to Eve's sin: "I permit no woman to teach or to have authority over a man; she is to keep silent. For Adam was formed first, then Eve; and Adam was not deceived, but the woman was deceived and became a transgressor."[120]

The Fall

In the Christian tradition, the sin of Adam and Eve is described as "the fall." The idea of a fall is itself an interpretation of the story. It is not part of the story itself. Within the narrative world of the story itself, there is an "inside" and an "outside" and a "before" and "after." Prior to sin, Adam and Eve are inside the garden; after their sin they are outside the garden. Before their disobedience all human needs are met; after their disobedience suffering and toil are their lot and the burden of everyone henceforth. The idea of a fall reflects theological speculation about human nature. It takes the external before and after of narrative time and places it into human nature. The early Christian writers will begin to contrast two states of nature: the state of original righteousness and—after the fall—the state of original sin.

In the time frame of more than a thousand years of Israelite history to Jesus, the idea of fall is "late." The interpretation of the first sin as a fall becomes prevalent in Jewish commentary near the first century C.E.[121] Paul and other New Testament writers may have thought of Adam and Eve's sin as a fall. The fall metaphor found in 2 Peter 2:4 occurs in relation to the angels, Claus Westermann points out, not Adam and Eve: "For if God did not spare the angels when they sinned, but cast them into hell and committed them to chains of darkness to be kept until the judgment...." The fate of the sinful angels is noted in Jude 1:6, too: "And the angels who did not keep their own position but left their proper dwelling, he has kept in eternal chains in deepest darkness for the judgment of the great Day." In these texts the fall occurs with the sin of the angels in the heavenly realm. Some religious groups in the ancient world think of the material world as the product of such a fall in the transcendent order. This usually means they think of materiality as evil. In the early church, some Christian theologians will vigorously refute this idea while others will be taken with it.[122]

Conclusion

The Hebrew and Christian scriptures are rich with insight into the relation between humankind and God. At the heart of their apprehension of sin is that human beings should seek and love God and, in doing so, evil would be transformed by good. Just what constitutes being in right relation to God is a matter of debate. In the scriptures are different views, as the example of contrast between priestly and prophetic voices illustrates. Jesus deepened the prophetic witness by using the eschatological symbol of the reign of God to critique the social order and to envision a restored creation. For the early Jesus followers, God validated Jesus' message by raising him from the dead. The praxis of their communities sought to embody Jesus' vision. Their preaching of Jesus' resurrection was an invitation to reorient one's life to God. Through Christ, God offers salvation to all.

It is this premise, that Christ's grace of forgiveness is necessary for all, that will lead to the emergence and development of the doctrine of original sin. Why is Christ's forgiveness necessary for all? For what? The idea of original sin will be an answer to these questions. To this development in the early patristic writers we now turn.

2. The Early Patristic Tradition

THE EMERGENCE AND initial development of the idea of original sin are found in reflections of bishops and theologians during the Christian church's first four centuries.[1] In this chapter we identify the fragments of tradition that in these first few Christian centuries were drawn into a compact theory of original sin.[2]

Early Christian writers often refer to the first sin as "Adam's sin," leaving Eve invisible. At other times Eve is made all too visible and blamed for the tragedy of the fall.[3] Either way, early in the tradition, it is not always the case that a reference to *Adam and Eve's sin* or even *first sin* means that the writer understands what the theological tradition came to designate by the term "original sin." Augustine fixed the meaning of original sin in the fifth century. The idea of original sin was incorporated into the church's doctrinal tradition by church councils of the fifth and sixth centuries. In this chapter, our focus is on the development of ideas about sin prior to Augustine.

An Interpretive Principle

Separating (1) Christian origins, (2) the early patristic period, and (3) the classical doctrine of original sin avoids two common errors in the history of interpretation.

One error presumes that the doctrine of original sin "has always been there." At its most extreme, this is the assumption that original sin is a universal belief. Less extreme is the more common view that original sin is "in scripture." To be sure, the story of Adam and Eve is in the Hebrew Bible, Paul refers to Adam's sin, and sin is a predominant theme in both testaments. But as scripture scholars and church historians insist, the idea of original sin is a post–New Testament development.

A second error asserts that Augustine "invented" original sin. No doubt Augustine's influence on the Christian understanding of original sin was substantial. The patristic church councils of Carthage (418 C.E.) and Orange (529) adopted his basic formulation of the problem in dealing with theological controversies of their time. But Augustine did not pull the idea of original sin out of thin air. He drew upon ways of answering questions found in the writings of his predecessors and contemporaries. From these fragments of tradition, Augustine developed a theory of original sin.[4]

The development of the idea of original sin is more complex than these two options in historical interpretation allow. The theology of original sin developed incrementally in the patristic writings. The idea of original sin was a response to a broad range of questions—the relation of God to evil, human nature, the reason for divine redemption, the necessity of Christ, the practice of infant baptism, and the role of the church in God's plan of salvation. Appeals to a first sin, to Adam's sin, to an original corruption, to an inclination to sin, or to a fall were ways of answering these questions. These appeals are not treatises but brief references and short discourses. They are the "fragments of tradition" that Augustine, in the fifth century, will consider an authoritative church tradition on original sin.

Early Fragments

The *Didache* is an anonymous manual of Christian instruction originating in the late first century or early second century, possibly in Syria.[5] It addresses several liturgical questions, including baptism. It assumes adult baptism.[6] Those to be baptized were to fast for one or two days before the ritual. The *Didache*'s assumption of adult baptism offers evidence that its author did not suppose human beings were in need of divine forgiveness at birth.

Clement of Rome (fl. 96) emphasized in his *Letter to the Corinthians* that Christ's redemption saves human beings from sin. He assumes both the universal need for Christ's redemption and the universality of sinfulness. Clement does not explain either by an explicit principle.[7]

Hermas, another apostolic father of the late first century and a contemporary of Clement of Rome, authored a work called *The Shepherd.* This work is a Christian apocalypse. It consists of a set of visions experienced by Hermas. The author writes that sin leads to death. This was a common belief in ancient Judaism. By sin, however, Hermas means personal sin, acts of wrongdoing resulting from personal choice. Infants are innocent of personal sin. Hermas makes no reference to Adam and Eve.

Similarly, another apostolic father, the first-century writer of the *Epistle of Barnabas,* argued explicitly that the souls of children are entirely innocent and born without sin. He alludes to Genesis 3. In his case, Adam is left invisible and Eve is responsible for sin. "The transgression was wrought in Eve through the serpent."[8]

Ignatius of Antioch (d. 107) was a second-century bishop and author of several pastoral letters held in high esteem in the early tradition. Ignatius's concern with sin was christological. Christ, the source of redemption, saves persons from sin. Like Clement of Rome, Ignatius did not go on explicitly to explain the universality of sin. He takes it for granted. For these early writers, church historian Henri Rondet notes, the conception of sin as an *inherited condition* was not yet on the horizon.[9]

Similarly, *Clement of Alexandria* (d. 215) dealt with sin in the context of redemption.[10] He proposed that sin was *inherited* from Adam but did not employ this idea as an explicit principle of solidarity in sin with Adam. Clement referred to inheritance more as humankind's inheritance of Adam's bad example, not the sin itself. In contemporary terms this would be described as a sociological rather than biological conception of the universality of sin. Further, Clement did not interpret Adam's sin in legal categories. He saw Adam's sin as his refusal to be educated by God, not his disobedience of a command. Adam's refusal debarred him from receiving God's Spirit.

Clement was among many early Christians opposing Gnostic views. Gnosticism was an amorphous but powerful religious movement in the Roman Empire.[11] Its worldview was deeply pessimistic. Henri Rondet describes the Gnostics as obsessed with evil.[12] Some Christian Gnostics proposed that the sin of Genesis 3 occurred in the heavenly realm.[13] The fall was the descent of the soul from the eternal realm into the historical realm. In the material world, human beings are incapable of avoiding sin. Sin is inevitable. In the Gnostic view, what human beings need is liberation from the material world. This liberation comes first in the form of a saving knowledge (Greek *gnosis*).

Clement and other early Christian writers thought the Gnostics rendered moral responsibility meaningless by their view of the inevitability of sin. For moral responsibility to mean something, Clement argued, human beings must have the freedom to sin or not to sin. Clement's understanding of human freedom and sin was rooted in an anthropology much like that reflected in the Hebrew notion of *yetzer ha-ra.* Desire can be either good or bad.

To oppose Gnostic determinism, Clement of Alexandria and others emphasized human freedom, self-determination, and moral responsibility. They argued that God could not very well demand human obedience to moral precepts if human beings did not have the capacity to obey such commands. While personal acts of wrongdoing "stain the soul" and weaken human nature, temptation could be resisted.

Further, Clement rejected the Gnostic view that the material world was the source of evil. He placed the source of evil in the misuse of freedom. While human beings have the capacity to choose either good or evil (freedom), they can and do misuse it. The misuse of freedom creates the fundamental human problem: sin. By sin human beings go astray; they are sick and blind. God's remedy for their sickness is the inner healing effected by religious conversion to Christ. Clement's notion of baptism corresponds with his conception of sin as sickness and conversion as healing. Baptism is a rebirth and regeneration.

Irenaeus of Lyons

The apprehension of sin we find in *Irenaeus of Lyons* (d. 200) stands in contrast to what became the dominant Christian perspective shaped by Augustine in the fifth century.

The purpose of Irenaeus's chief work, *Against Heresies,* was the refutation of Gnostic ideas.[14] He rejected an interpretation of Genesis 3 as the story of a cosmic fall. Irenaeus interpreted the story simply as one of disobedience. Adam's act was like the impulsive act of a child. Irenaeus thought of sins as growing pains and mistakes. Henri Rondet remarks that Irenaeus held persons responsible for sin, but he also thought of sin as somewhat inevitable in the life of humankind.[15]

Irenaeus took the process of maturation from childhood to adulthood as his image for history and salvation. Human history is a gradual process of maturation, an ascent toward the future. Historical achievement calls for development from imperfection to perfection. Irenaeus placed paradise not at the beginning of history but at its end, in the human fulfillment created by union with divine mystery.

Irenaeus drew from the Pauline letters to develop a Christology of *recapitulation*. Christ took up all things since the beginning into himself as the recapitulation of Adam. His obedience destroyed the effects of Adam's disobedience, reclaimed humankind from the devil, restored God's plan of salvation, and reestablished the process of divinization begun in Adam but interrupted by sin. Irenaeus saw divinization as the purpose of the incarnation. "The Logos [Word] was made man so that we might be made God."

In his theory of human nature, Irenaeus contrasted the *natural person* and the *perfection of the person*. The natural human being is composed of body and soul. The perfected human being is composed of body, soul, and spirit. The spirit—the personal Spirit of God—must be received. This gift is at the heart of Irenaeus's understanding of redemption. The idea of redemption as buying back or restoring something implied that humanity had lost something. Irenaeus interpreted this loss as humankind's *likeness to God*. Irenaeus differentiated between two terms found in Genesis 1:26, "image of God" and "likeness to God." He thought *the image of God* referred to human rational moral nature, that is, reason and freedom. Adam did not lose the image of God by his sin.[16] *Likeness to God* referred to Adam's spiritual similarity to God. It was this spiritual similarity, Irenaeus argued, that Adam lost by his sin.

Redemption restores what was lost by sin. It is a process of healing and rehabilitation. Through Christ's forgiveness and the gift of God's Spirit, redemption is both recreation and divinization. It becomes effective through the sacramental life of the church.

While Adam's sin was a factor in Irenaeus's theology of redemption, he was clearly more interested in the process of conversion and ascent toward divine union than in Adam. The cause of human solidarity in sin was not a question for him. "By the third century," Henri Rondet writes, "original sin is not part of Christian faith except in a general way."[17]

Prior to speculation about original sin was the gradual formulation of a distinctive Christian anthropology. A key element in this theory of human nature was the description of Adam's nature before and after his sin. Various terms were used on either side: *perfect, blessed, innocent, righteous, fallen, sinful, wounded, depraved.* The question "What was *lost* by Adam's sin?" asks what human nature was like prior to sin. At this early stage in the tradition, Irenaeus answered the question by contrasting what was given to nature by the image of God and the likeness to God.[18]

Two Apologists

Christian *apologists* were writers who offered philosophical justifications of the rationality of Christian beliefs to the larger Greco-Roman society. They often appealed for toleration of Christianity. By portraying Christianity as a moral set of beliefs, they sought to show that Christians were of benefit—or at least not a threat—to the empire. Two apologists are especially relevant for the early stages of Christian reflection on sin and redemption. The first is Justin Martyr, the founder of a Christian school in Rome. The second is Tertullian, one of the African church fathers.

1. Justin Martyr

In his *First Apology, Justin Martyr* (d. 165) advocated the necessity of infant baptism on the grounds that infants are born with wayward inclinations.[19] He does not make an explicit reference to Adam and Eve, however. In the *Dialogue with Trypho,* Justin referred to the sin of Adam, to fallen humanity, and to the power of sin and death but without further explanation. He brings out the relation between sin and death found in the ancient Hebrew writers and in Paul. By their sin, human beings brought death upon themselves.

Like other Christian thinkers, Justin acknowledged the sinful condition of humankind. Also like them, he was not concerned with developing an explicit principle explaining what he took as fact, the universality of sin.[20] The regularity of personal sins seemed reason enough for Justin. People sin. This is what separates them from God. This why they are in need of divine forgiveness and redemption.

Justin took Adam and Eve's sin as the prototype of personal sin. For everyone who follows, "each man sinned by his own fault."[21] The basic sin is disobedience against God's will. Two other second-century apologists, Tatian and Theophilus, shared Justin's view, finding in Adam's act nothing more than a type of the disobedience of the race.

In the *Dialogue with Trypho,* Justin interpreted the tragedy of Adam's sin and its consequence for humankind as the loss of deification.[22] Their capacity for becoming divine is given back through Christ's redemption.

Justin's questions about human nature, sin, and redemption were shaped by the particular historical conflicts in which he was engaged. His conception of human nature, for example, explicitly challenged deterministic features of Stoic philosophy. His anthropology reveals that elements of a theory of original sin were not yet general assumptions for Christian writers.

The Stoics acknowledged human freedom but took freedom only to mean the power to choose between alternative actions without external compulsion. The determinism of the Stoic anthropology showed in their tendency to make *nature* and *fate* synonymous. To the Stoics, Harry Wolfson writes, "Freedom means to act by the necessity of one's own nature, a nature which itself is prefated and predetermined."[23] The laws of nature are fate. Human decisions and actions fulfill what a person is bound to do.

Justin countered the Stoic anthropology of fate and predeterminism with an alternative of human freedom and responsibility. One resource was the work of the Alexandrian Jewish philosopher Philo (d. 50).[24] Philo had engaged Jewish thought with Greek philosophy on many issues, including the relations among freedom, human action, and evil. He agreed with the Greek theory that human reason and emotions were in conflict. Human action is a result of the relative strength of these forces. He brought the Hebrew notion of desire *(yetzer ha-ra)* to this dualistic anthropology, identifying reason with good desire and the emotions with evil desire. Against determinism, Philo argued that God had created human beings with the genuine power to choose among alternative courses of action. In his view, sin had not taken away the human ability to desire and to do the good.

Justin argued that even with sin and even though human beings had lost their capacity for deification, the capacity to choose and decide to live in ways acceptable to God remained. Human goodness or evil was not predetermined. Consequently, the responsibility for failure is greater. Justin took human rationality as evidence of human freedom. "Since we are reasonable beings, we are without excuse in God's eyes when we do wrong."[25]

Justin placed the root or origin of sin in free will.[26] What came from Adam is not Adam's sin but the taint of corruption. Adam's sin affected the moral character of his descendents for the worse. While his sin weakened human freedom, thus diminishing the power to resist evil, freedom was not completely lost by Adam's sin. Because of sin, human beings may be more in need of divine help to choose and act upon responsible choices of action, Justin thought, but they are not unable to do so.

Justin's understanding of the relation between Adam's sin and humankind is better described as a doctrine of *original corruption* rather than a doctrine of *original sin.* While the difference may appear incidental, it turns on the principle of explanation for the universality of human sin and whether a conception of solidarity of sin appeals to an inherited sin.[27] Justin Martyr does not. Later writers such as Julian of Eclanum (d. 454), a follower of Pelagius, will appeal to Justin Martyr to counter Augustine's arguments on human nature, grace, and the depravity of fallen humanity.[28]

Justin explained the origin of evil by a demonology. There are, he wrote, "malign demons...swarming everything, they have obsessed men's souls and bodies, infecting them with vices and corruption."[29] Justin's demonology shaped his conception of redemption. With the New Testament writers, Justin emphasized Jesus' activity as exorcist.[30] For Justin, the purpose of the Christ-event was to break the power of the demonic over humankind. It discloses a knowledge that restores to human beings the capacity to live by the moral law. Redemption is a victory over the demonic.[31]

2. Tertullian

Tertullian (d. 220) is one of the most prolific writers of the early Latin church.[32] His works include many apologetic and polemical writings. Tertullian intended to set forth Christian truth, engage the pagan world in dialogue with Christianity, and diminish the credibility of his opponents' views.

Tertullian knew and rejected the Gnostic reading of Genesis 3 as a cosmic fall. For him, the story revealed a historical sin and historical fall from which two consequences resulted, one in the historical realm, the other in the inner realm of human nature.

In the historical realm, Adam's sin caused the alienation of human beings from God. In nature itself, the first sin changed the human state from one of blessedness to one of moral wretchedness. To explain the relation between Adam and his descendents, Tertullian drew upon current theories in the ancient world of the origin of the soul.[33] He favored the *traducianist theory* that the body and soul were generated together in sexual intercourse. He also argued that Adam and his descendents shared an original unity: "We are linked with Adam because all souls were first of all contained in his."[34] This idea of an original unity of Adam and humankind is the emergence of a metaphysical or ontological principle of explanation for human solidarity in sin with Adam.

Tertullian thought that Adam's sin introduced an irrational element into human nature. While persons remain responsible for the misuse of freedom, the inclination to sin brought about by Adam's sin impedes freedom in fallen humanity and impels wrongdoing. Tertullian conceived of this bias toward sin as an impurity, stain, or corruption. It bears serious consequences for the historical realm. The problem of evil is the product of this irrationality.

Tertullian's *bias toward sin* is not the equivalent of original sin as *actual sin,* as it will be understood later in the tradition. A central clue is found in Tertullian's *Homily on Baptism,* the earliest known patristic treatise on Christian initiation. This treatise offers clear evidence that infant baptism was practiced by this time.[35] Tertullian attacked the custom as a novelty and rejected its necessity. Even with the corruption of human nature brought about by Adam's transgression, Tertullian did not see the need for baptizing infants. In other words, this inclination toward sin due to Adam was not itself a sin for which forgiveness was required.

Baptism for adults, Tertullian argued, removes the guilt of personal sin and thus the penalty for it. It washes the sins of blindness away, restoring human beings to the likeness of God lost through sin.[36] In advocating the deferment of baptism for infants and children, Tertullian encouraged a process of coming to know Christ:

> So let them come, when they are growing up, when they are learning, when they are being taught what they are coming to: let them be made Christians when they have become competent to know Christ. Why should innocent infancy come with haste to the remission of sins?[37]

Origen

In contrast with Tertullian, the great third-century Alexandrian theologian *Origen* (d. 299) correlated infant baptism with sin and explicitly named the sin "original sin."[38] He answered the obvious theological question raised by offering infants the forgiveness of baptism: What kind of sin could exist in an infant? "All are tainted with the *stain of original sin* which must be washed off by water and the spirit."[39] The premise of original sin shaped Origen's understanding of the purpose of redemption and the role of the church. "Certainly," he wrote, "if there were nothing in infants that required remission and called for lenient treatment, the grace of baptism would be unnecessary."[40] Origen grounded the necessity of the church's mediation of salvation in humankind's universal need for forgiveness. His claim was exclusivist: "There can be no salvation without this church."[41]

In seeking the rationale for infant baptism, Origen evoked scriptural evidence for humanity's sinfulness. He appealed to both Genesis 3 and the defilement texts in the Psalms and elsewhere. An example of a defilement text is the Psalmist's lament, "Indeed, I was born guilty, a sinner when my mother conceived me" (Ps 51:5). Origen interpreted these texts as divine revelation that all human beings are born with a stain on their soul in need of removal. Baptism cleanses this defilement, and the gift of the Holy Spirit generates a pure rebirth. But even with defilement, Origen believed that human beings retained the capacity to choose the good.

Both Origen and Tertullian draw upon ancient theories of the origin of the soul to deal with the question of the origin of evil and the character of human nature.

Though used in various ways, "soul" *(psyche)* generally meant the spiritual dimension of the person, specifically, the intelligent and moral capacities of human nature. "Body" *(soma)* referred to the material dimension of human being, the physical being. Questions about the relation between the body and soul were many. For example, how or when does the soul come to animate the body?

For Christian writers, the question of the origin of the soul was especially relevant to speculation about human solidarity in sin. Once the idea of inheritance was introduced, the proposal that Adam's descendents inherited his sin provoked much theological debate. As an act of disobedience, Adam's sin was a failure in his soul. How can the misuse of Adam's freedom—his failure to do what is right—be transmitted to the soul of others? Christian theologians drew upon three well-known theories on the origin of the soul for insight in their speculation.[42] These discussions became part of the larger debate about original sin.

A first theory, called *traducianism* or, alternatively, *generationism,* held that sexual intercourse and biological conception generated the body and soul together. Because Adam's sin caused a primeval defect in human nature, the body and soul Adam's descendents receive are defective. The appropriation of the traducian theory in Christian speculation created a doctrine of *original corruption* rather than *original sin* in the technical sense in which we understand the meaning given to the latter.[43] Tertullian favored this view that the body and soul are transmitted together because it best advanced a principle of human solidarity in sin with Adam. He explained this in terms of an ontological or metaphysical conception of unity with Adam: All human souls were "in Adam"; thus when Adam committed sin all committed sin and, consequently, all are guilty for the sin.[44]

Questions about the effect of Adam's sin on the souls of his descendents were bound to raise questions about the human nature of Jesus. In Ignatius of Antioch, belief in the virgin birth of Jesus permitted holding two contradictory assumptions in tension: (1) that all humankind enters by birth into a sinful condition, and (2) that Jesus, a human being, is without sin.[45]

A second philosophical theory appropriated by Christian theologians such as Jerome (d. 420) affirmed the *divine creation of the individual soul.* The human soul is not eternal but created by God at the time of physical conception. In relation to an emerging theory of original sin, however, the chief difficulty with this view is clear. How is Adam's sin transmitted to the soul of others if each soul came directly from God? Does this mean that God creates a defective soul at the time of creation? If not, how does the soul inherit the sin of Adam?

A third theory argued for the *preexistence of the soul.* Platonist in origin, this view held that all souls, human and angelic, were created at the same time. According to this theory sin occurred in the transcendent realm, not in the realm of historical existence. The punishment for sin was the descent—the *fall*—into the material world. Origen favored this theory. It provided the basis upon which he constructed his interpretation of original sin.

Origen read Genesis 3 as an allegory, transforming it as he did so into a cosmic myth.[46] Because the soul originated in the heavenly realm, not in an earthly paradise, the origin of sin was in the transcendent realm. In the transcendent realm, Origen argued, God had created rational essences endowed with free will (souls). Each soul had departed from the good in varying degrees. As a consequence, each was banished from the transcendent world to a material world. The fall was a descent of the transcendent soul into a material and historical body. The soul suffered defilement by this fall. Only through baptismal cleansing and rebirth through the Holy Spirit could the soul begin its ascent back to the transcendent realm from which it came.

While Origen's philosophical tendencies were Platonist, he considered his views about the soul and evil to be grounded in a principle of scripture and faith, namely, God's justice. Granted that God is just and God's creation is good, why is there such disparity among human beings? Why are some poor, others rich, some sick, others healthy? Why do some suffer every disadvantage while others dwell in advantage and privilege? Origen found his answer in the conjecture that each soul deserves its present existence because of prior choices in the transcendent realm. In *On First Principles,* Origen writes:

> Rational creatures were endowed with the faculty of free choice; and they were induced, each one by his own free will, either to imitate God and so to advance or to ignore him and so to fall.[47]

Origen's theory of original sin was not dependent on a principle of humankind's solidarity in sin with Adam. The defilement of the soul did not originate in an act of an historical person. As J. N. D. Kelly summarizes Origen's view: "If human beings are sinful from birth, their wickedness is the legacy of their own misguided choices in the *transcendental world,* and has nothing to do with the disobedience of any first man."[48] Yet Origen held, too, that Adam's bad example carried unfortunate consequences for his descendents. The personal sins of Adam's descendents result from following his example. To explain the problem of evil, Origen, like Justin, appealed further to a demonology. The experience of human beings in the material world is an "exposure to the continuous assaults of malign demons.... The story of Adam and Eve mirrors the experience of every man and woman."[49]

Baptism, Transmission, and Romans 5:12

Three views in the early church gradually contributed to the assumption that original sin had always been part of Christian belief. The first was a theological consensus that the church baptized infants because they were born with sin. The second explained the first. The sin for which infants require the forgiveness of Christ is Adam's sin. The appeal to the physical transmission of Adam's sin—through sexual intercourse—completed the circle. It explained the universality of human sinfulness and offered the critical principle required for a theory of original sin. In particular, Augustine will emphasize physical transmission as a fact to be accepted by Christians. The third view was a nuanced reading of Paul's reference to Adam in Romans 5:12.

Cyprian (d. 258), the third-century bishop of Carthage, contributed to the theological tradition on both the understanding of infant baptism and on the view that Adam's sin was inherited.[50] He described Adam's sin as a "primeval contagion" inherited by each person through their physical conception, that is, by sexual intercourse. Cyprian took the defilement text of Psalm 51:5 as evidence: "Indeed, I was born guilty, a sinner when my mother conceived me." Because each person is born with Adam's sin, each is in need of divine forgiveness. Baptism cleanses the stain of this contagion and imparts divine forgiveness for it. The description of effects of original sin as wounds comes from Cyprian.

Cyprian was influenced by Tertullian's theology but differed with him on the question of infant baptism. He clearly expressed the view that baptism should be done as early as possible:

> We ought not to shrink from hindering an infant, who being lately born, has not sinned, except in that, being born after the flesh according to Adam, he has contracted the contagion of the ancient death at its earliest birth, who approaches the more easily on this very account to the reception of the forgiveness of sins—that to him are remitted, not his own sins, but the sins of another.[51]

Augustine later relied on Cyprian's views, as Pelikan notes, arguing that infant baptism "*proved* the presence in infants of a sin that was inevitable but a sin for which they were nevertheless held responsible."[52] Like that of his predecessors, Augustine's argument worked backward from the church's sacramental practice to the existence of an actual sin for which the practice was needed. With Cyprian especially in mind, Augustine thought the church's teaching on infant baptism was an ancient, implanted opinion of the church. While the practice may not have been as ancient or even as implanted as Augustine thought, late second- and early third-century texts offer evidence that baptizing infants began quite early. In the *Apostolic Tradition, Hippolytus* (d. 236) writes that children are baptized without delay in the Roman church.[53] As Tertullian shows, opponents to the practice provide key evidence of the early appearance of the liturgical custom.

Didymus the Blind (d. 399), a fourth-century Alexandrian theologian, drew attention to an original fall.[54] He also contributed to consensus that Adam's sin was transmitted through sexual intercourse. The correlation between two Christian beliefs, virgin birth and original sin, is evident in Didymus's view of Jesus. Because Jesus' conception was not through the sexual intercourse of his parents, his nature was not stained with Adam's sin.

In contrast to later theological views, Didymus believed that baptism restored human beings to the way they were first made: "We had received the image and likeness of God, which scripture speaks of, and through sin we had lost it, but now we are found once more such as we were when we were first made: sinless and masters of ourselves (*De Trin.* 2, 12).[55]

Some patristics argued for the inheritance of sin, even calling it original sin, without holding that infants were *born* in sin. Contemporaries of Didymus the Blind, the Cappadocian Fathers, *Gregory of Nazianzus* (d. 389), *Gregory of Nyssa* (d. 399), and *John Chrysostom* (d. 407), share the view that humankind shares Adam's fall but that infants were exempt from sin.[56]

Gregory of Nazianzus believed that the whole human race participated in Adam's sin and fall. The weakness occurring in Adam's will as an act of disobedience became in his descendents a weakness of the moral will. This weakness Gregory called "original sin." Its consequences are particular wrongdoings and such evils as lust and greed.

Gregory of Nyssa described humanity as diseased. Sharing Adam's fall, human nature is too weak to do the good. The purpose of the incarnation and the redemption is to restore the primitive order destroyed by Adam's sin. The incarnation begins a new human race. New life is mediated to each believer through the sacraments.

The Antiochen theologian and biblical exegete *Theodore of Mopsuestia* (d. 427) saw in Adam's sin the beginning of sin and death for humankind, a view he grounded in a reading of Romans 5:12: "Just as sin came into the world through one man, and death came through sin...."[57] Even though he considered moral nature weakened as a consequence of Adam's sin, Theodore resisted the opinion that sin was inevitable. He remained confident that the moral capacity to choose to sin, thus also to choose not to, had not been lost with the first sin.

Scholars argue that Theodore's theology is more one of original death or original corruption than original sin as such. In fact, he explicitly denied original sin. His rejection rested on the principle of inheritance. In *Against the Defenders of Original Sin,* Theodore argued that only human nature could be inherited, not sin.[58] He did not accept the view that an act of free will—Adam's disobedience of the divine command—could be inherited. After the fifth century, when the word *Pelagian* stood for those who rejected original sin and expressed confidence in the capacity of moral nature to sin or not sin, Theodore's views became suspect—and in retrospect—as Pelagian.[59]

The anonymous fourth-century commentator on Paul, referred to as *Ambrosiaster,* derived original sin from his exegesis of Romans 5:12. His interpretation of this text was adopted by Augustine of Hippo and became a central component of the classical doctrine.[60]

In the modern NRSV, the Greek text of Romans 5:12 is translated this way:

> Therefore, just as sin came into the world through one man, and death came through sin, and so death spread to all because all have sinned....[61]

The Latin Vulgate translation Ambrosiaster used, however, rendered the latter part of the sentence "*in whom* all sinned," not *because.* Ambrosiaster took the *in whom* as an obvious reference to Adam and its meaning—"all have sinned in Adam"—as the metaphysical unity of all human nature with Adam. As scripture, the text was taken by him to be divine revelation of original sin both in Adam and his descendents. All humankind was in Adam as one. When Adam sinned, all humankind who shared his nature sinned with him.

This image of solidarity of humankind with Adam had already been utilized by others. Tertullian, for example, said, "We are linked with Adam because all souls were first of all contained in his." Ambrose of Milan offered a similar explanation of solidarity: "Adam existed, and in him we all existed; Adam perished, and in him all perished."[62]

Ambrosiaster used the image that all humankind sinned in Adam as in a lump *(quasi in massa)*. "For Adam himself was corrupted by sin, and all whom he begat were born under sin. Thus we are all sinners from him, since we all derive from him."[63] He identified two principal consequences of Adam's sin. The first was physical death. The second was spiritual; all are bound to personal sin. The whole race is infected with Adam's guilt. No one is without the tendency to sin.

For Ambrosiaster original sin is the problem for which Christ is the remedy. It is this historical situation, the inability of human nature to overcome its inclination to sin, that redemption by Christ meets and overcomes by the gift of the Holy Spirit. Ambrosiaster's anthropology reflects this difference. Human nature from Adam, he argued, is composed of body and soul. But human nature redeemed by Christ is composed of body, soul, and the Spirit. The Spirit enables persons to grow in likeness to the divine Trinity. Redeemed human nature is not, however, a return to the pre-sin or pre-fall status of Adam but an elevation of human nature. Redeemed nature is the gift of a new and better status.

Ambrosiaster's speculation shows the way claims about original sin are responses to questions about redemption. As we saw early on, the idea of original sin emerged from the confessional claim that Christ's redemption is universally necessary. Why? For what? Ambrosiaster's anthropology suggests an answer to yet another question. What did Christ's redemption do? What does it change? As other Christian writers, Ambrosiaster's answer directs us inward, to a transformation of human nature.

Fragments and Meaning

The sacramental practice of baptizing infants prompted questions about the kind of sin for which infants were forgiven. Appeal to the existence of Adam's sin in his descendents in turn generated questions about how sin could be transmitted. By what principle, in other words, could the solidarity in sin with Adam be understood?

Two distinct ways of conceiving solidarity surfaced in the work of the early theologians. Clement of Alexandria appealed to an ontological principle. Adam's nature, in some way, incorporated all humankind. When Adam sinned, all sinned. Each of Adam's descendents makes his sin actual once again. Cyprian appealed to a biological principle of inheritance. The physical transmission of Adam's sin unites his descendents to him in sin. In each case, the principle served to explain the universality of human sinfulness. But the reason for doing so was ultimately, as we have suggested, to account for the necessity of Christ's redemption for all humankind.

As we will find in the next chapter, Augustine of Hippo took the views of Cyprian and others as evidence of the antiquity of the church's teaching on original sin. What Augustine did not advert to are the different ways his predecessors used basic terms and the ways in which their explanations diverged.

For example, in the early patristic writers we find references to the *origin of sin,* to a *fall,* and to the *inheritance of sin,* but what is meant is often different from the meaning given to these terms in the later classical tradition influenced by Augustine. It is useful to note how the diverse opinions present in the early church contrast with those we find later in the classical tradition.

In the classical tradition, the *origin of sin* refers specifically to the *cause* of the universality of human sinfulness. Why does everyone sin? The patristics gradually answered by way of either an ontological principle of unity (all were in Adam and sinned with him) or the biological theory of physical transmission (Adam's sin is inherited).

But the crucial question of origin for the Hebrew writers and earliest Christian writers was more about the origin of *death* than of sin. Why are human beings created only to face death? Why is the created order, a product of divine goodness, the source of tragedy and suffering? These dilemmas invite a theodicy, an explanation of how God is powerful, good, and loving and yet there is evil. Death faces humankind as an evil. To attribute to sin the introduction of death into the created order places the blame for such evil on the side of humans, not God. By their rejection of God's will, it was argued in both the Hebrew and Christian traditions, human beings brought death into a world where it had been absent. Death is the punishment for sin.

In the classical tradition, an original *fall* serves as a cypher for two kinds of changes from more to less or better to worse, one in human nature, the other in historical existence. After Adam's sin the capacities of human nature are less than before. After the loss of paradisal conditions and the entry of suffering, domination, and death, human existence is worse than before.

But the early patristics do not agree about the location of the fall. Some writers, such as Origen, believed that the fall occurred in the transcendent realm. By rejecting God's will, angels and human souls were rejected from the heavenly realm. Their fall was a descent into the lower material realm of history. Irenaeus placed sin in history but conceived of the fall as the gradual spread of evil due to the inevitability of personal sin, not as a specific change in human nature itself.[64]

Finally, early writers appealed to the *inheritance of sin,* but the meaning of inheritance is not fixed. Some meant by *inheritance* that human beings enter into a world distorted by the sins of others. Other meant that humankind inherits the guilt of Adam and Eve but not their actual sin. All humankind suffers the consequences of Adam and Eve's wrongdoing in the same way that children inevitably suffer from the misdeeds of their parents.

These fragments of tradition, which Augustine unifies into a coherent theology, suggest again that the idea of original sin was always bound up with questions on other theological matters—God and evil, human nature, the reason and necessity for redemption, and the historical purpose of the church and its sacramental practices.

Some topics were more instrumental than others in generating the development of a theology of original sin. Accepting infant baptism as necessary practice of the church, for example, required an explicit answer to the question "For what sin?" Original sin was the speculative answer. It was not a synonym simply for the first sin but a differentiation of sin into personal sin and that which distorts human nature itself. The conception of the physical transmission of this sin grounded human solidarity in sin with Adam. It answered the question of why Christ's grace of forgiveness was necessary and for what the church's sacramental purpose was intended.

Conclusion

The concerns of the early Christian writers were soteriological—they emphasized what God had done for humankind through Christ. At the heart of their proclamation was the conviction that

Christ had overcome the estrangement of humanity from God caused by sin. Through his death and resurrection, Christ reconciled humanity with God. While much was said about sin, the theological interest of Christian writers was not primarily with the problem—sin—but with what they saw as God's remedy to the problem—Christ.

The sacramental development of baptism from an exclusively adult rite to that of infants is lost to historical record. But it is clear that the liturgical practice of infant baptism evoked the initial speculation about original sin. With personal sin as their only category of sin, writers such as Hermas did not find infants in need of baptism and dismissed the practice. Others such as Theodore explicitly rejected the idea of original sin. Early Christian anthropology did not include the conviction that Adam's sin had changed human nature or that this sin was inherited by each as an actual sin. But this anthropology will come. When it does, original sin will be the axis around which theologies of incarnation, redemption, and the church will revolve.

3. Augustine and the Classical Tradition

THE CLASSICAL DOCTRINE of original sin addresses the sin of Adam and Eve, the inheritance of sin, the universal sinfulness of humankind, Christ's redemption, the church as mediator of salvation, and the sacrament of baptism. These basic terms, however, do not always carry the same meaning for the early church writers as they do for a later tradition in which the classical doctrine took definitive shape. Rather than dismiss these nuances in meaning and begin with the classical doctrine, we have highlighted them as clues to the diversity and development of the Christian *idea* of original sin in the early stages of the theological tradition. While we must in retrospect today say that the fragments of tradition we have from early writers—references to Adam's sin, for example—do not mean what *original sin* eventually came to mean, *Augustine of Hippo* (354–430 C.E.) took these fragments of tradition as firm evidence of divine teaching on original sin as revealed to the church through scripture. To Augustine credit is rightly given for shaping the classical doctrine, but he neither started from scratch nor from a theological doctrine intact from scripture and early Christian belief.

Augustine's influence on the church and its theologies of sin, redemption, and grace has been incalculable.[1] Likewise for original sin, Augustine fixed the meaning of the basic terms of the doctrine. The distinctions he brings to a theology of original sin—key among them are *peccatum originans* (the event of original sin) and *peccatum originatum* (the condition of original sin in humankind)—remain standard to the present day.[2] Influenced by Augustine, the councils of Carthage (411–418 C.E.) and Orange (529 C.E.) brought theological speculation about original sin into the official lexicon of the church.

Like earlier theologians, Augustine's primary concerns were in the person and work of Christ rather than in the matter of the first human sin itself. His appeal to an inherited sin, for example, reflects Augustine's desire to ground the universal necessity of Christ's redemption.[3] It is the latter that Augustine considered the core of Christian belief. The idea of an inherited sin served an explanatory function for why sin is universal, and thus the universal need for redemption.

Early Thinking

Augustine's existential and intellectual journey toward religious conversion and acceptance of Christian faith occasioned his early thought about original sin.

Augustine documented this inner journey in his book, the *Confessions*. Writing the work as an autobiographical prayer, Augustine bared his experience of acute inner psychological conflict and the fragile and ambiguous character of human moral nature. He pointed to the inner psychological struggle as one between two parts variously named mind and body, reason and emotions, rationality and appetites, reason and passions. In the apostle Paul Augustine found a succinct description of this struggle of the rational and moral self. Paul writes:

> I can will what is right, but I cannot do it. For I do not do the good I want, but the evil I do not want is what I do. Now if I do what I do not want, it is no longer I that do it, but sin that dwells within me. (Rom 7:18–20)

Augustine located the profound dilemma of human existence in what Paul spoke of in quite personal terms. It was his experience, too. Human beings are unable to carry out what they will as good. This fundamental impotence underlies humankind's sinfulness. The good that God already knows and desires of human beings is not simply for them to will but to perform. How is this basic moral impotence to be overcome?

For Augustine, this question was answered in the freedom he experienced in his religious conversion. He came to believe that it was only through the gift and assistance of divine grace—what Paul described as the power of the Spirit—that human sinfulness could be overcome. God's gift of God's love is the redemptive solution to the problem of sin. Augustine's theology of original sin took the problem of moral impotence a step further back. Why moral impotence? Adam's sin had caused a disharmony in human beings. Because of sin, human reason cannot carry out what it has willed or properly dominate the passions. This is the condition of original sin.

Augustine scholars have traditionally placed the impetus for Augustine's thinking about original sin in his heated conflict over human nature and divine grace with the British theologian Pelagius (d. c. 425) beginning around 411 C.E. As Stephen Duffy notes, today scholars underscore evidence for Augustine's concern with original sin well in advance of the Pelagian controversy and in relation to other matters.[4]

The earliest occurrence of the term *originate peccatum* appears in the *Confessions,* written in 398 C.E.[5] Augustine distinguished between personal sins he had committed and another kind of sin, *original sin*:

> At Rome my arrival was marked by the scourge of physical sickness, and I was on the way to the underworld, bearing *all the evils I had committed* against you, against myself, and against others— sins both numerous and serious, in addition to the *chain of original sin* by which "in Adam we die" (1 Cor 15:22). You had not yet forgiven me in Christ for any of them, nor had he by his cross delivered me from the hostile disposition towards you which I had contracted by my sins. (5.9.16)

Augustine is not exact on what he means by *originate peccatum.* But three features stand out. First, with personal sin, original sin creates a "hostile disposition" toward God. Second, citing Paul, Augustine reinforces the link between sin and death found in the biblical tradition. The Pauline text also provides an allusion to the unity of humankind with Adam. Outside of using the theological term *originate peccatum,* Augustine's reference to Paul retains the sense of the original text. Sin causes death. All humankind suffers the consequences of Adam's sin. Finally, Augustine implies that both kinds of sins—personal and original sin—require the forgiveness of Christ.

Augustine's invocation of *originate peccatum* in the *Confessions* did not advance the theory that each human being inherits Adam's actual sin. In this context the term suggests the *entanglement of sin* or *sin from the beginning* more than inherited sin.[6] Like Paul, Augustine establishes a causal relation. The *reason why* human beings have the pervasive inclination to evil— evidence of their hostility to God— thwarting their moral decision and action is *because of* Adam's sin.

Personal sins are virtually inevitable given this bias toward sin. This bias once acted upon, individuals become entangled in sin.

Like earlier writers, Augustine's reflection on sin and human nature led him into philosophical speculation about the origin of the soul.[7] Early on, Augustine found the idea of the preexistence of the soul attractive. "Tell me, God, tell your suppliant, in mercy to our poor wretch," Augustine writes in the *Confessions,* "tell me whether there was some period of my life, now dead and gone, which preceded my infancy....Was I anywhere, or any sort of person?" Or again: "I ask you, my God, I ask, Lord, where and when your servant was innocent?" In this theory, the disobedience of the soul in the transcendent realm—not an historical sin—caused the fall. The fall was the soul's descent into the material world. Created existence in the material world is the soul's punishment for its sin. In the Book of Job Augustine found confirmation of a sinful impurity human beings acquired prior even to personal sin: "None is pure from sin before you, not even an infant of one day upon the earth" (Job 14:4–5).

Augustine later rejected theories of the preexistence of the soul and a transcendent fall, dismissing them as hangovers from his Manichean days.[8] He then found the traducian or generationist theory of the origin of the soul—the human soul is generated with the body through sexual intercourse—a better philosophical resource for explaining human solidarity in sin with Adam. Transmitted with the body and soul is Adam's sin.

Augustine's conflict with the Donatists sharpened his views about sin.[9] During Augustine's time in North Africa, the Donatists were the majority Christian church. Christians who had committed apostasy in the face of persecution—and who later desired reunion with the Christian community—were the object of severe criticism. The Donatists argued that the church consist only of those who were morally and spiritually pure. Augustine's anti-Donatist writings (c. 406 C.E.) reflect a theological position grounded in his existential experience of moral impotence and his developing theology of original sin. While Augustine believed that the gift of God's grace creates the conditions for moral and spiritual *development,* he considered moral and spiritual *purity* a human impossibility. The Catholic position argued by Augustine was that the inclination to sin remains a permanent feature of human nature even after original sin has been removed from the soul in the sacrament of baptism. The church cannot consist of those who are morally and spiritually pure, because such a state does not exist in the human race.

Redemption and Baptism

The church's sacramental practice of baptizing infants generated for patristic theologians both the question "For what sin?" and, eventually, an answer: "For the sin of Adam possessed by each." For Augustine, too, reflection on baptism became an important source for his theology of original sin.

Augustine considered the custom of infant baptism both ancient and valid. He took as authoritative the brief references of earlier writers linking baptism with an inherited sin. Following arguments fashioned by others, Augustine derived the existence of an inborn sin from a sacramental practice already in place.

Augustine's argument linking baptism with an inherited sin works backward from redemption to sin. It is fundamentally a christological argument: Every human being needs Christ's redemption. Infants would require divine forgiveness, however, only if an inborn sin exists. They are incapable of personal sins. If infants need Christ's redemption, their guilt must follow from the sin of another residing in them as real sin.

The scriptural foundation used by the patristic writers to ground infant baptism was not without ambiguity. Jesus' reply to Nicodemus, for example, implies adult conversion: "Very truly, I tell you, no one can enter the kingdom of God without being born of water and Spirit" (John 3:5).[10] Paul's references to baptism reflect the context of women and men who had made life changes because of their religious conversion. In reminding the Galatian Christians of the significance of their baptism, Paul speaks to adults:

> As many of you were baptized into Christ have clothed yourselves with Christ. There is no longer Jew or Greek, there is no longer slave or free, there is no longer male and female; for all of you are one in Christ Jesus. (Gal 3:27)

The same is true for the parallel invocation of baptism in Paul's letter to the Corinthians: "For in the one Spirit we were all baptized into one body—Jews or Greeks, slaves or free—and we were all made to drink of the one Spirit" (1 Cor 12:13).

But eventually Christian theologians took New Testament baptismal texts as references simply to persons—infants as well as adults. Matthew's portrayal of Jesus' command to "make disciples of all nations, baptizing them in the name of the Father and of the Son and of the Holy Spirit and teaching them to obey everything that I have commanded you" (Matt 28:19–20) lent itself especially to this interpretation.

The views of *Cyprian* on baptism were particularly important for Augustine in his prolonged struggle with the Donatists.[11] Cyprian argued that infant baptism was necessary because no one is without sin, citing one of the Johannine letters: "If we say that we have no sin, we deceive ourselves, and the truth is not in us" (1 John 1:8).

Ambrose of Milan (d. 397) was a chief resource in Augustine's later conflict with Pelagius. In his contemporary Ambrose, Augustine found an explicit biological principle grounding humankind's solidarity in sin with Adam. Ambrose wrote that Adam's sin is transmitted to all his descendents. When accused by others of innovation and novelty, Augustine defended his understanding of original sin as continuous with the tradition. He acknowledged particular debt to Cyprian and Ambrose:

> My instructor is Cyprian,...my instructor is Ambrose, whose books I have read and whose words I have heard from his own lips, and through whom I received the washing of regeneration....[12]

Augustine's biological theory of inheritance was also influenced by *Jerome* (d. 420), one of the great scholars of the patristic church.[13] Jerome's authority, in turn, was *Didymus the Blind* (d. 399). Didymus maintained that infants were born with a sin transmitted through physical procreation and thus in need of divine forgiveness.[14]

Augustine's theological sources were further buttressed by Ambrosiaster's interpretation of Romans 5:12 as divine revelation of original sin.[15] As noted earlier, the accurate translation of the Greek text is that "death spread to all *because* (or *inasmuch as*) all have sinned." Ambrosiaster's Latin Vulgate edition, however, translated the text "*in whom* all sinned." For Ambrosiaster, Romans 5:12 offered evidence of the inclusion of all human nature in Adam, thus grounding a principle of explanation for human solidarity in sin. But as the Pauline biblical scholar Joseph Fitzmyer argues, accurately translated the text does not advance a *principle of inclusion* in Adam as much as it advocates a *principle of causal determination:* From one event (Adam's sin), consequences have been incurred (death).[16] Paul appeals to Adam to answer the question, "Who brought *death* into the world?" His real interest is not with death, however, but with *life* now offered in Christ.[17]

Augustine did not have Fitzmyer's exegesis of Romans 5:12. Taking Ambrosiaster as his authority, Augustine grounded original sin in humankind's ontological inclusion in Adam. "The whole human race, which was to become Adam's posterity through the first woman, was present in the first man."[18] As did Paul's, however, Augustine's appeal to Adam served christological concerns. With Christ, human solidarity is no longer limited to solidarity in sin. The Christ-event opened up the possibility of human solidarity in belief. For Augustine, Christian belief was at its core belief in the gift of God's grace through Christ. This gift is the means of moral transformation—empowerment, in fact—and the reorientation of spiritual development toward the ultimate good of the human soul, God. Augustine writes that "the seed of our common human nature was present in Adam and thus we in him. By birth all men belong to Adam and his sin, just as all who are reborn belong to Christ."[19] Solidarity in grace—the religious community, those who belong to Christ, the church—is a fundamental dimension of God's remedy for meeting the problem of sin.

Augustine's Anthropology

Augustine's theology of original sin generated the distinctive characteristics of his theories of human nature and history. His views of the human condition are found in both his anthropology and his portrayal of history.

Augustine divided human beings into three categories: created, fallen, and redeemed. A distinct understanding of human nature corresponded with each: (1) a state of original blessedness, (2) a state of fallenness, and (3) a state of restored and graced nature. Each state has its own capacities and potentialities.

1. The Created State of Original Blessedness

Augustine assumed the historicity of Adam as well as the historical veracity of Genesis 1–3 as divine revelation. He understood the *image of God* (Gen. 1:27) as the intellectual and moral nature with which human beings were endowed. Human beings are like God inasmuch as they are rational and moral. They are unlike God when they are irrational and immoral. This is their sin. For Augustine these capacities are intrinsically and ultimately purposeful. They are created in human beings to bring them to knowledge and love of God, not simply to knowledge and love of finite things.[20]

In the state of original blessedness, Augustine argued, Adam had the capacity to choose to do what is good. Because God is the ultimate good, the choice of any good is the choice of God. Because Adam was also created with freedom, however, his choice of the good was not necessary.

Augustine argued that in Adam's original state he had the ability *not to sin (posse non peccare)*. He also possessed certain gifts in this prelapsarian state. These gifts were over and beyond what human nature as nature requires. Among these gifts were immortality, integrity, and knowledge. By sin, Adam lost these gifts. Consequently, Adam's descendents are born without them.

2. The State of Fallen Humanity

Augustine portrayed Adam's will in the state of blessedness as "entirely set on God." Adam's sin, then, creates something of a logical dilemma. Why would Adam sin if his will were oriented wholly toward God? Augustine did not resolve this conflict. He took scripture's revelation to be that Adam's created state was one of original blessedness and that Adam's sin had brought a state of fallenness for all humankind.

Augustine interpreted Adam's particular sin to be that of pride. Adam's disobedience of God's command reflected his desire to be God. His sin was the refusal to acknowledge absolute dependence on God.[21] The penalties for Adam's sin were (1) *death,* loss of the gift of immortality; (2) *ignorance,* loss of the knowledge and intimacy with God; and (3) *difficulty,* loss of the ability to accomplish the good one wills.

Augustine argued that in Adam and Eve's original state, the dominance of reason over the passions established a relation of harmony between the body and soul. Difficulty, the third penalty, reflects the loss of this inner harmony. Sinful nature reverses what should be. Now the passions interfere with and dominate rational thought. This disorder, *concupiscence,* distorts what was intended by divine creation.[22] Augustine writes in the *Confessions:* "For you have imposed order, and so it is that the punishment of every disordered mind is its own disorder."[23] Concupiscence is a defect in fallen nature created by Adam's sin.

Baptism removes original sin and the guilt for concupiscence. But it does not remove concupiscence, the disorder in nature caused by sin. Concupiscence remains in nature as punishment for Adam's sin. The inner disorder of human nature is a permanent condition experienced as inner struggle, conflict, and self-contradiction. While concupiscence is not itself sin, it inclines persons to sin. Even though grace will elevate human nature, as Augustine will argue, it does not destroy nature as distorted by the sin of Adam.

Augustine's conception of redemption was influenced by these assumptions about original sin and concupiscence. One of his primary images for concupiscence was of a sickness requiring healing. Christ is the source of healing and restorer of what was lost in nature by Adam's sin. Redemption remedies the sickness in human nature.

Sexual impulses and sexual passions were often Augustine's examples of disordered desire. His understanding of concupiscence, consequently, has often been identified with the dominance of sexual feelings and drives over the rational and moral self.[24] Augustine's *Confessions* contribute to this interpretation inasmuch as the book documents his difficulties and embarrassment with the power of sexual feelings and passions. But sexual passion is a characteristic symptom of concupiscence for Augustine, not the whole meaning of it.[25] Margaret Miles describes Augustine's understanding of concupiscence as "the primal and undifferentiated lust for pleasure without orientation to God."[26] In the *Confessions,* Augustine writes that his sin "consisted in this, that I sought pleasure, sublimity, and truth not in God but in his creatures, in myself and other created beings."[27] For Augustine, the unrelenting rebellion of human passions and drives against human rationality was the primary evidence of humankind's rebellion against God.

Augustine thought of the fall in two ways, one moral, the other metaphysical.[28] Morally, the fall was the result of Adam's pride. Adam failed to acknowledge that his existence was dependent on God. In Augustine's judgment, this refusal to acknowledge their absolute dependence on God as created beings is humankind's basic sin. Augustine put the fall in metaphysical categories as being and nothingness. God is the fullness of being. In the sinful falling away from God, human beings become less real. They have less being. Adhering to God makes one more human or genuinely human. Falling away from God makes one less human. For Augustine the human being is only truly human when oriented fully toward God. Inasmuch as that orientation shifts, the person is diminished in his or her own being.

Through his sin did Adam lose the image of God? That human beings are made in the image of God is a proclamation of scripture (Gen 1:27). Augustine interpreted *image of God* to mean the rational and moral capacities in human nature. He believed that Adam's sin damaged the image of God in human beings but did not destroy it. Sin wounded the potentiality of rational moral nature, changing human nature for the worse.

Augustine thought of humankind as blinded by sin in its fallen state. Because of concupiscence, human nature is predisposed toward wrongdoing. Adam's *ability not to sin (posse non peccare)* was lost, replaced by fallen humanity's *inability not to sin (necessitas peccandi).*[29] In their fallen state, human beings have lost their natural power to do what is right by human will alone.

Moreover, human nature possesses the actual sin of Adam, not just the penalty for it (concupiscence). Augustine utilized both the ontological and biological fragments of tradition on this question. Following Ambrose and others, Augustine conceived of all humankind as in Adam: When Adam sinned, all sinned. He cites from Ambrose's *Concerning the Resurrection* in the book *On Original Sin,* "'I fell in Adam, in Adam was I expelled from Paradise, in Adam I died....'"[30] Elsewhere, Augustine cites Ambrose's remark that "we all existed in that one man *(omnes fuimus in illo uno)....*We are Adam."[31] But human beings are also sinners by descent, *generatione non imitatione.* They inherit original sin through physical conception. Augustine considered the male seed the bearer of Adam's sin because he thought human nature was transmitted through it in the sexual act.

Even though human nature was corrupted by Adam's sin, Augustine believed that the vestiges of the image of God remain. Christ's grace rehabilitates the image of God in human beings, enabling believers to adhere to truth and love. Redemption heals nature and restores what had been lost.

The predicament of fallen humanity, then, is the inability to accomplish or perform what one wills as the good.[32] John Rist describes Augustine's view this way: "We are free and able to do evil of our own accord, but we are unable to choose the good freely."[33] Augustine argued that the only liberation from this bondage to sin is the divine infusion of the Holy Spirit, *caritas,* love for what is right and for doing what is right. Because of Adam's sin, fallen humanity is born without *caritas.* Human beings are servants of its opposite, *cupiditas.* Hence their tendency to choose evil, not good.

As Margaret Miles notes, Augustine thought of the spiritual life as the progressive victory over the concupiscence created by sin.[34] As grace heals nature, control over the passions and a strengthening of rationality replace the disorder brought about by concupiscence. With Christ as their example, persons discover God as their true source of happiness, as Augustine's opening in the *Confessions* submits: "You have made us for yourself, and our heart is restless until it rests in you."[35]

3. The State of Restored Humanity

To redeem means to "buy back." In its religious appropriation, redemption signifies that God has set the relation between humankind and God right again. Humanity has been *brought back* to its original direction and purpose. For Augustine, the recreation of human nature through Christ's redemption did not return human nature to its state prior to Adam's sin. Even with the sorry punishment of concupiscence for humanity to bear, grace raises human nature to a higher state.

The restoration of fallen humanity occurs historically and socially through a redemptive community. The church mediates God's offer of salvation and gift of grace. Through participation in the church's sacramental life and acceptance of its revealed truths, human beings are oriented toward the good and away from evil. Religious conversion and the subsequent power to do the good that one wills are effects of grace.[36] So, too, is faith in Christ. The church exists as a new means by which humankind may enter into a relationship with God and be healed of the inner contradictions imposed by sin.

The destiny of redeemed humanity is participation in God. In the beatific vision, human beings will achieve what was impossible even to Adam: the *inability to sin.* In this final state, human beings will be united fully in love with God, unable to turn away from God.

Augustine and Pelagius

With these features of Augustine's thought in mind, we turn to the conflict between Augustine and Pelagius. In his opposition to Pelagius's theology of nature and grace, Augustine brought the fragments of tradition and his own thinking on original sin into definitive form.

Pelagius, a British monk and theologian, is believed to have read Augustine's *Confessions* around 405. Augustine's later anti-Pelagian writings also appear to date their conflict to this date. But Augustine's silence about Pelagius until around 415 C.E. suggests this later date as the beginning of their antagonistic relationship.[37] Their friction continued until Pelagius's death in 420.

Pelagius came to Augustine's *Confessions* deeply concerned about the laxity of Christian morality. To him, Augustine's view of freedom and sin made sin appear inevitable for fallen humanity. He thought Augustine's portrayal of sin as virtually unavoidable would contribute to moral irresponsibility by making sin fated. If sin cannot be avoided, why should persons pursue a moral life?

At heart Pelagius's difficulty with Augustine was over what moral nature is capable of doing. Margaret Miles highlights their different anthropologies:

> Pelagius' teaching had its foundation in an anthropology very different from Augustine's. Instead of Augustine's view of the disastrously undermining effect of original sin in the human race, Pelagius saw the slight undertow of bad habits as being socially conditioned and reversible with effort and conscious reconditioning.[38]

Moral Nature

Augustine and Pelagius agreed on the three faculties of human nature: *capacity, volition,* and *action.*[39] They parted ways on how divine grace related to each.

By *capacity,* Pelagius meant moral ability generally. Moral ability means that humans can engage in moral deliberation about what is right, choose among alternative courses of action, and live moral lives. Moral capacity is the condition of possibility for volition.

By *volition,* Pelagius meant the activity of willing or deciding. It is the inner power that settles on a course of action as good. Just as capacity is the condition for volition, volition is the condition of possibility for action.

By *action,* Pelagius meant actual moral performance. Performance is the doing of a responsible course of action. By performance, persons not only do the good but become good.

Stoicism provided Pelagius with his philosophical theory of human nature.[40] The Stoics saw human beings as intelligent and rational. They are capable of discovering the law and acting in ways determined by reason to be right. Divine assistance is not required to move human willing and deciding toward the right course of action or its performance. What rational and moral persons are able to do is live according to their nature.

For Pelagius, God's primary gift of grace is moral nature itself *(bonum naturae).*[41] The image of God in human beings is this capacity for moral choice and performance. Choosing and doing the good do not require a further gift of divine assistance.

In Pelagius's view, God created moral nature in human beings so that they can know and do what is right. If they have such a nature, Pelagius reasoned, human beings must be able *not* to sin. Pelagius believed that Adam's ability not to sin *(posse non peccare)* exists still in his descendents and was not lost by his sin.[42] This view of Pelagius was particularly offensive to Augustine. He thought it suggested a "natural salvation," rendering Christ unnecessary for salvation.[43] It seemed to Augustine that Pelagius was saying human beings could merit their own justification by keeping the law and not sinning.[44]

For his part, Pelagius took the existence of human freedom as evidence that human nature can do either good or evil. If nature does not have the potential to avoid wrongdoing, Pelagius argued, how may a person be held morally responsible? If one by nature has the ability to avoid wrongdoing yet does not, the person is morally responsible for the failure to do what is right.

Natural and revealed law provide the guides for moral behavior. Pelagius described natural law as that which reason or conscience grasps as right. Revealed or Mosaic law is comprised of revealed commandments. Both types of law originate in the divine will. Sin is the deliberate disobedience of what God commands of human beings through natural and revealed law.

Pelagius believed, too, that God offered further graces as divine help in avoiding sin. He identified three such gifts. The first is the grace of the law itself, both natural and revealed. The command to love God and neighbor is the heart of the law. The second grace is Christ's teaching and personal example. It assists the faithful in orienting their lives to God. Pelagius called the third grace "redemptive grace." It is the forgiveness of sins mediated through the sacraments of the church.

Pelagius specifically rejected the inheritance theory of original sin advanced by Augustine. He did not believe that Adam's sin was transmitted to humankind through sexual intercourse.[45] He maintained that the spread of sin in human history was due to the imitation of Adam's bad example. Pelagius also rejected Augustine's idea that Adam's sin had caused a defect in human nature. Pelagius did not think that it could change human nature. He was aware of the way others derived an inherited sin from the church's baptism of infants but he justified the practice on the different grounds. Baptism enabled infants to participate in the kingdom of God (cf., John 3:5).

The conflict between Augustine and Pelagius sprang from their different conceptions of moral nature. Pelagius argued that moral nature is God's gift. It enables human beings to know and do the good. Human nature remains unchanged as nature by Adam's sin. Augustine agreed that nature was God's gift, but contended that Adam's sin had changed nature. Moral nature is not the same after the fall as it was in Adam prior to sin.

Augustine described the effect of Adam's sin as wounding nature. These wounds are ignorance, concupiscence, weakness, suffering, and the inevitability of death.[46] As we noted previously, Augustine argued that Adam's original nature possessed an internal harmony between reason and the passions. But concupiscence, as the consequence and punishment for Adam's sin, replaced harmony with disharmony in sinful nature.[47]

Concupiscence prohibits true freedom until nature is liberated by grace. In Augustine's judgment, human nature is not neutrally open toward good or evil. It is biased toward evil. While human beings retained freedom of choice *(liberum arbitrium)* after Adam's sin, it is free choice in bondage to sin. In fallen nature what free choice does easily is choose evil. More difficult, perhaps even impossible in Augustine's opinion, is choosing and doing the good. By Adam's sin human beings lost true freedom *(libertas),* the freedom to direct themselves wholly toward their true good, God. Freedom was weakened by Adam's sin. Now the will was misdirected.[48]

The differences in Augustine's and Pelagius's anthropologies also reflect different existential experiences. Augustine experienced inner struggle, conflict, and contradiction as fallen nature. He thought Pelagius was too optimistic in his portrayal of moral nature. For his part, Pelagius must have experienced moral potentiality. He certainly valued it. Augustine had experienced and despaired of moral impotence. Augustine countered Pelagius's optimism with a pessimism emphasizing the corruption of human nature by its inheritance of Adam's sin.[49]

Sin and Grace

Augustine agreed with Pelagius that the law and Christ's teaching were external graces. But his personal experience led him to correlate divine grace first with the healing transformation of the self effected by religious conversion. The infusion of the Holy Spirit, the gift of charity—love for what is right and strength to do it—generates this transformation. Charity then motivates moral action. It is charity that creates conformity between moral knowing and doing:

> By such grace it is effected not only that we discover what ought to be done, but also that we do what we have discovered—not only that we believe what ought to be loved, but also that we love what we have believed.[50]

In Augustine's terms, religious conversion is operative grace. God operates through conversion to redirect a person's orientation away from sin and back toward God.[51] This experience is objectified as faith in Christ. Cooperative grace is God's assisting human freedom with the moral strength to resist sin, to choose what is good, and to perform the actions willed as good.

Augustine based operative and cooperative grace on several scriptural texts. He cited Philippians for a divine grace going beyond the gift of moral nature itself: "For it is God who is at work in you, enabling you both to will and to work for his good pleasures" (Phil 2:13). In John, he found evidence of the absolute necessity of Christ: "Apart from me you can do nothing" (John 15:5). For charity as the inner transformation of human nature Augustine cited Romans: "God's love has been poured into our hearts through the Holy Spirit that has been given to us" (Rom 5:5).

The Origin of the Soul

Augustine's and Pelagius's divergence on the question of an inherited sin was matched by a similar divergence on the question of the origin of the soul.

Pelagius preferred the theory of *creationism*.[52] This view held that God created each human soul independently, infusing the soul into the body at the time of conception. In contrast, *traducianism*—also called *generationalism*—held that the body and soul are generated together in physical conception.[53] While traducianism can accommodate the idea of an inherited sin, creationism does not. If each soul comes directly from God, to argue that it is born with a sin of nature implies that God creates each soul with sin.[54]

Early on Augustine was attracted to a theory of the preexistence of the soul. He later leaned toward the traducian theory for the same reason that Pelagius rejected it.[55] Traducianism offered the philosophical base from which to derive a theological principle of human solidarity in sin with Adam. In contest to creationism, traducianism accommodated the view that Adam's actual sin could be transmitted to all his descendents by sexual intercourse.

Conciliar Opposition to the Pelagians

In the fifth century, *Pelagian* views—later tradition will use the term as synonymous with heresy—were one side of a highly charged divergence of theological opinion. Both sides could cite scripture. Both sides could cite influential patristic figures in their favor. Pelagius even cited Augustine's earlier anti-Manichean writings as support for his own position.

Four theological positions were suspect to those who opposed the Pelagians: (1) a rejection of the biological transmission of sin or the inheritance of original sin *(de traduce peccati);* (2) a rejection of the purpose of infant baptism as the forgiveness of a pre-personal inherited sin; (3) a belief that human solidarity in sin, the universality of sin, or the spread of sin occurred through imitation of Adam's example; and (4) an optimism about created moral nature and the capacity of human beings to live a moral life.

Pelagius considered himself an orthodox theologian of the church advancing authentic Catholic teaching. To his mind the danger was not optimism about moral nature but pessimism. He thought Augustine's view that human nature was corrupt and sin as virtually inevitable diminished human freedom.

The Council of Carthage (411–418) debated Pelagian views, specifically the teachings of one of Pelagius's associates, Celestius.[56] Taking Augustine as their theological authority, the council identified a number of Celestius's teachings that were at odds with Augustine's.[57] Among these views are that: (1) Adam was created mortal and would have died whether or not he had sinned; (2) the whole human race did not have to die because of Adam's sin; (3) Adam's sin was not transmitted to his descendents; (4) infants are born in the same state as Adam prior to his sin; and (5) the Law (the Old Testament) was as sufficient for salvation as the gospel.[58]

Against Celestius's teaching that death is a natural part of human existence, Carthage affirmed in its first canon that Adam had been given the gift of immortality but lost it by his sin.[59] Their second canon concerned the state in which human beings were born.[60] For the Pelagians, the theory of the inheritance of original sin *(de traduce peccati)* was an open theological question. The council cited Romans 5:12 to close the question. Following Augustine and his sources, particularly Cyprian and Ambrose, the council derived the existence of original sin from the sacramental practice of baptizing infants. With the Council of Carthage, the theological speculation that infants are born with Adam's sin was established as a normative element of Christian belief.

Augustine's distinction between the event of Adam's original sin *(peccatum originale originans)* and the condition of original sin in which infants are born *(peccatum originale originatum)* became a permanent feature of the doctrines of original sin and redemption. In the early church, as today, reference to the "problem of original sin" refers to the sinful state brought about by Adam's sin, *peccatum originale originatum.*

Carthage did not adopt all of Augustine's views, however. For example, they laid aside his theory of the predestination of the elect. But the council followed Augustine in their repudiation of Pelagian optimism about the natural goodness of human nature. With Augustine, the council affirmed that human nature is sinful from birth. Human nature requires the healing grace of Christ's forgiveness for salvation as well as to live a moral life.

Pelagius was only indirectly involved in the deliberations of the Council of Carthage. But he was summoned personally to the Synod of Jerusalem in 415 to defend himself.[61] He avoided condemnation by signing a declaration of orthodoxy, explaining his own position later in two books, *On Free Will* and *On Nature*.

Almost a hundred years later, the Council of Orange (529) was convened in southern France to address the difficulties presented by those who were taking Augustine's theory of the corruption of human nature to an extreme.[62] Faustus of Riez (d. before 500), a major figure in this controversy, argued against both sides in *De gratia et libero arbitrio*. He assailed those who held that human freedom remained completely intact after Adam's sin (the Pelagian position) and against those who held that human freedom had been completely destroyed (the extreme Augustinian position).

Orange countered the Augustinian extremists by disavowing the view that human freedom had been completely lost by Adam's sin. The council countered the Pelagians by rejecting the view that only the body had been changed for the worse by Adam's sin (by concupiscence), not the soul (human freedom). Orange affirmed that original sin changed both the body and the soul.[63] Although human freedom had not been completely destroyed, Adam's sin had diminished it. In its conclusion, the Council of Orange emphasized its understanding of the effect of original sin on free will:

> Through the sin of the first man free will had been bent *(inclinatum)* and weakened *(attenuatem)* in such a manner that consequently no one can love God as he ought, or believe in God or do good because of God unless assisted *(praevenerit)* by the prevenient grace of God's mercy.[64]

With the Council of Orange, patristic debates over human moral nature and original sin reached an end. Augustine had triumphed. Further conciliar pronouncements on the matter would not appear for ten centuries. Oddly, the Council of Orange was apparently unknown to medieval theologians.

Conclusion

Augustine's conception of an inherited sin provided a principle explaining human solidarity in sin with Adam. This principle is the core element of the classical doctrine of original sin. Like Paul, Augustine's primary interest was with Christ, not Adam. While his assumption of original sin shaped his conceptions of redemption, grace, baptism, and the church, Augustine's starting premise was the necessity of Christ's redemption for all humankind, not original sin. His speculative appeal to an inherited sin answered both the christological and the sacramental questions. Why Christ? Why baptize infants? "If Christ is the savior of all," Augustine wrote, "he cannot have saved only adults but infants as well."[65] Because of the sin received by inheritance, Christ's grace of forgiveness is necessary for everyone.

Without an alternative available, Augustine presumed the historicity of Adam and Eve. His theological anthropology pivots on the Genesis story. Yet Augustine's insights into sin can be detached from the story. It was Augustine's inner psychological experience—as much as his reading of Genesis 3—that led him to interpret the paradigmatic human sin as pride. For Augustine, sin originates in the human refusal to acknowledge created dependence on God and do what God wills as good through fidelity to natural and revealed law.

Augustine fine-tuned his theology of original sin through his rejection of Manichean views, his controversy with the Donatists, and his engagement with Pelagius. Against Pelagius's optimism, Augustine's view of human nature looks more like the determinism opposed by earlier Christian theologians such as Clement of Alexandria.[66] The threat of Gnostic determinism prompted Clement to emphasize human freedom and the capacity to sin or not sin in order to highlight moral responsibility and offset fate. The Donatists of Augustine's time asserted the possibility of not sinning, provoking Augustine's reaction and more practical view that such was unlikely for fallen nature.

In Pelagius, Augustine perceived the threat to Christian faith in an overconfidence in human freedom, an underemphasis on divine grace in moral decision and action, and a minimalizing of the necessity of the Christ's redemption. Pelagius's appeal to the neutrality of human freedom toward good and evil led Augustine to emphasize the impotence of moral nature and its bias toward evil. By doing so, Pelagius thought, Augustine portrayed sin as virtually inevitable.

In his theology of grace, Augustine transposed the symbolic language of the Spirit and religious conversion found in Paul into the more technical categories of operative and cooperative grace. The medieval theologians will transpose Augustine's descriptive language of original sin into the metaphysical definition of original sin as the ontological privation of original justice.

In his own time, Augustine's influence was such that theological speculation about original sin was integrated into official conciliar language by the councils of Carthage and Orange. With that move, original sin became a church doctrine in a more formal sense. Augustine had appealed to those he considered theological authorities—Cyprian, Ambrose, Jerome—to defend his views as ancient and traditional. After these patristic councils, however, appeal could be made directly to church teaching itself.

What was adopted by the patristic church was more than the idea of original sin. Adopted as the church's teaching about Christ's redemption and the church's sacramental life was a particular interpretation of Genesis 3 and Romans 5:12 as divinely revealed teaching about original sin, an anthropology of rational moral nature, and an historical worldview encompassing original blessedness, fallen nature, and restored nature.

4. Anselm, Thomas, the Reformers, and Trent

THE FIFTH-CENTURY COUNCILS of Carthage and Orange confirmed Augustine's theology of original sin as a core belief of Christianity. Completed by the doctrines of creation and redemption, original sin anchored a distinctive Christian account of history and human destiny that would prevail unquestioned for a thousand years.[1] Beyond the patristic age, further technical developments in the theology of original sin occurred in the work of the medieval scholastic theologians. Of the medievals, the work of Anselm of Canterbury and Thomas Aquinas is especially significant. The Reformer Martin Luther reacted against theoretical speculations of the scholastics and a metaphysical explanation of original sin. He recovered Augustine's existential apprehension of original sin. Luther's understanding characterizes subsequent Reform reflection on original sin. For Catholics, the Council of Trent (1545–1563), responding to Luther, brought medieval developments to closure by its definition of original sin as a dogma of the church. The sixteenth-century Tridentine explanation of original sin remains that of Roman Catholic doctrine today. These medieval deliberations are the subject of our discussion in this chapter.

Medieval Theology

Medieval theologians assumed the historicity of paradise, the persons of Adam and Eve, a first sin, and a fall from divine friendship. They took for granted the idea of original sin forged by the patristic theologians. Why Christ's redemption was necessary and why baptize infants were explained with reference to Adam's sin and the consequences it bore for humankind.

Medieval theologians exhibited no particular difficulties with original sin.[2] The idea was assumed as a core component of the divine truths revealed to the church. Speculation about original sin customarily occurred in the context of medieval anthropology. What was human nature before and after Adam's sin? Medieval theologians posed this question philosophically as a contrast between two states: the essence of original innocence and the essence of original sin *(quid sit originale peccatum).*

In their theological anthropology, the medievals drew upon a philosophical concept of the hierarchy of natures—lower to higher natures—to address a number of questions. The technical differentiation between natural and supernatural helped to conceive of the relation between divine grace and human nature.[3] Though a medieval achievement, the distinction built upon the patristic idea that God had bestowed on created nature certain gifts "over and beyond nature" that were lost by Adam's sin. The medieval theology of original sin is embedded in a metaphysical theory of the faculties, powers, and capacities of human nature.

Medieval theologians argued that rational and moral capacities are proper to human nature as created. The capacities of intellect and will belong to the natural order. Divine grace, however, is supernatural. Divine gifts can be given to human nature that reflect capacities or powers proper to divine, not human, nature. Because these gifts properly belong to the divine order of reality, they may be taken away from human nature without destroying it. Without these divine gifts, human nature is not less than human but left only with what is proper to it as created.

Anselm of Canterbury

For *Anselm of Canterbury* (d. 1109)—Benedictine monk, theologian, and archbishop—the most significant of these supernatural gifts bestowed on human nature was that of justice. Anselm's understanding of original sin was shaped by his assumption of what original justice contributed to human nature and the consequences in nature due to the loss of this gift.

Anselm was the preeminent theologian of the early medieval period.[4] Unlike Augustine's, Anselm's thinking on original sin was not forced into clarity by a situation of theological conflict over questions of grace and nature. His interest in the doctrine owed more to the desire to provide intellectually satisfying answers to his contemporaries' questions about the purpose of the incarnation and redemption. Among the results of Anselm's searching intelligence are the classic theological works *Cur Deus Homo* and the *Monologion.*

Like his patristic predecessors, Anselm saw Christ's redemption as God's remedy to the problem of sin. The way Anselm thought about sin and redemption was influenced by the assumptions, ideals, values, and ways of living characteristic of the social and cultural world in which he lived. The monastic order of Anselm's religious world mirrored in miniature the hierarchically structured social and political world of medieval kings, lords, knights, vassals, and subjects.

Of all medieval feudal values, honor and obedience were given highest place. To disobey one's superior withheld honor where honor was due. Disobedience dishonored that person. Repayment to the one dishonored and punishment of the one committing the dishonor were both due.

Anselm's reading of Genesis 3 reflected the influence of this feudal world. With Augustine, Anselm concurred that Adam had disobeyed God. For Augustine, Adam wanted to be God. That is why he wanted to eat from the tree of knowledge of good and evil, and that was his sin. For Anselm, however, Adam's disobedience had insulted God. This insult was Adam's sin.

As a creature and God's subordinate, Anselm argued, Adam owed God submission of his will. By violating God's command in the garden, Adam flaunted God's will. He failed then to give honor where honor was due. For this insult, God deprived Adam of the special gifts given to his nature.

Adam's sin required repayment to the one dishonored. The repayment required for dishonoring a divine being, however, was too large for an individual or even humankind as a whole to meet. But, Anselm argued, as both *God* and *man,* Jesus Christ could satisfy this debt owed to God. Anselm's *Cur Deus Homo (Why God Became Man)* worked this argument out in detail. Because of Christ's commensurate status and by his perfect obedience (in contrast to Adam's disobedience), he restored to human beings the possibility of reaching ultimate union with God. This was the end for which human nature had been created.

The incarnation was the *means of,* and redemption the *repayment for,* satisfying the infinite debt owed to God by Adam's insult. Anselm derived the reason for the incarnation from original sin.

Original sin is a pivotal factor in Anselm's theological anthropology. The central element in his theory of human nature, and especially for his conception of original sin, was the divine gift of *justitia.*

1. The Supernatural Gift of Justitia

Anselm argued that Adam and Eve were created *just* by God. He used the term *justitia*—often translated "integrity"—to designate a supernatural gift possessed by Adam's nature prior to sin. By *original justice,* Anselm meant the rational and moral ability of human nature to will what God wills, namely, that which is right.[5] Rectitude, the moral integrity of the will, is constituted by willingness to do what is right *because* it is right. What is right conforms with the divine will.

In Anselm's conception of created nature, Adam was also oriented toward union with God by possession of the supernatural gift of *blessedness* or *beatitude.*[6] The gifts of justice and blessedness assisted human nature toward its intended transcendent end, but as *supernatural gifts* they were not essential to nature. They could be taken away without destroying human nature. Possessed, the divine gifts complement the purpose of the highest powers of human nature.

This notion of purpose was important to medieval speculation. The essence or nature of things was understood in relation to their purpose. When the purpose of the highest powers of human nature—reason and will—are understood, the essence of human nature is grasped. What, then, is the purpose of intellectual and moral capacities?

Anselm first highlighted the relation of reason and will to one another. God gave human beings reason (the capacity to know what is true) in order that they might will rightly. What should they know is true? Anselm's answer signals his feudal setting: *Human beings should know they owe obedience to God.* These powers of human nature serve a moral and a transcendent end. Reason and will first conform to the divine will by knowing and doing what is right because it is right. This is their moral end. Second, they orient human beings to seek and attain union with God. This is their transcendent end. Anselm described this end as "keeping justice."

Anselm defined true human freedom as the absence of sin. His understanding of sin evoked the contours of the feudal world of his experience. The absence of sin is the absence of disobedience to the divine will. Sin is the absence of dishonor to God. Anselm's insights into human experience were formulated negatively and abstractly. As a medieval he lacks the explicit language with which to describe psychological experience. But his concept was positive. Human beings become fully human by living in accord with their built-in capacities for rationality and moral choice. As did Paul and Augustine, Anselm's description of sin was metaphorical. The achievement of the transcendent end of human nature is a journey, and it can be thwarted by straying from the right road. Human beings lose their way by servitude and bondage to sin, he writes poignantly:

> But this absence is not a negative quality: it is the power to do that which fulfils the nature of Man as a rational being. So long as a man is following the law of his nature—that is to say, so long as he is on the road to final beatitude—he is free. When he deviates from this road, he becomes unfree, and unfree in a double sense: unfree in having lost his way without a plan to guide him, and even more unfree in being unable, having no plan, or at least not the right plan, to find the right road. Though lost, he may still have an illusion of freedom because he has a choice between various possibilities. But since none of them can be the right road, his freedom is illusory, and his bondage deeper than he can understand.[7]

2. The Loss of Justitia

Anselm's conception of original sin subtly but significantly reoriented the doctrine shaped by Augustine in the fifth century. Augustine described the condition of original sin *(peccatum originale originatum)* as a *something*. It is the culpable inclination of the will against God *(amor sui, cupiditas)*. In this sense, Augustine's definition of original sin was positive. It was the definition of a something— a bias, tendency, or inclination toward evil. Anselm's definition, in contrast, was negative. The condition of original sin is not something but a *privation* in nature. That which had been possessed as a supernatural gift was now *absent* due to sin.

Anselm argued that Adam had lost the supernatural gift of *justitia* by his disobedience of God's command. Disobedience was *injustitia:* willing what was wrong. In Anselm's view, disobedience was the paradigmatic sin. *Injustitia* is the absence of owed justice. The condition of original sin *(peccatum originale originatum)* is the absence, privation, or deprivation of original justice.

What Augustine described in metaphorical terms as the impotence of the will, Anselm put in technical terms as the privation of original justice *(privatio justitiae originalis)*. By this deprivation, Adam lost the ability to will what is right. The consequences were also described in terms of deprivation—loss of the relation of harmony with God and loss of harmony within human nature itself. Sin introduced disharmony within nature.

Anselm's understanding of personal sin follows the paradigm set by his theology of original sin. Again his description of the experience of sin is put in an abstract analysis of the relation between the human and divine wills. By willing to do what is incompatible with what is right, human beings act against God's will. They dishonor God by failing to give God the obedience—rational moral choice and action—that is God's due as Creator.

Anselm's theological anthropology and theology of original sin established the framework for his Christology. God created human beings to seek God and to take their places in heaven with God. Adam's sin had thwarted this original transcendent purpose. For human beings to achieve this end now required divine redemption. In Anselm's view, the saving benefit of Christ's redemption was returning to humankind the possibility of reaching the divine end for which their nature was created. Christ put right what human beings had made wrong in the created order. His perfect obedience offset Adam's disobedience. Obedience gave honor where honor was due. And, most significant, as both God and man, Christ could repay the debt incurred by Adam's grievous insult to God, which no mere human being could do.

Anselm understood the effect of redemption first as an interior change. Redemption changes human nature by restoring what was lost. Anselm described this technically in terms of a faculty psychology of reason and will. Through Christ's healing grace, the capacity of reason to know what is true and the ability of the will to choose and do what is right are reestablished. Once again, reason and will conform to the divine will. Once again, human beings are able to obey God. This obedience is the condition for moral rectitude. In turn, moral rectitude is the prerequisite for attaining the transcendent end of human nature.

For Anselm, the traditional reading of Romans 5:12, "in Adam all sinned," confirmed humankind's solidarity in sin with Adam. Following patristic writers such as Ambrose of Milan, Anselm interpreted this text as divine revelation of the metaphysical unity of humankind in Adam. The idea that Adam was humankind implied that (1) all human beings were created at the same time in Adam, (2) all human beings sinned when Adam sinned, and (3) all were guilty with Adam of dishonoring God. The nature inherited from Adam is a nature deprived of the supernatural gifts of original justice and blessedness. The condition of original sin *(privatio justitiae originalis)* is an ontological defect in human nature. At conception, original sin is in the human soul, paradoxically, as a privation. Yet it is a real sin. "Above all," writes Henri Rondet, for Anselm "original sin is a *sin of nature*. In Adam, the person tainted the nature; in us, it is the nature that taints the person."[8]

Questions about infant baptism and original sin also arose in the medieval context. The speculative question was posed in terms of God's justice. If unbaptized infants are damned to eternal punishment because of original sin, isn't God unjust? Anselm's definition of original sin as a sin of nature served as his defense of God's justice:

> Although in the eyes of men, infants who died before baptism had committed no sin and should not be condemned, God judged differently and condemned them justly, "not for Adam's sin but for their own."[9]

For Anselm, as for the earlier thinkers, interest in original sin was motivated by soteriological and ecclesial concerns. He derived the purposes of both Christ's redemption and the church from original sin. At issue in both concerns were questions of universality and necessity. Because all humankind shares this sin of nature, Anselm argued, Christ's forgiveness mediated through the church's sacrament of baptism is necessary for salvation. Redemptive grace meets both the moral and transcendent problem introduced by the loss of original justice. Christ's redemption restores to human beings the ability to will and perform the good that God desires and to achieve the divine end for which they were created.

Thomas Aquinas

A century and one-half later, *Thomas Aquinas* (d. 1274), the best-known of the medieval schoolmen, brought together into one synthesis the Augustinian and Anselmian conceptions of original sin.[10] Like Anselm, whose theological themes reveal the contours of the feudal social world around him, Thomas, too, was inspired by factors beyond Christian scripture and spirituality. For him the primary influence was the work of Aristotle, the ancient Greek philosopher, most of whose writings had been lost to Western culture for many centuries and had only recently been reintroduced.

While Anselm was likely unaware of the influence of feudalism on his theological speculation, Thomas deliberately employed Aristotle's metaphysics, logic, and ethics to shape a coherent systematic framework for Christian belief. Aristotle's understanding of nature, for example, was helpful for clarifying the theological distinction between the natural order and the supernatural order.[11]

Thomas's best-known work is the *Summa Theologiae.* The heart of its conceptual framework is *exitus et reditus:* humankind comes from and returns to God. In this extended work and others, Thomas constructed an order for Christian doctrines individually and in their relation to one another. His theoretical appropriation of the meaning of Christian beliefs moved beyond the expression and perspective of the biblical and early Christian theological tradition. A contrast with Augustine suggests a feature of this development.

Augustine introduced technical terms such as *operative* and *cooperative grace* into Christian reflection, but his theological expression often shared the predominantly metaphorical character of the biblical tradition. He describes the problem of sin, for example, as the enslavement of the human will to evil ways. The will is impotent to do the good. The fall stands at the center of Augustine's explanation of why human beings are morally impotent and from what they are freed by Christ's redemption. Grace delivers human beings from bondage to the power of sin, enabling human beings not only to will the good but to carry it out as well.

For Thomas, a metaphysical theological anthropology and theology of grace serve as an explanatory foundation for reflection on both sin and redemption. At the center of his theology is not the fall but the supernatural destiny of human nature.[12] Sin is an ontological problem—a problem of nature—rather than exclusively a moral problem. Because the transcendent goal intended for human nature is disproportionate to the ends that its natural capacities can achieve, humankind is in need of divine aid—assistance Adam's nature originally possessed—over and beyond its own powers.[13] Thomas transposed the metaphorical language of the power of sin and the Spirit and the beginning of a theoretical appropriation of grace found in Augustine into a metaphysical conception of divine grace as the means for finite nature to reach its supernatural end.[14]

Finite ends are proportionate to finite nature, for example, self-preservation, marriage, community, and the desire to know God. With the exception of the latter, natural means have been created to fulfill each of these natural ends. But the natural desire to know God cannot be fulfilled by natural means, because the fulfillment of the desire—knowing God, being with God, union with God—is a transcendent end.[15] Moreover, human reason cannot independently discover the truth that human existence is only fulfilled by union with God. This truth must be disclosed to reason. That God alone constitutes human happiness is revealed through Jesus Christ. The church mediates revealed truths of salvation and offers the means by which salvation is achieved.

Thomas's theological anthropology distinguished between natural and supernatural principles of operation. The virtues are natural principles of moral agency. They are habits of acting in the right way. Proportionate to the ends of the natural order, virtues are disproportionate to the supernatural end to which human nature is ultimately oriented. For this transcendent end, grace reorients the person to God by a new set of supernatural habits and acts, new powers for moral and religious agency. The supernatural principles of operation are the theological virtues of faith, hope, and love.[16] Thomas's theology of grace is a metaphysical theology of religious conversion.

The powers of faith and hope transform the potentiality of human reason. Wounded by sin, human reason is blind to the truth. Faith and hope reorient reason to its proper goal: God. They provide knowledge of God and of all things relevant to salvation. The supernatural principle of charity transforms the potentiality of the human will. It restores what was lost by Adam's sin: the capacity of the moral will to do the good because it is good. Through these supernatural gifts, human beings are empowered to observe the moral law and to love God above all things.

Quentin Quesnell writes that for Thomas, grace "is a new habitual orientation of the whole person toward God as personal goal and life."[17]

Thomas understood the purpose of the incarnation in this light. The Incarnate Word of Christ bestows grace in order that human beings attain the supernatural destiny ordained for them. The church is the Mystical Body, with Christ its head and Christ's followers the body. With the tradition, Thomas believed that baptism forgives and removes original sin. But in medieval reflection the eucharist had taken on a more central place than baptism in an understanding of the redemptive role of the church.[18] The sharing of Christ's body and blood in the eucharist unites the body with its head.

While the fall was not central to Thomas's concerns, it remained a matter of speculation. Thomas took the basic contours of the theological tradition as his starting point. Following Anselm, Thomas held that the divine gift of *justitia* established the state of original innocence enjoyed by Adam prior to his sin. Original justice had kept Adam from disharmony in his soul as well as from suffering and death.[19] These—concupiscence, suffering, death—are now part of the natural order as penalties humankind endures for Adam's sin.

For Anselm, *justitia* referred specifically to the supernatural capacity of the human will for moral integrity. By this gift Adam was able to will—and, more important, to do—the good. Thomas elaborated the meaning of original justice in his theological anthropology.

For Thomas, original justice established internal harmony in human nature by holding "all the soul's parts together in one."[20] The right order in nature is a threefold subjection: (1) the subjection of human reason to God, (2) the subjection of the moral will to reason, and (3) the subjection of the powers of the body to the powers of the soul (will and reason). Prior to sin, Adam's nature was characterized by this threefold subjection.

Thomas adopted Anselm's ontological and negative concept of original sin. Original sin is the loss of original justice.[21] This loss renders the soul unable to achieve the threefold subjection required for internal harmony. Because of sin, God had removed the gift of *justitia* from the soul, leaving nature to itself. Now absent was the condition necessary for moral integrity.

In his anthropology, Thomas designates pre- and post-sin states by the terms integral and fallen nature. Integral nature is human nature before the fall, exemplified by internal harmony and order. Fallen nature is nature after the fall, beset by disharmony and disorder. Without the threefold subjection *justitia* establishes, human beings cannot sustain their orientation to God.[22] The fall inflicts the wounds of ignorance, malice in the will, and disordered inclinations on human nature. These wounds replace knowledge, moral integrity, and the conformity of body and will with reason.[23]

Thomas further elaborated Anselm's notion of original justice by specifically identifying its cause, sanctifying grace.[24] Thomas conceived of the *gift* and its *cause* as distinct realities. Formally, original sin is the loss of *original justice,* not the loss of *divine presence*—what is meant by sanctifying grace—to the human soul. For Thomas, Brian Nolan notes, "only a graced human nature, free and prone to sin, has ever existed."[25] Subsequent to Thomas, however, Catholic teaching collapsed the distinction between gift and cause.[26] Original sin was described as the privation of *sanctifying grace,* not the *privation of justitia.* Due to Adam's sin, the manuals held, human beings are born without sanctifying grace.

That the theological tradition began the fusion of what were two distinct realities for Thomas is evident in one example of resistance against it. "The definition of original sin as the absence of sanctifying grace is first mentioned by William of Auvergne (d. 1249), who rejects it as erroneous."[27] But from the time of the Council of Trent and the further influence of the Catholic Reformation theologian Robert Bellarmine (d. 1621), Catholic teaching explained original sin as the loss and the continued privation of sanctifying grace.[28]

The Aristotelian categories of formal, material, agential, and instrumental cause enabled Thomas to bring together Augustine's and Anselm's very different ways of understanding original sin.[29]

The *formal cause* of original sin, Thomas argued, was the privation of original justice. He took Anselm's conception of original sin as his primary meaning, namely, that original sin is the absence of that which establishes moral integrity in the will and provides the condition for friendship with God.

Thomas characterized concupiscence as the *material cause* of original sin as a sinful state.[30] As a sin of nature *(peccatum naturae),* original sin exists in human beings as a corrupt habit, a disordered disposition or inclination toward evil.[31] This corrupt habit should not be present, according to the original intention of God.[32] Baptism forgives this sin of nature, but it does not eliminate concupiscence as the inclination toward wrongdoing.

Thomas located the *agential cause* of original sin in the human heart. Adam opposed God's command freely and voluntarily. In like manner, Adam's descendents voluntarily do what is wrong. In his theology of original sin, Thomas left unaddressed the paradox that Adam could or would sin when the gift of original justice oriented his nature wholly toward God. He raised the question in the context of his metaphysics of evil, specifically in his discussion of free will as the cause of evil.[33] When human beings fail to attend to reason and divine law as the rule and measure to which their actions should conform, there is a "free defect" in the will, a privation or failure in being. The moral evil is in the action, but its root is in the voluntary failure of free will to conform to reason and divine law. There is no further prior cause to be sought for moral evil other than freedom. This is sin, and in the end it is inexplicable.

Finally, Thomas identified the *instrumental cause* of original sin as the transmission of Adam's sin through physical generation or sexual intercourse.[34] What is received as human nature through birth is not *integral nature* but *fallen nature.* Fallen nature has been deprived of what was essential for moral integrity, the supernatural gift of original justice. Each of Adam's descendents receives a nature wounded by what Adam lost.

Thomas's understanding of redemption followed from the foundation laid by original sin. Continuing an established theological tradition, Thomas assumed the metaphysical unity of humankind with Adam. Adam and his descendents were as one person, *unus homo,* with Adam the head and humankind the body.[35] But Adam had lost what divine creation intended as the *means* for reaching the supernatural end destined for humankind. It was this loss that redemption remedied. Christ's redemption both elevated and healed human nature. Redemption elevated nature by infusing the supernatural means for attaining union with God. It healed a nature disordered by sin by enabling it to do what it could not do on its own.

No further distinctive changes to the doctrine of original sin were made by medieval Catholic theologians. In the sixteenth century, the reformer Martin Luther recovered Augustine's existential grasp of the problem of original sin and discarded Anselm's metaphysical conception. With only slight modifications, the Council of Trent (1563) affirmed Thomas's synthesis of the Augustinian and Anselmian under-standings of original sin and defined original sin as a dogma of the Catholic Church.

Martin Luther and the Council of Trent

The fifth-century councils of Carthage and Orange adopted Augustine's theology of original sin as a means of defending their theological positions against those of others. But it was not until the sixteenth-century Council of Trent that the Roman Catholic Church formally defined original sin as a dogma of the Roman Catholic Church.[36] In its original Greek context, *dogma* means "what seems right." The designation of a belief as a dogma in the Christian tradition served a twofold function. It first marked a truth affirmed by the church as grounded in divine revelation. Second, it denoted a belief necessary for salvation that must be accepted by believers.

The Council of Trent, named for its location in the northern Italian city of Trent, met in sessions called by Pope Paul III from 1545 to 1563. By 1545, when Trent undertook its deliberations, the conflict with Martin Luther was already two decades old. The 1520 papal bull *Exsurge Domine* had censured Luther's works. The 1521 pronouncement of *Decet Romanum Pontificem* effected his excommunication. In 1546, only a year after Trent began, Luther himself died. By this time, the opportunities and expectations for reuniting Catholics and Protestants had disappeared. Reformers refused to attend the council. With the split in medieval Christendom irreparable, Catholics understood their task at Trent to be one of internal reform and clarification of Catholic dogma.

Of primary concern to those at Trent were matters of doctrine raised by the Reformers. In particular, Martin Luther's assertion of justification by faith alone required an explicit theological response from Catholics.[37] Trent's consideration of original sin was a preliminary to its counter to Luther's position on justification and laid the groundwork for it.[38] How are justification and original sin related? We turn first to Luther's perspective.

1. Luther's Existential Perspective
Martin Luther's (d. 1546) appeal to justification by faith alone was not simply rhetorical. Nor did Catholics hear it as such. Deriving the

language from Paul, this idea of justification reflected Luther's personal experience of religious conversion. It also functioned as a theological axiom, signaling for Luther a different ecclesiology and a new principle of salvation. Luther's assertion that persons are justified by their faith alone challenged the church's longstanding position that the church sets the relation between God and human beings right again through its sacramental mediation of divine grace. Catholic opponents did not deny a relation between conversion and justification, nor did they dispute obvious scriptural sources from which Luther derived his principle, but they did balk at the radical religious independence Luther's theological axiom promoted.[39]

Luther also caused a stir by criticizing the Catholic theologies of original sin and justification as Pelagian.[40] This was a damning charge, given that Pelagian had been used interchangeably with heretical for a thousand years. Luther's understanding of original sin broke from the dominant scholastic paradigm of his day. The theological tradition had long distinguished between two realities—original sin and concupiscence. Luther collapsed these into one.[41] Going further even than Augustine, Luther asserted that concupiscence is a real sin *(peccatum, culpa)* after baptism. This had never been the position of the church. The tradition had been consistent that all sins are forgiven in baptism. Concupiscence was an *effect* and *punishment* of original sin, not sin itself.[42]

Luther's position that believers remain real sinners after baptism followed directly from his theology of justification. He argued that sinners were justified by God not because they are without sin, but only because God *considers* them just. This is the meaning of Luther's famous and paradoxical formulation, *simul justus et peccator:* at once just and sinner.[43]

Luther's theology was shaped by years of teaching the New Testament letters of Paul. Paul's metaphorical language of the power and bondage of human beings to sin and the transformative power of the Spirit spoke to Luther's own interior experience. Gradually Luther found the metaphysical description of sin and grace vacuous. Starting from God as Creator, he thought of sin in relational terms. Robert Kolb writes that Luther depicts the root of sin in his *Small Catechism* as a "failing to fear, love and trust God above all things..., a broken relationship with the creator of human life."[44] Kolb continues, "Inheriting sinfulness from Adam and Eve, sinners are born, according to Luther, with wills completely bound to oppose God and to flee from him." In contrast to a theology of original sin removed from personal experience, Luther's was existential. For Luther, Alfred Vanneste writes:

> The doctrine of original sin is not an abstract theologoumenon, an object of school disputes, but rather, the expression of an essential moment of his deepest religious experience. For Luther, original sin is the irresistible tendency toward evil which we experience in all our life even after being baptized.[45]

Luther's understanding of original sin drew from Augustine's explanation of sin as an evil inclination of the will. While he rejected the Anselmian definition of original sin as the loss of the supernatural gift of original justice, Luther did not abandon the notion of privation. He wrote that original sin "is a total lack of uprightness and of the power of all the faculties both of body and soul and of the whole inner and outer man."[46] But like Augustine's, original sin for Luther was a *something,* not an absence. Original sin, he writes:

> is a propensity toward evil. It is a nausea toward the good, a loathing of light and wisdom, and a delight in error and darkness, a flight from and an abomination of all good works, a pursuit of evil, as it is written in Ps. 14.3: "They are all gone astray, they are all alike corrupt"; and Gen. 8.21: "For the imagination and thought of man's heart are evil from his youth."[47]

Original sin, Luther writes, is "the deep root sin which I possess."[48] By collapsing the distinction between cause (original sin) and effect (concupiscence), concupiscence *is* original sin.[49] In Luther's judgment, the inner experience of disharmony, disorder, self-contradiction, and moral impotence the early church writers named "concupiscence" is the root sin—in the sense of *original*—with which human beings are always afflicted. The chief manifestation of this root sin, in his view, was the last of the prohibitions of the ten commandments, coveting. Original sin is "this universal concupiscence by which we become disobedient to the commandment 'You shall not covet' (Ex. 20:17; Deut. 5:21)."[50] Original sin for Luther, Alfred Vanneste writes, is "the radical and fundamental self-centeredness which characterizes all our actions even if externally they conform with current morality."[51]

Luther's theological anthropology of *simul justus et peccator* remains decisive for Protestant theologians to this century. In his

Church Dogmatics, the twentieth-century Protestant theologian Karl Barth refers to the *person of sin.* By this, Barth means that sin is not a something removable from the person but is the person. George Van-dervelde writes that "in line with certain elements of Augustine's doctrine of original sin the mainstream of contemporary Protestant theology distilled from the traditional doctrine the notion that in his deepest being man stands in conflict with God."[52]

2. Trent's Definition

Given the theological orientation of Martin Luther's teaching, one of the Council of Trent's central tasks was the reassertion of an ecclesial theology of justification that would emphasize the necessity of participation in the church's sacramental life for salvation. Given Luther's indictment of Pelagianism in scholastic theologies of sin and grace, it was imperative, too, that Trent formulate its doctrines of original sin and justification in a clearly anti-Pelagian manner.

The Council of Trent's foundation for its original sin decree was the synthesis fashioned by Thomas Aquinas. Thomas brought the Augustinian and Anselmian theologies of original sin together through the use of Aristotelian categories. The *material* element of original sin is the bias toward evil (Augustine), and the *formal* element of original sin is the privation of original justice (Anselm).[53] In an Aristotelian philosophical analysis, the formal element answers the question "What is it?" By appropriating the Thomist explanation, Trent gave dogmatic status to a metaphysical conception of the answer to the question "What is original sin?"

By locating original sin in what human nature lacks for salvation and by what must be restored for eternal life, Trent also defined original sin in sacramental and ecclesial terms. This was a deliberate counter to Luther's theological principle of justification by faith alone. Inasmuch as Adam's actual sin is transmitted to each human being through propagation,[54] each human being is born with a sin that can be taken away only through the mediation of Christ's grace by the church's sacraments.[55] The introduction to the 1546 *Decree on Original Sin* emphasizes this ecclesial dimension of redemption: "Our Catholic faith, 'without which it is impossible to please God' (*cf.* Heb. 11.6)" marks the necessity of the church for salvation. By linking original sin, redemption, and the sacramental mediation of grace, Trent reinforced the ecclesiology articulated by Origen in the third century: "Outside the church there is no salvation."[56] The Christian exclusivism that characterized the patristic and medieval doctrine of the church—rooted in the doctrine of original sin—remained dominant in the Catholic Church until Vatican II.[57]

Trent appropriated the tradition's exegesis of Genesis 3 and Romans 5:12–21 to ground human solidarity with Adam in divine revelation. While questions about the historicity of Adam and Eve would not arise for several centuries after the Council of Trent, concerns had risen already regarding the theological use of Romans 5:12 in the doctrine of original sin.

The sixteenth-century Catholic theologian, scholar, and exegete *Desiderius Erasmus of Rotterdam* (d. 1536) questioned using Romans as a proof-text for original sin. Among his many scholarly works, Erasmus produced a New Testament edition in 1516, translating the Greek into Latin himself. In a critical study of the Greek, Erasmus demonstrated the exegetical untenability of the Vulgate translation of Romans 5:12, which provided the critical phrase "in whom all sinned." In the tradition, this text was taken by some to mean that humankind was—in some way—in Adam as one. When Adam sinned, all sinned with him. Neither Adam's sin nor his guilt was his alone.[58]

Erasmus demonstrated that the Greek was better translated "that sin came into the world, and through sin death, *because all have sinned*."[59] While those at Trent knew of Erasmus's work, they retained the common interpretation since Ambrosiaster, citing the text twice in the Decree on Original Sin.[60] The primary function of the text as a revelatory principle of explanation for original sin remained undisputed.[61]

In its Decree on Original Sin, the Council of Trent addressed the questions of the essence of original sin, its effects, transmission, and remedy.

With regard to the *essence* of original sin, Trent affirmed that Adam's transgression of the divine command was a true sin in him and for each of his descendents.[62] Trent defined original sin as the privation of original justice and sanctifying grace. By his sin, Adam lost holiness (*sanctitatem,* sanctifying grace) and original justice *(justitiam),* with which he had been created.[63]

Trent identified three *effects* of original sin resulting from the loss of supernatural gifts: concupiscence, suffering, and death. By the privation of original justice, the powers of Adam's body and soul had been changed for the worse.[64] While changed, the powers of the soul (reason and will) are not totally corrupted. Trent specifically rejected Luther's collapse of original sin into concupiscence. Concupiscence is described as from original sin and that which inclines persons toward sin, but not sin itself.[65]

On the *transmission* of original sin, Trent adopted the view influenced by Augustine. Original sin is transmitted through sexual intercourse.[66] All human beings inherit the actual sin itself as well as the effects or penalties for Adam's sin (concupiscence, suffering, death). Inasmuch as sin requires forgiveness, and original sin is transmitted as a true sin in each, original sin requires divine forgiveness.[67] Trent's assertion that original sin spreads by inheritance directly refuted the view that it spreads by imitation of Adam's example.[68]

Against unidentified protagonists, Trent rejected the view that children of baptized parents do not require baptism. Presumably those whom Trent countered had speculated that if Christian baptism removed original sin in parents, they would have no sin to transmit through sexual intercourse.[69]

Lastly, the *remedy* for original sin: Trent argued that the possession of the gift of original justice established the relation of friendship between Adam and God. Adam's loss of original justice through sin destroyed this relation, putting both himself and his descendents under the power of the devil.[70] The remedy for restoring this relation of friendship is mediated through Christ.[71] Infants are born without holiness (sanctifying grace) and original justice. The sanctifying grace necessary for eternal life is restored sacramentally through baptism.[72] If infants die without baptism, they are unable to enter the kingdom of God.[73] Freed of original sin, baptized persons are new persons, recreated in the image of God, with nothing holding them back from eternal life.[74] For the universality of Christ's redemption, Trent appealed to Acts 4:12: "There is salvation in no one else, for there is no other name under heaven given among mortals by which we must be saved."[75]

Protestant and Catholic Perspectives

With Martin Luther and the Council of Trent, the Reform and Catholic traditions reflect two Christian interpretations of original sin. They diverge in their theological anthropologies as well as accounts of justification, grace, and the church. Posing four answers to four questions suggests the lines of their differences.

1. Wounded or Corrupted?

Is human nature wounded by original sin or corrupted by it? With the medieval theologians, Trent described human nature as wounded by original sin. While original sin had changed the powers of the body and the soul for the worse, it had not destroyed them completely.

To distinguish between human nature before and after sin, medieval theologians utilized the categories of natural and supernatural orders.[76] Human nature is constituted by the capacities or powers proper to it. Adam's original state, however, the state of original righteousness, was constituted by the possession of supernatural gifts. These gifts established a twofold harmony, that resulting from the subjection of the human mind to God, and that resulting from the subjection of the physical body to the rational mind. These subjections sustained Adam's relation of friendship with God. But while the possession of supernatural gifts perfected human nature, they were not essential to nature.

On this basis, medieval theologians distinguished original righteousness from the image of God. The scriptural text that had generated the initial differentiation was Genesis 1:26. Two terms appear in the text: "Then God said, 'Let us make humankind in our *image,* according to our *likeness...*'" (emphasis added). The scholastics maintained that by Adam's sin and the loss of the gift of original justice, the supernatural state of original righteousness—likeness to God—was lost. But Adam's sin did not lose in human nature the image of God. The image of God belongs to nature. After sin, without original justice, and with the end of the state of original righteousness, the image of God remains in human nature as proper to it.

Luther opposed this theological anthropology. He took the metaphysical distinction between natural and supernatural to mean, in effect, that Adam's sin lost something inessential to human nature. He maintained that original sin deprived human nature of something essential to it. Adam's sin had corrupted human nature.

Luther rejected both the metaphysical distinction between natural and supernatural orders as well as Thomas's philosophical distinction between the formal and material elements of original sin. In his view, the two terms of Genesis 1:26, *likeness to God* and *image of God,* referred to the same state—the state of original righteousness. Adam's likeness to God was a state of holiness, an internal harmony of desire, reason, and will empowering Adam to obey God's will. Adam's sin destroyed this. Because Luther equated *likeness* and *image,* he then concluded that original sin had thus destroyed in Adam and his descendents the image of God. Nothing in human nature was left untouched by sin. Human nature is depraved.

Not all Reformers agreed with Luther. John Calvin believed that even with the corruption of nature brought by original sin, human beings possessed the image of God.

Other Reformers, however, shared Luther's judgment that the Catholic explanation of original sin as the absence of grace was not radical enough. This definition appeared to make original sin incidental to human nature. With Luther they argued that human nature was corrupted by original sin. Everything in human nature was infected by sin. There remains no natural goodness untouched by sin, as Luther thought the Catholic position implied. Stephen Duffy writes that "to define sin merely as the absence of grace did not, to the Reformers, do justice to the awesome dark power of the proclivity to evil that bedeviled human nature."[77]

Luther criticized Catholics for retaining too much confidence in human nature. This was his Pelagian indictment. In return, Catholics rejected Luther's portrayal of depraved human nature as too pessimistic. While they did not want to assert that human beings could avoid sin, Catholics also did not want sin to appear inevitable. Each side's theological anthropology implied an ethical stance about the possibilities—or lack thereof—inherent in human nature. For his part, Luther took Augustine at face value. Unless aided by grace, human beings cannot do the good.[78]

2. Different From or the Same as Concupiscence?

Is original sin different from or the same reality as concupiscence? Trent's separation of original sin from concupiscence drew from the Aristotelian distinctions introduced by Thomas and his synthesis of the Augustinian and Anselmian conceptions of original sin.

For Thomas, *formally* original sin is the privation of the supernatural gift of original justice. *Materially,* original sin is the disorder of concupiscence. The latter is the consequence of Adam's sin, its punishment. Through the forgiveness of baptism, the sin of nature (original sin) is removed but its punishment (concupiscence) remains. Concupiscence is from original sin and leads to personal sin, but is itself not sin.[79]

Trent and Luther understood concupiscence in similar ways—an evil internal disposition, a perverse tendency toward sinful cravings, the propensity toward evil, a fundamental self-centeredness. Catholics portrayed the separation of original sin and concupiscence as distinct realities as the indisputable teaching of the tradition. But the relation between them had long been a speculative question in theology. Luther's view reflected one pole of a longstanding divergence among theologians on the matter. Following Augustine and *Peter Lombard* (d. 1160), Luther identified concupiscence with original sin itself. To put it in the Aristotelian framework of medieval theology, Luther met the question *"What* is original sin?" with the answer, "Concupiscence." He held that *formally* original sin is concupiscence.

In fact, Augustine had differentiated between original sin and concupiscence. Yet his portrayal of one may be easily mistaken for the other. The difference between them often appears indistinguishable. For example, Augustine described *concupiscence* as the disordered desire that turns one away from God and *original sin* as an active culpable inclination of the will against God *(amor sui, cupiditas)*. The nuance of meaning differentiating the two realities is subtle, to say the least.

Anselm of Canterbury clearly separated original sin from concupiscence. But Peter Lombard, an influential medieval theologian, equated them, claiming Augustine as his authority. The widespread use of Peter's *Sentences (Libri quatuor Sententiarum,* 1155) as the leading manual in theological schools from the twelfth through the sixteenth centuries prompted the identification of original sin and concupiscence by many. The tradition Martin Luther claimed for his view on this question was a dominant strain in medieval thinking.

Adopting Peter Lombard's Augustinianism, Luther granted that baptism took away the guilt for original sin. But he insisted that original sin remains as sin in the baptized.[80] The disordered desire that persists after baptism is real sin, original sin.[81]

Luther's preference for Augustine and Lombard was due, in part, to his rejection of the metaphysical categories of the scholastic theologians. He spurned the explanation of original sin as the privation of a supernatural gift, thinking that the Catholic view implied that sin did not affect nature.[82]

3. Removed or Permanent?

Is original sin removed by baptism? Martin Luther and Catholics came down differently on the question of the relation between original sin and concupiscence. Their views governed how they each thought about the effect of baptism. One reason for their divergence was different conceptions of original sin as a problem.

Medieval theologians presented original sin not only as a *moral* problem, as Augustine had, but also an *ontological* one. The moral problem original sin creates is moral impotence. Fallen nature is unable to know and do the good on its own. The ontological problem is that fallen nature can no longer achieve the supernatural destiny for which it was created. Divine grace is the remedy for both problems. The grace mediated through the sacramental life of the church restores to believers the power to live a good life (the moral problem) and to reach the supernatural end for which they are drawn by God through faith (the ontological problem).

In Luther's judgment, baptism removes only the guilt for original sin but not the sin. As he writes in his *Lectures on Romans,* "This concupiscence toward evil remains, and no one is ever cleansed of it, not even the one-day-old infant. But the mercy of God is that this does remain and yet is not imputed as sin to those who call upon Him and cry out for His deliverance."[83] Luther argued that the problem of original sin is a radical self-centeredness unremovable from human nature by baptism because it is fundamental dimension of human being. Luther's theological axiom, *simul justus et peccator,* captures the paradoxical nature of God's relation to humankind. Though persons are sinners, and remain sinners, their relation to God is set right—*justified*—through their faith in Christ. Human nature remains corrupted, however, by an irresistible tendency toward evil.

For Luther, original sin is not first a moral or an ontological problem but a *religious* problem. The paradigmatic sin he saw in Adam's disobedience was the lack of faith. When Luther employed the notion of privation, he did not mean, as the scholastics did, the absence of a supernatural power or habit, but the absence of faith in God. Faith in Christ and original sin are shorthand for two ways of being. "Faith in Christ" objectifies the existential stance of *belief.* "Original sin" objectifies the existential stance of *unbelief.* Each person stands in conflict with God—sin—until belief replaces unbelief. Where Trent presented justification in sacramental and ecclesial terms, Luther saw justification occurring in and through the persons of faith becoming aware, and remaining aware, of their own sinfulness.[84]

Trent was acutely aware that Luther's insistence on justification by faith alone bypassed the Roman Catholic Church's sacramental mediation of divine grace. Its treatises on original sin and justification uphold the necessity of the institutional church for salvation. The reference was obvious: No other entity or means could mediate the salvation and eternal life desired by all. This conclusion, however, the Reformers had already rejected.

4. Is Adam Essential?

Is an historical Adam essential to the theological meaning of original sin? The historicity of Adam, Eve, paradise, and the fall was not a question for Trent or the Reformers. Both sides assumed the historicity of the first parents. Yet the Genesis story was more crucial to the Catholic interpretation of original sin than it was for Luther. One reason lies in their different apprehensions of original sin as a problem.

Trent's apprehension of the problem was both moral (a propensity in the will toward sin) and ontological (a privation in nature of original justice). The inheritance of original sin as a sin of nature depended specifically on the postulate of an historical sin that was transmitted through sexual intercourse.

Luther did not reject the historicity of Adam. Nor did he deny the solidarity of humankind in sin with an historical Adam. He retained the patristic image of the inclusion of all human beings in Adam and the idea that all sinned when Adam sinned.[85] But, more significant for Luther, original sin was the existential and religious problem of *unbelief* that puts each person in conflict with God. As we have seen, Karl Barth put this viewpoint plainly: The person is sin. Given this apprehension of the reality, Luther's theology of original sin depended less on the historical Adam and an inherited sin than did the Roman Catholic doctrine.

While this point of difference was something to which the sixteenth-century opponents did not advert, it gradually became significant. When the Christian doctrine was assailed by modern theories about human origins and the literary character of the Bible, the Protestant existential interpretation of original sin was less affected than the Catholic historical interpretation. In the modern period, the Roman Catholic teaching office has struggled to preserve the legitimacy of doctrine against increasing doubt in the historical reliability of the biblical narratives upon which the church made its foundational claims.

Conclusion

One mark of the Council of Trent's significance is the fact that another general council would not be convened for 300 years.[86] In part, Trent's subsequent influence was due to a widely used catechism commissioned by the council. For the Roman Catholic tradition, Trent is the source of the definitive conciliar statement on original sin. As a rebuttal to Martin Luther, Trent emphasized the necessity of the ecclesial mediation of grace.

A subtle shift occurs in the way theologians derive the meaning of original sin in post-Tridentine explanations of original sin. Anselm and Thomas, pre-Trent theologians, derived the meaning of original sin by starting from the *past* and Adam's loss of the supernatural gift of original justice. Post-Tridentine theologians started from the *present*—from what baptism *gives*—to derive the meaning of original sin as the privation of sanctifying grace.[87] While the difference may appear inconsequential, the shift in the basis from which the definition of original sin is derived clouded Thomas's distinction between gift of original justice and its cause, sanctifying grace.

For both Protestants and Catholics, the assumption of original sin shaped a concept of redemption. Trent's perspective was ecclesial. The council secured the relation between original sin and Christ's redemption: All human beings need the church because they require Christ's forgiveness of Adam's sin. Martin Luther secured this relation christologically: All human beings need belief in Christ to overcome the problem of original sin as unbelief.

For whatever differences existed between Protestant and Catholic conceptions of original sin, the idea of original sin was taken for granted until the modern age. Modernity posed a fundamental challenge to the foundation of original sin as an historical reality. A first line of defense sought to prohibit the question itself. In a 1955 teaching manual, *Fundamentals of Catholic Dogma*, Ludwig Ott argued that "since

Adam's sin is the basis of the dogma of Original Sin and Redemption the historical accuracy of the [Genesis] account as regards the essential facts may not be impugned."[88] Sustaining this position, however, proved more difficult than Ott's confident statement suggests. We turn now to modernity and the challenges a new worldview posed for the doctrine of original sin.

PART II

MODERN AND CONTEMPORARY MEANINGS

5. MODERNITY

THE PROTESTANT REFORMATION and the Council of Trent are part of a momentous cultural transition from the medieval to the modern world.[1] They occur between the Renaissance, as the renewal from the thirteenth to sixteenth centuries is called, and the Enlightenment, the designation given to the seventeenth and eighteenth centuries. These later centuries inaugurated resistance to the cultural dominance of the Christian church and its beliefs. Questions put to the doctrine of original sin had to do, in part, with newly founded doubt about the church's reliability for knowledge of the past.

Two Different Worlds

The world of the Reformers and Trent was still medieval. The culture was ecclesial and Christian; it shaped the church and religious beliefs. Medieval scholarship and science assumed the Bible as an authoritative source for knowledge of the past and for the disclosure of the meaning and destiny of human existence. Theological inquiry, still the queen of the sciences, was guided by the church's past doctrinal decrees and the writings of its most influential theologians. Among those theologians, Thomas Aquinas had given medieval Christendom a rational and coherent worldview by appropriating the intellectual tools—logic, ethics, metaphysics—of the Greek philosopher Aristotle.

The medieval intellectual perspective was *theocentric*—God-centered. In culture dominated by religion, all inquiry is oriented toward the divine. Renaissance and Enlightenment artists, philosophers, scientists, and scholars reconfigured medieval theocentricism into an *anthropocentric*—human-centered—perspective. The secularism of modern culture severed human inquiry from ecclesial domination and diminished the contribution of theology to human knowledge.[2]

Modern empirical sciences and historical disciplines eschewed biblical revelation as a source of knowledge of the natural world. In contrast to revelation, modern thinkers celebrated human reason as the exclusive source of knowledge. The object of scientific inquiry, they argued, was not God but empirical data. Truth was a matter of verifiable hypothesis, not a gift of revelation. Those who did treat religion did so philosophically and without the burden of appeal to the church's theological or doctrinal tradition. The German philosopher Immanuel Kant exemplified this approach in his *Religion within the Limits of Reason Alone* (1793).

The critical and rational spirit of modern thinkers increasingly sought knowledge independently of religious tradition, authority, and dogma. Great scientists—Nicholas Copernicus (d. 1543), Johann Kepler (d. 1630), Galileo Galilei (d. 1642), and Isaac Newton (d. 1727)—personified the achievement of reason in their advancements in mathematics, physics, and astronomy. Cumulatively, modernity produced alternatives to a long-assumed Christian cosmology, history, and articulation of the meaning and purpose of human existence.[3]

For Christianity—perhaps religion in general—the transition from the medieval to the modern age was painful. A hostile critique of religion often accompanied the separation of the natural sciences, scholarship, and philosophy from religious assumptions. Even more damaging than direct hostility was the quiet dismissal of Christianity. The French philosopher, Françoise Voltaire (d. 1778), opined that Christian beliefs were a good thing for chambermaids and tailors, but for the elite he advocated a simple deism.

The Critical Spirit

Renaissance humanists ushered in new critical methods for literary interpretation. Interest in classical antiquity, for example, motivated the development of textual criticism. By comparing multiple manuscripts, textual critics sought to reconstruct the original form of a text. Desiderius Erasmus, the Dutch humanist and priest, produced critical editions of Greek and Roman classics and the Fathers of the Church, in addition to translating the Greek New Testament into Latin (1516).

Humanist scholars also developed historical-critical methods for the analysis of biblical and other literary texts. The scholarly understanding of texts dramatically expanded by raising and answering questions about literary genre, historical setting, author, audience, and narrative purpose.[4] These new insights were not without consequence, however. In some cases, a new understanding of a biblical text conflicted with the church's use of it in the tradition as a basis for doctrinal affirmations. Original sin will be a primary case.

The Reformers' principle of *sola scriptura* contributed to the weakening of the institutional church's dominance over scriptural interpretation. Against the long-held ecclesial position that biblical interpretation was the church's exclusive prerogative, Martin Luther argued that scripture was its own interpreter and authority. He rejected the Roman Catholic contention that the Holy Spirit worked through the *magisterium,* the church's teaching authority. On the contrary, Luther proposed, the Holy Spirit works through the *reader's* discovery of the text's literal sense—its meaning. For this purpose, Luther brought biblical scholarship into the heart of religious life and theological reflection. As Edgar Krentz writes, "Luther used all the means that the humanists had developed to discover this literal sense: Hebrew and Greek philology, the Erasmus Greek New Testament, and the historical background of a book."[5]

Still, Luther was medieval. For him, too, the Bible remained an *historical* source. It established certitude about the origins of the universe and human beings as well as that of sin. From it could be culled an historical chronology from the first human beings to Jesus and a chronicle of salvific events.[6] While medievals granted many difficulties with biblical texts, they trusted the narratives revealed history through the events about which they told.

The assumption that the Bible was a reliable historical source was among the first to be dismissed by modern scholars. Edgar Krentz notes, "At the beginning of the seventeenth century the Bible was the universal authority in all fields of knowledge, but by the end of the century that authority was eroded."[7] The work of Isaac de la Peyrere (d. 1676), for example, questioned biblical chronology and proposed a theory of pre-Adamites. The nongeocentric physical universe discovered by Copernicus and Kepler stood at odds with the biblical conception of the world. Developments such as these contributed to a growing sense that the Bible was an unreliable source for knowledge of the natural and human worlds.

For modern historians, critical evaluation is a central task. In contrast to the medieval trust of biblical texts, the methods of objective history demand that documents meet certain conditions to be considered reliable historical sources. Is the text what it purports to be? Was it actually written as a letter, for example, or does the letter genre merely provide a useful form for the author? Can events narrated by a text be confirmed by external evidence? Is the text purporting to say "what happened"? Or is the text doing something other than history?

Evaluation of the usefulness of a text for historical knowledge involves a determination of its literary genre. If the genre is fiction, the historical truth of its statements is not at issue.[8] It is pointless, for example, to ask questions about Jonah's surviving being swallowed by a fish. The meaning of the story lies elsewhere.

Modernity's unrelenting questions about the historical reliability of the biblical stories of the origins of the universe and humans in Genesis 1–3 bore directly on the doctrine of original sin. The church presented Genesis 3 as a divinely revealed historical source for the origin of human sinfulness and, consequently, for the universal necessity of Christ's grace of forgiveness. The characterization by modern literary scholars of Genesis 1–3 as myth or as a kind of parable, as the seventeenth-century Dutch philosopher Baruch Spinoza described it, was initially scandalous.[9] As myth or parable, the text would no longer serve as historical knowledge of "what really happened." Like Jonah, its point lies elsewhere. Moreover, modern scrutiny of the expulsion story sometimes proposed a meaning quite at odds with the church's reading. The remarks of the nineteenth-century German philosopher Friedrich Nietzsche (d. 1900) offer an example. "At the beginning of the Old Testament we find the famous story of God's agony. Man is represented as God's error: work, necessity, and death are presented as God's 'legitimate defense' established to keep man in a debased state...."[10]

While the work of twentieth-century thinkers—the French philosopher Paul Ricoeur and others—deepened the appreciation of the symbolic power and cultural function of myth, the early modern characterization of Genesis 3 as a myth had already inflicted great damage on a doctrine that had long purported to be based on history as it happened.[11] In early uses of the term *myth,* still the case today in popular language, history and myth are posed as opposites. If Genesis 3 is myth, modern thinkers argued, then the doctrine of original sin cannot be true. Some modern interpreters—Jean-Jacques Rousseau, for example—gave original sin and the fall a new historical meaning. But others dismissed both ideas as relics of premodern thought.

As modern sciences and scholarship expanded knowledge of the physical and human worlds, acceptance of the Bible as an historical source for knowledge shrank. Dismissal of Genesis 1–3 as history invited, in turn, dismissal of the truth of the doctrine of original sin. If the doctrine's scriptural foundation was not historical, how could it explain the historical origin of sin? A more urgent question was implied. Without this historical and doctrinal foundation for universality of human sinfulness, on what was the necessity of Christ based? Or, to put it in the ecclesial framework already initiated by the Reformers, was the mediation of Christ's grace by the church necessary? Opened up for scrutiny and debate were the theological anthropology and historical worldview of the medieval scholastics assuming the historicity of Adam and Eve, an original state of perfection, the possession and loss of supernatural gifts, the first sin and its penalties, and the inheritance of a sin of nature by all humankind through physical procreation.

Anthropology, Knowledge, Perfection

Medieval Catholics and Reformers shared the judgment that original sin had changed human nature, either wounding the intellectual and moral capacities of human beings (Catholics) or corrupting human nature completely (Reformers). Modern secular thinkers challenged this conception of human nature and history. Some rejected the proposal that human nature had once been other than it is. Others rejected the view that human nature lacks something that it should have.

Modern theories of human nature often projected an optimism, opposing the Augustinian pessimism embedded in Christian theology. Human nature was viewed as good or, if not entirely good, then at least capable of great achievement. Some placed great hope in universal education, arguing that if they were enlightened, human beings could solve the problems besetting their existence. To the theocentric principle of the Christian tradition—*Grace perfects nature*—modernity substituted an anthropocentric one—*Reason perfects nature.*

Modernity parted ways with the medieval world on the nature of knowledge, too. Theologians had long appealed to reason and revelation as two distinct and complementary sources for human knowledge. Divine revelation of some truths was necessary because Adam's sin had distorted reason and limited its potential. For moderns, however, the only source for knowledge was human reason. Disciplined inquiry and empirical investigation, not revelation, produced truth. Objectivity was derived from verified hypotheses, not from correspondence of scientific or historical judgments with church doctrine.

The modern attitude toward revelation is captured by the well-known remark of the French astronomer and mathematician Pierre Simon Laplace. When asked by Napoleon what part God played in his celestial mechanics, Laplace reportedly said, "I have no need of such a hypothesis."[12]

Finally, medieval and modern thinkers differed in their images of human perfection. The doctrine of original sin located an original perfection in the distant past. While redemption did not recreate this nature, it did enable human beings to attain their transcendent destiny. For moderns, perfection was future. Their future was not transcendent but immanent—history itself as the arduous process of incremental advances in human intelligence and virtue. Or, as Karl Marx forcefully argued in the nineteenth century, perfection is achieved through a reordering of social relationships. The problem of sin does not disappear entirely for Marx. His idea of ideology or false consciousness transposes into secular terms the theological judgment that human reason is distorted by sin.

Modern Theories

The doctrine of original sin suffered the brunt of modern hostility to Christian belief. In it was everything that moderns resisted—a precritical historical worldview, an abstract anthropology, and a solution to the human problem controlled by the church's mediation.[13] Paradoxically, however, the extensive attention opponents gave to Genesis 1–3 in order to refute their reliability as history contributed to the rise of modern biblical scholarship and the development of critical biblical methods.

Criticism of original sin among secular thinkers created an unexpected kind of community. Their rejection of the Christian doctrine did not mean they ignored it. Speculation was widespread. The twentieth-century philosopher and historian Ernst Cassirer noted that "the concept of original sin is the most common opponent against which the different orientations of Enlightenment philosophy unite."[14] Without the explanatory function of the doctrine, however, the question of evil was opened up. As Stephen J. Duffy writes, "The doctrine of original sin had been debated from the time of Augustine but with the Enlightenment it began to undergo total eclipse. Many ceased to view evil as a religious or theological problem."[15]

Blaise Pascal (d. 1662), the seventeenth-century French scientist and mathematician who late in life turned his attention to religious philosophy, was a central figure in the Enlightenment discussion of original sin.[16] In opposition to widespread rejection of the doctrine, Pascal made original sin the cornerstone of his Christian apologetic.[17] He understood original sin much as Augustine had done. But Pascal's method for affirming the reality of original sin was thoroughly modern, even as he turned the method on its head.

Pascal was influenced by René Descartes's ideal of the "clear and distinct idea." As a scientist, he took this principle to mean that the test of a hypothesis was whether it adequately accounted for the object or phenomenon under inquiry. Pascal argued that exact observation was just as important for theological reasoning as it was for scientific reasoning. In the case of original sin, the phenomenon to be observed is human nature. In humans, Pascal maintained, we observe a being who is not complete and harmonious but divided within and burdened with contradictions, capable of self-transcendence but also of degradation, a being both great and wretched. "Nature points everywhere—both within the human being and outside of him—toward a God who has been lost and a nature that has been corrupted," he wrote.[18]

The ideal of reason, Pascal held, was to explain observed phenomena. But the contradictory character of human nature defies explanation. Human nature becomes comprehensible only by virtue of the mystery underlying it. This mystery, Pascal argued, is original sin. Because human reason is powerless and incapable of arriving at knowledge of this mystery, it can be grasped only as a revealed truth, apprehended in the surrender of faith.

Pascal's interpretation of original sin offered a "middle way," honoring methodical reason and the ideals of scientific observation yet privileging divine revelation as the explanatory source for the mystery of human nature. But it is exactly at this point of revealed truth that modernity separated from its medieval and Christian roots. Modernity's cardinal trademark was its denial of divine revelation and its affirmation of methodical reason as the exclusive source for truth.

But denying revelation also shifted the burden of the explanation of evil to reason.[19] The doctrine of original sin functions as a theodicy, answering the question of God's relation to evil. By locating the origin of evil in human freedom, the Christian doctrine absolves God of blame for evil. Without the doctrine, how is evil to be explained? Without the doctrine's theocentric perspective, blame could shift from human beings to God. As Cassirer writes, "When evil cannot be attributed to an original sin, then God himself must carry the burden for permitting it to exist."[20]

Françoise Voltaire, the French philosopher of the eighteenth century (d. 1778), attempted to avoid blaming God while still bypassing the Christian doctrine. He rejected Pascal's account of original sin, but over the course of his life returned to it again and again. That Voltaire did so signals the difficulty of developing an explanatory understanding of human subjectivity and evil.

Voltaire argued that moral evil is inevitable to human nature. He turned Pascal's contradictories into evidence of human nature's strength, versatility, and creativity. Cassirer writes of Voltaire's view that "were it not for our weaknesses, life would be condemned to stagnation, since the strongest impulses of life arise from our appetites and passions, that is, ethically considered, from our shortcomings."[21] To allow for possibility of human creativity, God permits evil.

Friederich Schelling (d. 1854) developed a philosophical analysis of the narrative of the fall in his doctoral dissertation.[22] He argued that evil's origin must ultimately be sought in God. Evil is not a consequence of an original failure in human nature but rather that which constitutes it as human. In Promethean fashion, the fall was "before time," when the human being "became human" by virtue of its opposition to God. Peter Henrici writes that Schelling believed that it is "only by being able to oppose its own personal will to the Universal will, that is, by being able to be evil, does the human being distinguish itself from God."[23]

Modern difficulties with the doctrine of original sin came from all angles. The Christian portrayal of human nature as intrinsically corrupt or impaired conflicted with secular excitement and confidence in human reason and goodness. The idea of an inherited sin, a mixture of biological and religious categories already a theological problem, received fresh doubt. The doctrine struck some as burdening God with injustice and cruelty, as Christian Duquoc writes, appearing "outrageous that for an archaic fault, whose content is unknown, men are made guilty before God and hence punished by all kinds of evils—a curse on the soil, the disordering of desire, the alienation of woman, the burden and brutal character of labor, and death itself."[24]

Moderns were closer to the intellectual orientation of Pelagius than to that of Augustine. Like Pelagius, they felt the idea that human beings were born already guilty of sin was morally reprehensible. Their confidence in human goodness was matched by the conviction that persons are responsible for their own wrongdoing. Persons are guilty—sinners, in religious terms—for what they do wrong through their own moral agency and freedom, not for the violations of others. Moderns considered the doctrine of original sin unsound on ethical grounds, not only historical ones.

As Cassirer notes, even theologians, especially in Germany, were among the voices of rejection of the traditional doctrine of original sin. Advocates of the Enlightenment-influenced "new theology," he writes, considered "the idea of an original sin which is visited upon succeeding generations as absolutely absurd, as an insult to the first laws of logic and ethics."[25] Their theological rejection was all the more significant because they did not abandon dogmatic theology altogether. But aligning themselves with modern sentiments, and echoing Pelagius, these theologians opposed "the opinion that man through the fall has lost all his ability to attain the good and the true without divine grace."[26]

Two Interpretations

Without accepting the divinely revealed status of the doctrine of original sin taken for granted by the patristic and medieval writers, modern thinkers were in new territory. Two philosophers offer useful illustrations of modern reinterpretations of original sin: Jean-Jacques Rousseau, the Swiss-French philosopher and political theorist, and Immanuel Kant, the German philosopher.

1. Jean-Jacques Rousseau

Reinterpretation of original sin was at the heart of *Jean-Jacques Rousseau*'s (d. 1778) theories of ethics and politics.[27] He rejected Blaise Pascal's Augustinian argument that an original perversity of the human will causes the misery of human existence. But he did take Pascal's description of the contradiction in human nature, its "greatness and wretchedness," quite seriously. For Rousseau, the question of moral evil belonged to the context of law and society.

Against Pascal and an original corruption, Rousseau affirmed an original goodness. In his philosophical essay, *Discours sur l'origine de l'inegalité des hommes* (1754), Rousseau assumed first that human beings are good by nature. They are not good, however, in society.[28] Differentiating between the *natural man* and the *civilized man,* Rousseau located the problem of evil in the latter. Historical development had "compelled man to adopt a compulsory form of society, thus exposing him to all moral evils; it had fostered in him all the vices of vanity, arrogance, and boundless greed for power."[29] Rousseau shifted the theological idea of concupiscence from an inner realm of subjectivity to the social arena of empirical, historical existence.

While Rousseau rejected the Christian story of original sin, he retained its notions of both an original innocence and an original fall into moral evil. Unlike Schelling, he did not put the fall into primordial history or before time. The fall was a *social* occurrence within history. For Rousseau the *original fault* was the distortion of relationships brought about by the introduction of private property, an historical occurrence that at the same time is at the origin of civil society, in contrast to the life of nature:

> The first man who, having enclosed a piece of land, took it into his head to say, "This is mine," and found people simple enough to believe him, was the true founder of civil society. The human race would have been spared endless crimes, wars, murders, and horrors if someone had pulled up the stakes or filled in the ditch and cried out to his fellow men, "Do not listen to this imposter! You are lost if you forget that the fruits of the earth belong to everyone, and the earth to no one!"[30]

Like other modern thinkers, Rousseau severed transcendence from his interpretation of the fall and redemption. The fall was not an individual act of disobedience against a transcendent reality. The idea of private property and its acceptance as an irrevocable right created the distortion of human relations within history. The acceptance of the usurpation of property into an irrevocable right, Rousseau writes, "for the advantage of a few ambitious men, subjected all others to unending work, servitude, and poverty."[31] He puts the human problem succinctly in opening his essay on the social contract: "Man is born free, and is everywhere in chains."[32]

The historical responsibility for the distortion of inequality created by privilege produces guilt. Human beings need redemption, but it is to be sought in the world, not in a transcendent order. They, not God, have to bring it about. The redemptive solution for the evils of inequality is the transformation of society and the rise of a new form of ethical and political community, as Rousseau argues in the *Social Contract* (1762).[33]

Rousseau's rather sweeping reinterpretation of original sin did not go unnoticed. It was the cause of his break with the Roman Catholic Church. The Archbishop of Paris condemned Rousseau's work *Emile*—where Rousseau argued that humankind's first impulses were always innocent and good—pointing specifically to Rousseau's divergence from the church's understanding of human nature and its doctrine of original sin.

2. Immanuel Kant

Immanuel Kant's (d. 1804) philosophy of religion, *Religion within the Limits of Reason Alone* (1793), offered a rational explanation for religion, the origin of evil, and the solution to evil.[34] Regarding the solution, Kant believed that the remedy to the problem of evil was more reason, not divine grace. Kant's work provoked an ecclesiastical order demanding that he desist from any further writings on religion.

As an adult Kant turned away from the Protestant tradition of his upbringing. He rejected a religious anthropology focusing exclusively on the corruption of human nature. Kant countered with a theory of human nature more akin to the ancient Jewish conception of two interrelated orientations co-existing in human persons—*yetser ha-tov*, the inclination to do good, and *yetser ha-ra*, the inclination to do evil—than that of Augustine or Martin Luther.[35] Kant, too, described human nature as both good and evil. "By nature, man is neither good nor bad, or rather he is by nature at once good and bad. There is in him a twofold natural inclination, for good and for evil. This holds for human nature taken in general, for every man whoever he may be."[36] Kant rooted the natural inclination toward the good in what he called the "categorical imperative," the capacity to act *as if the maxim from which you act were to become through your will universal law.*

Kant rejected Augustine's judgment that human beings are unable to do the good without the assistance of divine grace. He agreed, however, that the tendency toward evil experienced in human nature was a stronger force than the inclination toward good. His anthropology was not emptied of the pessimism carried by the Augustinian conception of original sin. Kant described the human proclivity toward evil as self-love or the instinct of self-interest. It is this that causes evil. In Kant's opinion, persons most often act out of self-interest to the detriment of others. Self-love creates a moral disorder and a perversity within human nature, what the biblical writers described metaphorically as an evil heart. This moral perversity is Kant's equivalent to what the Christian theological tradition called the condition of original sin. He identifies *peccatum originatum* as the problem of radical evil.

Radical evil originates in freedom. The will is free to act against what reason would objectively affirm as morally right. While Kant dismissed the historicity of Genesis 3—as well as the Christian claim of the revelation of original sin and the inheritance of Adam's sin based upon the text—he thought the story served well as a symbolic representation of the fallenness of all humankind.[37] Adam's sin is the human experience. But in retaining the idea of a fall Kant did not appeal to Adam or an historical event. The historical beginning of evil remains closed and inscrutable. For Kant, the fall into evil occurs through temptation. His fall is a metaphysical, not an historical, one.

The proclivity toward evil created by self-love answered the questions of a theodicy for Kant. God created human nature as good, including the instincts whose function urges nature toward harmonious development. But because human beings are free, instead of following their instincts properly, they can go willfully against them in wrongdoing. Even so, Kant insisted that human nature itself is good. It remains capable of moral improvement.

While the question of evil is prominent in Kant's work, understanding the mystery of human nature did not require a surrender in faith to a revealed truth, as it had for Pascal. For Kant, redemption occurs in performance, that is, in obeying the inner categorical imperative that sustains moral living. Kant saw the function of religion in moral terms.[38] While morality does not need religion, still morality leads to religion. Religion is the recognition of the inner moral law—the categorical imperative—commanding assent. Religious living should proceed to true morality. In Kant's view, doing the will of God means obeying the command of reason and living rightly. Worship of God should be what he described as a "rational worship." Kant gave a minimal role to institutional religion, however, believing that it served only to lead the weak.

The World of Modern Science

The medieval and modern worlds exhibit widely disparate views of knowledge and truth. For medievals, truth was twofold. Truth is both divinely revealed and discovered through human reason. Because it is the guardian of divine revelation, the church is the highest authority in matters of truth. Its revelatory source, the Bible, is the chief means for knowledge of the past. The emergence of modernity bore consequences for these views assumed in medieval Christendom. Empirical methods of inquiry narrowed the sources of truth to reason alone—and then often to scientific reason alone. Modern thinkers rejected the authority of the church over human knowledge. And finally, modern sciences and historical disciplines undermined the reliability of the Bible as a historical source for knowledge of the past.

Jean-Jacques Rousseau, Immanuel Kant, and others separated the origin and problem of human evil from its Christian explanation. Their philosophical theories of human nature severed redemption from its religious interpretation, too. Philosophy was not alone in disengaging the dominance of Christian explanations of human experience and the universe. Modern science—especially evolutionary theories—produced alternative stories to the biblical and Christian stories of creation and human origins.[39] A popular epistemology or theory of knowledge followed. Modern empirical science and history were *true*. Religious doctrines were *belief*. Religion was relegated to an interior realm of morality or personal piety.[40]

1. Early Conformity
While modernity's impulse was to sever historical and scientific truth from the church and divine revelation, early modern theories were

sometimes scientific versions of the biblical and Christian worldviews. Nineteenth-century geologists, for example, assumed a limited historical or geological time that put the Earth's origins at about 6,000 years ago. This time frame was consistent with biblical interpretation even though the biblical chronology had been subjected to critical scrutiny already.

Correspondence is evident, too, between Christianity and early modern science in two interrelated scientific ideas about creation. The first idea was that of a special creation at the beginning of the universe of "things as they are," or the theory of the *fixity of species*. The second idea explained changes in the Earth's geological development by appeal to the theories of *catastrophism* and to *successive* or *multiple creations*.

The theory of catastrophism held that at certain intervals in the Earth's past all living things had been destroyed by cataclysms (earthquakes, floods). It was at these times that geological changes in the Earth's development (such as mountains) and changes in the species (through extinction of some and creation of others) had occurred. This theory fit quite neatly with the biblical account of Noah and the flood. Its scientific acceptance by a majority of geologists was due to the influence of French geologist *George Cuvier* (d. 1832). While the scientific method employed by modern biologists, geologists, paleontologists, and others was thoroughly empirical, their explanations did not always avoid invoking supernatural rather than natural causes.

This drift beyond the empirical was even more prominent in the theory of successive or multiple creations. Fossil evidence indicated to scientists that some species no longer existed and that new species had emerged at certain points in the Earth's history. The theory of the fixity of the species appealed to divine intervention to account for the fossil data. In continuity with the Christian doctrine of creation and the biblical account of the flood, scientists argued that the Earth had been destroyed and restocked with new species a number of times. In each divine creation, species had been created "specially and individually" as they are, thus the designation *fixity* or *permanence* of species.

Some promoted a "rational Christianity" to achieve a *rapprochement* with eighteenth- and nineteenth-century scientific developments. A metaphorical interpretation of Genesis 1 replaced the church's literal interpretation of the Genesis story of creation. Even while designating Genesis story's seven days symbolic, however, scientists argued that the design of each species required its special creation. An influential book of this sort was William Paley's *Natural Theology: or Evidences of the Existence and Attributes of the Deity* (1802).[41]

2. The Displacement of Religion   117 to 126   Roman Catholic

By the end of the nineteenth century, however, the Christian explanation of creation, the Earth's development, and human origins had been thoroughly displaced. The chief reason lies in the 1859 publication and widespread acceptance of the book *The Origin of Species.* Its author, *Charles Darwin* (d.1882), was not the first to introduce evolution as an account of the origin of species. Darwin's immediate forerunner was the French naturalist *Jean Baptiste Lamark* (d. 1829). More remotely, the ancient Greeks had proposed that life originated in a primordial slime. Darwin's extraordinary achievement lay in the coherence and persuasiveness of his scientific explanation in terms of natural—rather than supernatural—causes. His scientific theory answered questions about the extinction of species, the emergence of new species, and the resemblance of species to one another.

Darwin was influenced by the English geologist *Sir Charles Lyell* (d. 1875), whose work *Principles of Geology* (1830–1833) challenged catastrophism and facilitated acceptance of *uniformitarianism.* This explanation had been promoted in the1785 work *Theory of the Earth* by Scottish geologist *James Hutton* (d. 1797). But because of the influence of Georges Cuvier and his support of the catastrophism theory, uniformitarianism did not became widely accepted until advocated by Lyell. It contended that past changes in the Earth's surface were due to the same kinds of causes that effect changes at the present.

As explanation, uniformitarianism went as much against the grain of religious beliefs as catastrophism went with them. It assumed an immensely long period for changes in geological process to occur. The earliest rocks in the Earth's development were thought to be about 4 billion years. This judgment was at obvious odds with the long-assumed biblical chronology of about 6,000 years. Uniformitarianism also discounted cataclysms as a primary explanation for geologic developments. It did not posit events such as the biblical flood to account for the fossil evidence of the extinction of species and the emergence of new species.

Darwin was convinced by Lyell's theory that the Earth's development required an immense amount of time. His research led him to reject the fixity of species, a special creation, and successive creations in favor of an evolutionary conception of the Earth's development and the mutability of species. The resemblances of species to one another suggested to Darwin the possibility of a common ancestor. Adopting uniformitarianism, Darwin explained the origin and development of species strictly in terms of natural laws. His explanatory principle was that the transmutation or evolution of species had occurred—in the now-famous phrase from *The Origin of Species*—through natural selection. By natural selection, Darwin referred to the accumulation of heritable variations useful in the species' struggle for existence, their preservation through reproduction, and the eventual spread through the species as a whole. Nature was not *fixed* at the moment of creation. It is variable, in process, dynamic rather than static. Darwin bracketed the questions of the ultimate cause and purpose of the universe as beyond the limits of empirical scientific inquiry. As theological questions, they were proper to the realm of religion, not science.

Scientific theories of immense geological time and the mutability of species contradicted the church's image of an historical Adam in the not-so-distant past. Geology, paleontology, and physical anthropology, among other disciplines, produced studies sustaining and advancing Darwin's evolutionary theory of human origins set forth in *The Descent of Man* (1871). The imaginable several thousand years of the biblical chronology were replaced by assertions of an immense—and unimaginable—geological time of billions of years. The biblical and doctrinal portrayal of Adam and Eve was at odds with the view that the earliest primates appeared about 70 million years ago, the emergence of *homo erectus* more than 1 million years ago, *homo sapiens* about 300,000 years ago, and the type of *homo sapiens* physically indistinguishable from modern human beings about 35,000 years ago.

Fossil evidence of the concurrent presence of the earliest *homo erectus,* followed by *homo sapiens,* in Africa, Asia, and Europe challenged the religious assumption that all humankind descended from one set of ancestors. To use terms introduced by modern evolutionary theories, the doctrine of original sin assumed *monogenism,* the original emergence of two human beings from whom all others descended. Modern scientific theories advanced *polygenism,* the original emergence of a number of human beings, or *polyphyletism,* the original emergence of several disparate groups of human beings.

More than Protestant doctrine, the Roman Catholic doctrine of original sin highlighted monogenism in its account of the universality of sin. From the time of Augustine, the explicit explanatory principle accounting for human solidarity in sin was the biological inheritance of an actual sin from humankind's first parents. The transmission of the sin of Adam and Eve *(peccatum originale originans)* through sexual intercourse causes the condition of original sin *(peccatum originale originatum)* in all humankind. The idea of a single set of parents appeared indispensable to the Catholic doctrine.[42]

Evolutionary theories were not limited to the physical world. Edward Burnett Taylor established the scientific use of the term *culture* in the late nineteenth century to distinguish human societies from animal groups. Paleontologists, cultural anthropologists, and archeologists accumulated evidence of the cultural evolution accompanying humankind's physical development. Studies demonstrated that every dimension of human living had evolved—not only the social, economic, and political relations that structure human living generally, but also religious apprehensions of the divine and cultic life.

Without the insights of modern historical and scientific disciplines, human beings had presumed the past to be much the same as the present. The Christian doctrines of creation and original sin portrayed Adam and Eve as intellectually and morally developed persons. This image of human origins gradually clashed with physical and cultural evolutionary theories tracing a complex process of human development from pre-human ancestors to primitive hunting and gathering groups to settled agricultural peoples to ever-more complex social arrangements.

Moreover, in both modern philosophical and cultural reflection, appeal to an original fall from perfection appeared less and less compelling as an explanation of the fundamental human problem of evil. In various ways, modern thinkers tended to think of evil in the context of intellectual and moral development. This recovered, without explicit intention, the orientation of Irenaeus in patristic theology.[43] Unlike the later Augustine, Irenaeus put the problem of sin in terms of humankind's growth from immaturity to maturity. The framework of development became explicit in the modern age as thinkers sought to understand the dynamics of human development not only in individual categories—human nature—but in social categories as well. New attention was given to social groups and the social construction of human institutions and structures such as the family, law, government, and religion.

Ecclesial Reaction

More than Protestant churches, the Roman Catholic teaching office resisted early scientific theories of human evolution. Rejection of evolution was not derived from an evaluation of the scientific interpretation of data but from *a priori* doctrinal and ecclesial judgments, specifically the dogmatic status of original sin defined by the Council of Trent. The magisterium insisted that the historicity of Adam and Eve, their first sin, and the biological inheritance of an actual sin by their descendents were not topics open for debate. While the magisterium could restrict discussion, Roman Catholic theologians could not avoid intellectual difficulties presented by evolutionary theories. Cumulative evidence from the sciences increasingly made the historicity of Adam and Eve as well as monogenism unlikely.[44]

A central question was whether *doctrinal judgments* could rule out of court *scientific judgments* arrived at by methodical observation of empirical data. The Roman Catholic Church in the modern age—after a somewhat bumpy start with Galileo—had not rejected empirical scientific method. It accepted many conclusions derived from scientific research. But the relation between the religious doctrine of original sin and scientific evolutionary theories of human origins was an especially sensitive one. Original sin was the pivotal element in a Christian theology of redemption. It answered the question why Christ came. And especially for Catholics, original sin was an equally pivotal element in the church's self-understanding, in its ecclesiology.

The Christian depiction of salvation history—creation, fall, and redemption—had dominated Western consciousness for nearly two millennia. The new data of evolutionary development and human origins disrupted this worldview, taken for granted by premoderns. Christian theological claims were now placed against a different and more complicated backdrop. The church's claim that the universality of human sinfulness was caused by the inheritance of an actual sin required explicit acceptance of the creation story of Adam and Eve. The church's proclamation of Christ turned on acceptance of original sin. The church's announcement of the human problem (original sin), the divine remedy (Christ), and the necessity of ecclesial mediation in salvation now required acceptance of historicity of the first couple, the biological inheritance of their sin, and monogenism. It was not immediately clear how this web of theological convictions could be sustained with the conceptions of human origins as polygenistic or polyphyletistic advanced by modern scientists.

Modern evolutionary theories presented immense difficulties for the Roman Catholic doctrine of original sin. They challenged the church to discuss original sin in relation to questions not raised during the development of the doctrine. The historicity of Adam and Eve was taken for granted, for example, until an alternative conception of human origins was introduced by modern historical and scientific studies. Patristic and medieval thinkers did not consider human origins and development, much less debate the choices of monogenism, polygenism, and polyphyletism as explanations of fossil data. Given the foundational importance of a single set of parents for Catholic doctrine, it is not surprising that much of the nineteenth- and twentieth-century concern of the Roman Catholic magisterium has to do with the question of monogenism.

The first explicit rejection of a "theory of descent" came in 1860 from a local Catholic synod in Cologne only a year after publication of Charles Darwin's *Origin of Species*.[45] Several Catholic writers, including *P. Zahn,* who wrote a book titled *Dogma and Evolution* (1899), were instructed to retract their views affirming *transformism,* a term for human evolution. Grounds for the instruction were doctrinal, specifically that transformism was considered contrary to scripture and the revealed doctrine of original sin. This ecclesial objection to the theological accommodation of evolutionary theories continued into the twentieth century.

The *First Vatican Council* (1869–1870) considered original sin in response to Darwin's evolutionary theories. The council specifically defended monogenism in affirming Adam as the origin of the human race. Key elements of the traditional doctrine were reinforced: the possession of preternatural gifts in Adam's original state, the loss of these gifts through Adam's sin, and the condition of original sin as the privation of sanctifying grace. In 1909 the Pontifical Biblical Commission clearly set out the church's position on evolution and historical-critical approaches to the Bible. The commission rejected both evolutionary theory and critical methods of biblical interpretation, insisting on the literal interpretation of Genesis.

It was not until the 1943 encyclical, *Divino Afflante Spiritu* that the Roman Catholic magisterium acknowledged the value of modern historical-critical biblical methods for the church's understanding of its scriptures. The encyclical marks an intellectual turn in Roman Catholicism. An abstract use of scripture to proof-text doctrines would give way to a contextual appropriation of the Bible derived from judgments regarding literary genre, author, historical setting, original purpose, intended audience, and literary features. The Second Vatican Council's decree on Revelation opens with the directive that "those who search out the intention of the sacred writers must, among other things, have regard for 'literary forms.'"[46] The scholarly understanding of Genesis 1–3 as symbolic narratives will gradually become the church's language, too. This will be easier, however, with the creation stories of Genesis 1 and 2 than the expulsion story of Genesis 3.

But almost a hundred years after publication of Darwin's *The Origin of Species,* Pope Pius XII's 1950 encyclical *Humani Generis* shows still the predicament that evolutionary theories presented for the traditional formulation of the doctrine of original sin.[47] By the time of *Humani Generis,* attempts had already begun at new theological interpretations of the meaning of original sin in light of modern scientific conceptions of human origins and development. A notable example was the work of the French Jesuit paleontologist and philosopher *Pierre Teilhard de Chardin.* Teilhard taught at the Institute Catholic in Paris from 1920 to 1923, returning in 1925 after two years in China. Ecclesial opposition to Teilhard's understanding of original sin in light of evolutionary theory forced his return to China in 1926.

One question raised by *Humani Generis* was whether church doctrines could be formulated in language other than the metaphysical terms of the scholastics. The encyclical answered the question: *No.* Scholastic terminology was defended as necessary to the meaning of church doctrines. Reaffirmed was the subordination of reason to revelation. The acceptance or rejection of scientific theories was to be based on their conformity to dogma. The encyclical made this explicit, declaring, "If any such conjectural opinions are directly or indirectly opposed to the doctrine revealed by God, then the demand that they be recognized can in no way be admitted."[48]

Humani Generis intended this twofold point to be clear: (1) Doctrines are *truths* assured by revelation; (2) scientific theories are *opinions* to be rejected if they do not coincide with revealed truths. Included among conjectural opinions was polygenism. While the document granted Catholic scientists and theologians freedom to inquire into human origins and physical evolution, they were prohibited from acceptance of a scientific theory of human origins proposing the descent of humankind from more than a single pair of ancestors. The prohibition followed from the intrinsic relation between monogenism and the universality of human sin:

> When, however, there is question of another conjectural opinion, namely polygenism, the children of the Church by no means enjoy such liberty. For the faithful cannot embrace that opinion which maintains either that after Adam there existed on this Earth true men who did not take their origin through natural generation from him as from the first parent of all or that Adam represents a certain number of first parents. Now it is in no way apparent how such an opinion can be reconciled with that which the sources of revealed truth and the documents of the Teaching Authority of the Church propose with regard to original sin, which proceeds from a sin committed by an individual Adam and which through generation is passed on to all and is in everyone as his own.[49]

Humani Generis's ban on holding certain scientific positions created difficulties for Catholic thinkers. Were scientific theories derived from empirical research to be ignored on the basis of *a priori* doctrinal judgments? Can church dogma dictate scientific conclusions about empirical data? However compelling the empirical evidence, is *polygenism,* for example, to be rejected by Catholics because *monogenism* is dogmatically necessary for the church's conception of the universality of sin?

Humani Generis assumed that the Council of Trent defined monogenism as a revealed teaching of the church. Whether this was the case would later become a question for theological debate. The preeminent German theologian, Karl Rahner, for example, defended monogenism as necessary to the revealed doctrine in his early writings, but later took the view that it was not. The Dutch theologian Piet Schoonenberg, whose reinterpretation of original sin was at the forefront of Catholic efforts, addressed the need for theological principles—analogous to those considered fundamental in biblical studies—to guide the interpretation of magisterial documents and genuine recovery of their teaching.[50] If the historicity of Adam and Eve was taken for granted by those at Trent, is it an intrinsic dimension of their teaching? Is the *historicity* of Adam and Eve what Trent declared dogma?

What exactly had Trent taught? Schoonenberg and other Catholic theologians insisted that the teaching of a magisterial document must be understood in relation to the specific questions it addressed. It must not be used to answer questions it did not address. These questions, in turn, must be situated in relation to the intellectual and cultural horizon of the document's setting, not that of a later time.[51] Debate about fossil evidence and human origins is a nineteenth-century problem reflecting recent discoveries in the natural sciences. It was not an issue for the Council of Trent in the sixteenth century. Medievals could talk without self-consciousness about an historical Adam and Eve because an alternative view had not yet arisen in biblical interpretation or from a scientific understanding of human origins.

Trent confirms the elements of the patristic and medieval theological tradition—an original paradise and time of innocence, an historical first couple, an event of disobedience, a loss of divine grace, and the redemptive remedy of Christ's grace. Because the question of monogenism was absent for Trent, Schoonenberg argued, it cannot be asserted that Trent is teaching monogenism. If monogenism is not Trent's point, it cannot be a doctrinal judgment binding on the faithful. In Schoonenberg's view, the binding aspects of the council's teaching reside elsewhere, for example, in the enduring need of human beings for redemption and the desire of a compassionate God to be in relation with humankind.

Official Catholic pronouncements often bracket contemporary biblical and theological judgments in continuing the language of the tradition. Biblical scholars concur, for example, that the genre of Genesis 3 is a symbolic narrative and not history. *Divino Afflante Spiritu* and Vatican II's *Decree on Revelation* acknowledge the necessity of respecting literary forms. Pope Paul VI's *Creed of the People* in 1968, however, speaks of an historical Adam from whom all have inherited an actual sin. The creed cites Romans 5:12 in the tradition following Ambrosias ("*in whom* all have sinned"), a translation that has met dogmatic purposes, but, in the view of biblical scholars as early as Erasmus, is unwarranted by the original Greek.[52]

The 1994 *Catechism of the Catholic Church* echoes Trent while also adverting to more recent insights into the biblical texts cited as sources for the doctrine of original sin.[53] While the *Catechism* notes the figurative character of Genesis 3 and its symbolic features, it employs the text as an *historical* genre, deriving from it paradise, Adam and Eve, and the first sin as historical realities. All are implicated—participate—in Adam's sin because of the metaphysical unity of the human race: "The whole human race is in Adam 'as one body of one man.'" The reason for infant baptism is the inheritance of a sin from Adam by all humankind.

The dogmatic centrality of original sin is evident in the reaction of Pope Paul VI and the Sacred Congregation for the Doctrine of Faith to a new *Rite of Baptism for Children* issued by the Sacred Congregation for Divine Worship, along with a new *Rite of Christian Initiation for Adults,* in 1969. Changes in the wording of the baptismal rite are instructive.[54] For adults, the new rite of initiation placed the emphasis on the change of heart or conversion involved in becoming a member of the body of Christ. As Paul Turner notes, the document makes reference to personal sin but none explicitly to original sin. For children, the 1969 edition of the *Rite of Baptism for Children* put less emphasis on the guilt of original sin, shifting attention away from original sin (as the old rite had emphasized) to the child's incorporation into Christ and the family of God.

The document's absence of reference to original sin was noticed by Pope Paul VI and the Sacred Congregation for the Doctrine of the Faith. The 1973 version of the rite for children reflects the concern of Paul VI and the congregation. Several changes in wording reassert the relation of infant baptism and original sin. The revised 1969 rite speaks of the *natural human condition.* The 1973 rite substitutes the phrase *power of darkness,* a metaphor traditionally used for original sin. The 1969 rite speaks of baptism as washing away the *stain of sin,* without explanation of the sin. The 1973 rite specifically identifies the stain of sin as original sin. Lastly, in the 1969 rite, preceding baptism, the prayer for exorcism and anointing asks for freedom from the *power of darkness,* again, the common metaphor for original sin, but not an explicit identification of it. In the 1973 rite, the prayer asks for freedom from original sin.

Conclusion

The modern world no longer shares the Christian tradition's supposition of original sin as an undeniable event and dimension of human history. From some quarters came hostility to the doctrine and doubt in its explanatory power. From other quarters came new interpretations of the doctrine's foundational texts. From still others, new insights into human origins and development. This new intellectual setting demanded more from theologians than simply repeating the words of the tradition. The theological task of rediscovering the meaning of original sin has been undertaken with great intensity by some of the best-known twentieth-century Protestant and Catholic theologians. To their efforts we now turn.

cf Celia Deane-Drummore
in "Evolution all die", pp 23 ff.
BS 649 E96 2017 Bgro

Gabriel Daly

6. Original Sin in a Contemporary Context

MODERN THINKERS left little unquestioned about original sin. The Christian doctrine was assailed for its biblical foundation, theological anthropology, and historical worldview. What patristic writers forged and medieval theologians assumed, moderns dismissed.

The acute problem that modernity presented for Christianity was not the selective dismissal of this or that detail of its doctrine but a threat to the Christian conception of the mystery of divine salvation. Early in the tradition, a theology of original sin had unified the central beliefs professed by Christians. Original sin explained not only the universality of human alienation from God and the origin of evil but also the reason for Christ's incarnation and the grace of forgiveness, the necessity of infant baptism for salvation, and the role of the church as mediator of Christ's redemption. With this pivotal doctrine under siege, the whole of the Christian creed appeared vulnerable.

The New Situation

Once under siege, Christians had to meet these intellectual difficulties. Their strategy tended to take one of two options.

The first option was to hold firm against the onslaught of modernity. The classical formulation of the doctrine of original sin was defended as intrinsic to the divine revelation of sin and redemption. Theological language continued to distinguish between a *prelapsarian* state of human innocence and friendship with God and a *postlapsarian* state of estrangement from God. Changes in the literary and biblical understanding of the literary genre of Genesis 3 remained invisible in

127

the announcement of the doctrine's fundamental claim that Adam's sin had changed human nature itself. The fact the modern insights had rejected the historicity of Genesis 3—thus leaving the prelapsarian and postlapsarian states without an historical foundation—was left unaddressed. Catholic teaching manuals repeated the dogmatic formulation of the Council of Trent with little or no advertence to modern questions.[1] If modern scientific and historical conclusions were mentioned, they were characterized as hypothesis, conjecture, or opinion, in contrast to the true, certain, and divinely revealed Tridentine dogma.

The other option, characteristic of the theologians discussed in this chapter and the two that follow, acknowledged that the conception of original sin belonged to a different age with different questions and a different apprehension of the world than shared by persons today. A deep and profound consideration of the doctrine was in order. Theologians argued that the meaning of the doctrine is true—there is a root sin that alienates humankind from God, generating personal and social evil—but that the insight into what this means and how to express it adequately to modern believers requires more than repetition of its classical formulation.

This is the question contemporary theologians would eventually raise: Is the classical *formulation* of humankind's sin—cast in the language of Adam and Eve, an historical fall, and an ontological change in created nature—equivalent to the *meaning* of humankind's alienation from God?[2] Are Adam and Eve the *reality* of original sin, to push the question even deeper, or are the origins and character of human alienation and evil something that can be grasped and expressed through a completely different conceptual framework? Can we talk about original sin without appeal to Adam's sin as an historical event? In light of a critical apprehension of history, scripture, and the human person, how do we understand the root sin of humankind?

Biblical Narrative

Contemporary theologians start with the view that religious practices, beliefs, doctrines, and texts are shaped by and reflect particular historical settings. In contrast to a static conception of religion, contemporary theologians think of religion dynamically, as a process of religious experience, conversion, questions, conflict, and development.

Religions are shaped by and in turn shape the cultures and social systems in which they are embedded.

Our review of the emergence and development of a theology of original sin in the Christian tradition reflects such a historically conscious approach. The idea of original sin developed in and through the experiences of individuals—the sacramental experience of baptizing infants, the inner psychological experience of moral impotence, polemical debate and differences over human nature, grace, and redemption. Questions Christians faced—about God and evil, Christ and redemption, sin and grace, the church and the world—were answered by explanatory appeal to original sin.

New insight into doctrinal development does not eliminate divine revelation. But it has invited a reevaluation of the conception of revelation. In the case of the doctrine of original sin, this has taken place through a consideration of the way scriptural sources have been used as proof-texts for the revelation of original sin.

One way the question is put is exegetical. Is original sin "in" scripture? The initially scandalous modern charge that Genesis 3 was myth was gradually appropriated by biblical scholars as an accurate evaluation of literary genre.[3] The Genesis story is symbolic narrative, not history. Like other myths in the ancient world, it raises fundamental questions. Why are we subject to such suffering? What is the cause of our misery? Why do we die? Why is our survival so difficult? Why are women subject to male rule? The story, situated in a primordial time and place of perfection, mediates an answer to these questions.

Biblical scholars point to the unity of the expulsion story with the creation story preceding it.[4] The Genesis 2 creation story portrays human beings as fulfilled only when the one creature is no longer alone and there exists a solidarity between two. The expulsion story shows this solidarity as one also of sin. Evil is a present dimension in the narrative world inasmuch as Adam and Eve are tempted by another to do what has been forbidden to them. The story of sin is not focused so much on what happened but on what is always happening in human existence.

The larger narrative context of which the expulsion story is a piece is concerned less with historical beginnings than with Israel's historical present. Adam's sin of infidelity is Israel's infidelity *now*. Early Christians, however, increasingly turned to the Genesis story as one of history as it happened. The symbolic meaning of the story, grasped by its original recipients, was submerged as the story came to be seen as a primary historical and revelatory source for the origin of humankind's solidarity in sin and the reason for the incarnation.

Exegeting Paul

Similarly, scripture scholars evaluated the meaning of the second of the biblical texts cited as a foundation for the doctrine of original sin, Romans 5:12–21. As Pauline scholar Joseph Fitzmyer has insisted, the idea of original sin *(peccatum originale)* belongs not to Paul himself but to theological and doctrinal developments from the patristic church to the Council of Trent. "Paul's teaching is regarded as seminal and open to dogmatic development, but it does not say all that the Tridentine decree says."[5] The patristic writers appealed to Romans 5:12 specifically as the revealed source on the origin of sin. How did sin begin? Fitzmyer notes that Paul's own concern lay with the *origin of death,* not with the origin of sin. Paul took sin for granted. Its origin was not a question for him.

With other Jews, Paul believed death was a punishment for sin. The universality of death gave sufficient evidence of the universality of sin. Paul's attention was not on the past but on the eschatological present and future. With the resurrection of Christ, he argued, death has been overcome. The punishment for sin has been set aside. The contrast between Adam and Christ is one between death and life. Adam's disobedience is the source of death. Christ's obedience is the source of new life. Paul's teaching in Romans 5:12 is directed toward the advent of redemption, not the origin of sin. Paul proclaims access to divine redemption, not only for Jews but now also for Gentiles, through faith in Christ.

Paul's thinking "works backward" from Christ's redemption to Adam's sin, not the other way around. Christ's offer of redemption signals the universality of sin. If through faith in Christ *all are saved* (the universality of redemption), then *all are sinners* (the universality of sin).[6] Pauline interpreters suggest it is more accurate to say that Paul had a theology of *solidarity in sin* rather than of *original sin.* The key component in the later patristic theology of original sin is the inheritance of Adam's sin. As a Jewish thinker, Paul does not think of human sinfulness in relation to biological inheritance. It is simply a fact of human existence.[7]

Paul treated Adam and Christ as equally historical individuals. But his teaching is not *about* Adam's historicity. That was not a question for him as it is for us. The problem of historicity arises in the context of uniquely modern concerns that do not belong to Paul's first-century horizon. Assumptions about biblical chronology and human beginnings were unquestioned until scientific and historical research presented data from which a new understanding of the past emerged. Then references to Adam's historicity became problematic.

Finding Other Foundations

The Christian understanding of Christ's redemption and the self-understanding of the church have been intimately bound to the affirmation of original sin. Contemporary theologians have discovered that rethinking the meaning of original sin invites a reexamination of the theologies of redemption and church, too.

The views of Roman Catholic theologians on the doctrine of original sin extend from a continued defense of its traditional formulation to a rejection of it altogether. At the latter end of the continuum, theologian Matthew Fox calls the doctrine of original sin a false theology of sin and redemption. The foundational truth of Christianity, in his view, is not original sin but original blessing, the affirmation of the goodness of creation and humankind.[8]

Protestant and Catholic theologians alike have voiced concern that original sin be disengaged from premodern assumptions incompatible with empirical scientific and historical knowledge. This is perhaps easier for Protestants than Catholics. For the latter, the dogmatic formulation of the Council of Trent remains the standard against which any reinterpretation is judged. Any rethinking of the meaning of original sin at conceptual odds invites questions of orthodoxy. Where in a new interpretation is the state of original innocence? Where is Adam's sin, *peccatum originale originans?* Where is the sin of nature inherited by each, *peccatum naturae?* Where is original sin as the inheritance of Adam's sin and a nature wounded by sin, *peccatum originale originatum?* Where is original sin as the privation of sanctifying grace? Where is the disharmony of nature, *concupiscence,* and how is it conceived?

While it is true that in the modern world there has been an "eclipse of original sin," in Stephen Duffy's words, the doctrine has not been ignored by theologians.[9] The doctrine is too central in the religious worldview of Christianity to be ignored.

Two distinctive interpretations of original sin have come from the twentieth-century religious thinkers, Catholic theologian Piet Schoonenberg and Protestant social ethicist Reinhold Niebuhr. Both men devoted serious attention and thought to the challenges modernity presented to Christian doctrine. Each sought to express the meaning of original sin in categories appropriate for today. In addition, we will also consider relevant features of recent liberation theologies. With these theologians and those in chapters ahead, our intent is to capture the outlines of what is distinctive to each. For the nuances and details of each reinterpretation of original sin, each should be read as a primary source.

Piet Schoonenberg

The Dutch Jesuit *Piet Schoonenberg* offered one of the first reconstructions of the doctrine of original sin among contemporary Catholic systematic theologians. His work became well known in the English world through the 1965 book *Man and Sin: A Theological View* and such articles as "Original Sin and Man's Situation."[10]

Schoonenberg took modernity's challenges seriously. He placed original sin against a new intellectual and cultural horizon constituted by the evolutionary worldview of modern empirical science, historical consciousness, and critical biblical scholarship. While he acknowledged difficulties with the classical doctrine, Schoonenberg also affirmed the reality of universal sinfulness to which the doctrine points. The problem remains if the classical formulation is rejected, as he suggests: "Even if we prescind from any original sin and its influence on each of us, this solidarity exists."[11]

For Schoonenberg, reinterpreting the traditional doctrine required recovery of the questions answered in the early tradition. It meant readdressing these questions in a theology conversant with modernity. This meant Schoonenberg, as a Catholic theologian, would shift from the abstract metaphysical categories of scholastic theology to categories that would reflect an apprehension of human historicity and becoming.

One difficulty for a contemporary theology of sin is the divergence between the religious perspective of the biblical writings and the secular perspective of modernity. The biblical world took sin for granted, but, as Schoonenberg wrote, "it has no such place in modern thought."[12] Modernity has its own blind spots, which are to blame for some of the eclipse; but Schoonenberg placed responsibility with the particular historical development of the church's theology of sin, too.

In the Christian tradition, a theology of sin developed in tandem with the sacrament of penance and the preparation of confessors. The model was Roman law. Theologians thought of sin in relation to the individual and as a violation of law. The prism through which early church theologians read Genesis 3, for example, was the law and categories of obedience and disobedience. Adam's sin was a crime for which punishments were dispensed. Along with Schoonenberg, prominent moral theologians such as Bernard Häring and Louis Monden were instrumental in raising awareness of the existential and theological limitations of an individualistic and juridical theology of sin.[13]

A juridical conception of sin presents human sin as the violation of divine commands, just as crime breaks the laws of the city or state. Primary attention is placed on individual wrongdoing without attention to social context or situation. Punishment sets right the order broken by crime and the relation to the divine broken by sin. When sin is crime and the sinner a criminal, the dominant images of God are judge and ruler.

Modeling a theology of sin on Roman law and situating it within penitential practices gradually restricted sin in Christian thought to personal sin. Christian theology lacked the means of integrating insights about social sin found in the Hebrew prophets. The doctrine of original sin extended the individualism of personal sin to account for universal sin. Each individual inherits Adam's sin, and sinful individuals collectively constitute the universality of sinfulness. The remedy is also perceived in individual categories. Each individual is restored to right relation with God through the personal reception of grace in baptism.

Schoonenberg argued that legal categories are incapable of capturing the personal relationship that exists between human beings and God. He portrayed the inherent drawback to understanding of sin as disobedience of law. A juridical concept of sin overlooks the central feature of sin, namely, the failure of persons to seek and love God. In traditional terms, this absence of loving God is the privation of sin. It is the meaning of humankind's alienation from God. But as Schoonenberg emphasized, the refusal to enter into a relationship of love with God is a social as well as an individual reality. Alienation from God is manifest in evil.

Refusal to love God shapes the orientation of persons' lives. It affects the values that persons apprehend and appropriate. It influences the choices they consider, the decisions they make, and the acts they commit or fail to carry out. Individual decisions and acts are constitutive elements of the historical situation. They are not self-contained but affect others. "As a free person I cannot be deprived of my freedom by the free decisions of others, but they may place me in a situation which may determine me inwardly even in my freedom," Schoonenberg wrote.[14]

What makes sin really sin, Schoonenberg asserted, is the *guilt* resulting from the *decision to do evil.* Even if actual guilt does not pass from one person to another, the influence of guilt does. The historical situation is conditioned and shaped by the freedom of others. Among free acts are persons refusing to seek and love God. Because refusal of God (sin) has entered the world already, each person meets it in some way.[15] Inevitably, persons are situated in a sinful world. The world is a "fellowship in sin."[16]

The classical doctrine of original sin accounted for this fellowship in sin by way of its theory of physical transmission. All human beings inherit the actual sin of Adam. To emphasize original sin as a *real* sin and not simply the influence of bad example, medieval theologians called original sin a *sin of nature.* Schoonenberg agreed that original sin was an internal reality, but he disagreed that the inward element was caused by physical inheritance. In his view, what the medievals had understood through a compound of biological and metaphysical categories could be grasped as the existential determination of *being-situated.* This notion of *situation* or *being-situated* is Schoonenberg's primary category in his theology of original sin. He expresses it in various ways:

- Human existence is *situatedness;*
- The free acts of human beings are unavoidably *situated;*
- The *situated character of human existence* is an inner reality in each human being;

- As an existential determination, *being-situated* is a universal and permanent feature of human existence.

Schoonenberg acknowledged that his concept of being-situated corresponded with the classical doctrine's *peccatum originale originatum* (the condition of original sin) but not with *peccatum originale originans* (the event of Adam's sin). He also conceded that his anthropology did not accommodate the medieval concept of original sin as the loss of supernatural gifts. But in his judgment the theological anthropology of the classical doctrine poses a dilemma in an evolutionary world. As Schoonenberg puts it, "There would seem to have been a higher form of humanity at the wrong end of man's evolution."[17]

In his reconstruction of original sin, Schoonenberg deliberately shifted biblical and theological sources.[18] From the Hebrew Bible, Schoonenberg grounded the problem of alienation and evil in texts that speak of Israel's sinfulness as a people or the sinfulness of humanity as a whole rather than in the story of Genesis 3. While the prophetic writings are the obvious source for this perspective, the Psalms offer a rich resource, too.[19] One benefit of this change is that difficulties regarding the historicity of Adam, a fall, and monogenism lose their primacy in the debate over the meaning of original sin. The fall remains historical in Schoonenberg's thinking, but not in the sense proposed by early church writers. The fall is existential. It occurs in each person, occasioned by the refusal to seek and to love God.

From the New Testament, Schoonenberg appealed to the Johannine *sin of the world* as an affirmation of the social and ideological dimension of human sinfulness.[20] The existential reality the gospel writer named the *sin of the world* and early church theologians defined as *peccatum originale originatum,* is humankind's solidarity in the refusal to love God and the evil incurred as a consequence of this refusal.

Schoonenberg boldly advocated retrieving Pelagius as a theological source. He proposed to extend the "Pelagian doctrine of bad example until it is orthodox once more."[21] What Schoonenberg sought to avoid in reappropriation of Pelagius were numerous problems associated with Augustine's pessimism about human nature and the biological theory of inheritance he advanced as an explanatory principle for the universality of human sin.

In his own time, Pelagius was criticized as implying that persons could be without sin. If they are without sin, they are without need for Christ's redemption. Augustine's opposition to Pelagius was rooted in this concern. But just as Pelagius's views invited questions, so did Augustine's theory of inheritance. How could a failure on the level of freedom be transmitted from one person to another?

Schoonenberg believed he had "extended the Pelagian doctrine to orthodoxy" through his concept of being-situated as an internal determination of human freedom. Being-situated is a universal feature in human nature operative in all acts of freedom. Each person makes decisions and lives in a world already shaped by refusal of God. It is impossible to be outside this existential and social context. This dimension of being situated in a world alienated from God, Schoonenberg thought, is what the early church writers named humankind's original sin.

The theological tradition grounded the revealed status of the doctrine of original sin in Genesis 3. Schoonenberg turned to John 1 to uncover what is revealed in Christian gospel. The Christian proclamation is of God's love and redemption, not original sin. Schoonenberg highlighted these themes:

- God's love for us is revealed (4:16);
- This revelation is mediated by Jesus (4:9);
- Jesus reconciles us to God (4:10);
- Jesus is the Savior (4:14);
- God lives in those who confess Jesus as the Son of God (4:15);
- God has sent God's Spirit to be in us (4:13);
- Those who love God must love their brothers and sisters (4:21).

Revelation of God's redemptive act points to humanity's fundamental sin. The root—basic, core, original—sin is the refusal to love. The juridical language of the tradition characterized sin as an offense against God. This is true, Schoonenberg argued, but the offense is situated historically in the human realm. God is offended when human beings disregard God's summons to love others.[22] Where love is absent, there is refusal to do what love would demand. Love would invite responsibility, compassion, and concern for the well-being of others. In this light, Schoonenberg derived an existential meaning for the metaphysical definition of original sin as the privation of grace in the classical doctrine. The privation of grace refers to the absence in a person of an interior life of faith and love of God. Positively, the presence of this interior life is the indwelling presence of God in friendship and love. This is what the tradition defined as God's gift of love, sanctifying grace.

Where this interior life of love exists, it is disclosed through response to the needs and well-being of others. Because the interior life of faith and love is a being in relation to God, it is God's grace that is mediated through human decisions and acts of persons doing what is right. The church facilitates the mediation of divine grace through the lives of its members. Its life is shaped by listening to the gospel and living out its message. In its proclamation of the gospel, the church calls human beings to conversion.[23] The purpose of the sacrament of baptism, Schoonenberg says, is to bring the baptized into a "community of the redeemed."

Where there is no interior spiritual life, there is no grace to mediate. The refusal of faith and love of God creates a grace-less situation.[24] Evil against others reflects the absence of love. Just as good examples influence persons and expand the good, evil examples raise the probability that more evil will follow. The deprivation of good examples further restricts the possibility that people will be able to recognize or do the good. Such a warped historical situation is made worse by social pressure. Human beings become blind to values, unable to grasp genuine values, hardened by their rejection of God. It is this existential and historical situation of humankind as a community in sin, Schoonenberg thought, that the early Christian writers tried to capture by the theological category of original sin. Originals is not personal, actual sin, but it is real sin nonetheless.

The historical situation is simultaneously one of being-situated by sin and being-situated by redemption. Schoonenberg's view was shared by Karl Rahner, his fellow Jesuit theologian. Rahner described original sin and being redeemed as two existentials of the human situation. They are both always there, at all times determining human existence.[25]

Reinhold Niebuhr

A charismatic speaker and prolific writer, theologian *Reinhold Niebuhr* (d. 1971) was influential in American religion and politics from the 1920s until his death. He was educated as a minister in the Evangelical Reformed tradition. As a professor of social ethics at Union Theological

Seminary in New York, Niebuhr became one of the best-known religious thinkers of the century. Larry Rasmussen, a prominent interpreter of Niebuhr's work, describes him as a "theologian of public life."[26]

Niebuhr commented on religious, social, and political issues in a wide range of journals. He also created one, *Christianity and Crisis*. One of Niebuhr's earliest books, *Moral Man and Immoral Society* (1932) is now a classic of American religious thought. It forcefully presents one of Niebuhr's pivotal assumptions in his social analysis, namely, that human beings are incapable of rising above group interests in the social realm.[27] In later life, Niebuhr became less optimistic about the morality of individuals than the title given to this early work suggests.

Niebuhr's most systematic examination of original sin appears as a theological anthropology and theory of history in his two-volume magnum opus, *The Nature and Destiny of Man* (1941–1943).[28] Several shorter works also provide valuable entries into Niebuhr's understanding of original sin, including *Beyond Tragedy* (1937) and *Christianity and Power Politics* (1940).[29]

1. Placing Sin at the Center

As a social ethicist, Niebuhr sought to address the modern eclipse of the doctrine of original sin. He did so by reinterpreting the doctrine through the lens of contemporary theories of personal and social existence. In Niebuhr's view, reflection on sin is central for theology: "A theology which fails to come to grips with this tragic factor of sin is heretical both from the standpoint of the gospel and in terms of its blindness to obvious facts of human experience in every realm and on every level of moral goodness."[30]

Inasmuch as sin is a factor in the dynamics of historical existence, Niebuhr argued that it must be included in a social analysis of the human good and evil. In a social ethics, the categories of good and evil correspond to those of justice and injustice. The roots of injustice are in the psychological reality of individual and collective egotism. Egotism, Niebuhr wrote, is "sin in its quintessential form."[31] Egotism results in "life taking advantage of life."[32] It generates social conflict. Those whose interests, privileges, and advantages are backed by power undermine the well-being and welfare of those without power. Sin—egotism—constitutes the basic problem of history, its "tragic dimension."[33]

For Niebuhr, understanding the relation between egotism and injustice requires a theoretical grasp of human freedom.[34] Human beings are distinctively human because of the self-transcending capacities that constitute their freedom—capacities for reason, moral choice, and decision. These capacities are the source of the human good as well as evil. The source of good is *other-regarding tendencies.* Niebuhr denotes an inner normative orientation toward the other by several terms—mutuality, the law of love, the law of being, and essential nature. In tension with this orientation, and the source of evil, are *self-regarding tendencies.* Niebuhr also uses a range of terms for these tendencies—egotism, self-regard, self-concern, self-centeredness, and selfishness.

For Niebuhr, egotism is not simply individual self-regard. Human existence is intrinsically social. Individuals live within communal contexts. Social reality influences and determines individual development in both positive and negative ways. Positively, communities foster individual self-realization and fulfillment. Negatively, communal existence generates parochial loyalty or tribalism, a kind of spontaneous attachment of individuals to one another.[35] Tribalism—collective egotism— divides human reality into "we" and "they" in a way parallel to the primordial distinction between the self and the other. The need, claims, interests, and even the humanness of others is never quite as real as ours. In Niebuhr's judgment, collective egoism is the chief cause of humanity's callous brutality and inhumanity. Self-regarding tendencies foster tribal limits to mutual obligation.[36]

It was this psychological and social experience of egotism, Niebuhr thought, that the early theological category of original sin referred. The "universal inclination of the self to be more concerned with itself than to be embarrassed by its undue claims," Niebuhr wrote, "may be defined as 'original sin.' "[37] He found the comment of French philosopher Henri Bergson an apt description of original sin: "When the self first begins to think of itself it thinks of itself first." What Augustine and Luther called "the bondage of the will" is the bondage of human reason and moral decision to self- or group interests. Niebuhr defined original sin as the persistence and universality of man's self-regard.[38]

2. Evaluating Traditional Elements of the Doctrine
Like Piet Schoonenberg and other twentieth-century religious thinkers, Niebuhr's reassessment of the doctrine of original sin was

generated by a new intellectual setting shaped by evolutionary theories of modern science, contemporary theories of history, and historical-critical biblical scholarship. He considered original sin a powerful religious symbol of the basic contradiction at the heart of human being. But in the contemporary situation, Niebuhr acknowledged that the doctrine's pre-modern historical and anthropological assumptions threatened to obscure a genuine grasp of its meaning. He thought some elements of the traditional doctrine should be rejected outright. For others, the existential meaning was to be reestablished.

Not surprisingly, Niebuhr rejected a literal interpretation of the story of Adam and Eve. In his view, such a reading opens the way to bad science and obscures the story's genuine insights:

> Religious literalism seeks to preserve childlike profoundity in religion by giving simple and childlike answers to childlike questions. It thinks that the mythical answers to childlike questions are adequate scientific answers. It tries to insist that, because the idea of creation is true, it is also true that God created the world in six days; and that because the story of the Fall is true, therefore the account of the serpent and the apple in the garden is actual history. Thus it corrupts ultimate religious insights into a bad science.[39]

Niebuhr agreed with contemporary biblical scholars that the literary genre of Genesis 3 is myth. Yet it is true myth. The story discloses genuine insight into the human condition. Unlike other myths in the ancient world, Genesis 3 did not place the origin of evil in a defect of creation or in a divine principle of evil. It did not blame the body for evil by demonizing human desires and passions. In Niebuhr's view, the story rightly locates the origin of evil in human freedom. Evil is a possibility because human beings have the capacity to choose between alternatives. They can decide for evil and against good. By such choice and action, they disobey the divine desire that human freedom choose the good.[40]

In a similar way, Niebuhr acknowledged the Christian idea of an historical fall as myth but true event. The event is not found by looking back to the distant past. It is known empirically by self-reflection. The fall is apprehended in the psychological introspection belonging to adult moral experience.[41] It is an internal existential event. In human consciousness there is a difference between the rational and moral grasp of *what ought to be done* and *what is actually done*. The fall occurs—each and every time—in the *failure to comply* with what should be done. The *ought* is grasped as an ideal. This ideal, the law of love, is an inner transcendent criterion of human moral activity. The *actual* fails all too frequently to meet the law of love.

Niebuhr derived the meaning of original perfection, as he did the fall, from psychological experience. In the theological tradition, original perfection represented a time prior to the first sin. In Niebuhr's view, a time of original perfection is just as mythic as the fall. He found it odd that contemporary theologians such as Karl Barth, who explicitly rejected the historicity of Adam and Eve, continued to regard original perfection as a historical time prior to sin.[42] In contrast to the historical understanding of the classical doctrine, Niebuhr understood both the fall and original perfection as existential, psychological realities.

For Niebuhr, original perfection denotes the *psychological experience of the law of love* as a transcendent criterion of human morality. The law of love is the "perfection before the act," an experience as yet uncompleted by action. Original perfection is the apprehension of *what ought to be*. This apprehension functions as the criterion for decisions and actions. The fall is experienced in an uneasy conscience that acknowledges that *what is* has failed to meet this transcendent criterion.

In the theological tradition, Catholics explained original perfection as the possession of supernatural gifts. The condition of original sin was the privation of these gifts. Human nature now possessed only the capacities proper to it. Niebuhr rejected this anthropology. To conceive of original sin as an ontological change in human nature whereby that which was lost was *unnecessary* to nature led to the conclusion, in his view, that human reason was essentially unaffected by original sin.

This question was important to Niebuhr as a social ethicist. In the Christian moral tradition, the relation between original sin and reason was posed as a question about natural justice. The question was of the capacity of human reason. Can reason, after sin, know what is just?[43] Is the effect of original sin such that reason is not only *darkened,* as Catholics held, but *corrupted,* as Martin Luther argued? If human reason is corrupted by original sin, human beings are *unable* to transcend self- or group interest to grasp what is truly just.

Niebuhr parted ways with both Catholics and Protestants on this question. The Catholic position—thought overly optimistic by Niebuhr—was that human reason remained capable of knowing what is just even after sin. The supernatural gifts possessed by Adam *over and beyond* human nature had been lost, but the capacity of reason, proper to nature, remained. Even if threatened by inner disharmony of concupiscence, Catholics argued, the capacity of reason to know justice can be fulfilled. But knowing is not doing. The ability to do what is just is thwarted by the moral impotence effected by original sin. Divine grace restores *ability*.

Niebuhr followed the medieval Reformers. Martin Luther had rejected the metaphysical explanation of original perfection and original sin. He thought that the Catholic position that reason had been "wounded" or "darkened" was too optimistic. In Luther's judgment, Adam's sin had corrupted human reason. In part, Niebuhr agreed with Luther. But he did not equate the corruption of reason with an historical Adam. Niebuhr drew his insights from a contemporary intellectual field, the sociology of knowledge, and the influential social thinker, Karl Marx.[44]

A core idea from these sources is that human knowledge is socially and historically situated. There is no transcendent vantage point from which human beings stand above their situation to grasp *the* truth or *the* good. Granted, individuals and groups are capable of knowing. But human knowledge is always ideologically tainted by self- or group interest. Embedded in the very process of knowing is a powerful desire to protect personal advantage and privilege. Human beings are skillful at shaping truth to advance prerogatives they already possess. As human, ideas and values are social products masking various kinds of interests, particularly the interests of the powerful. The "ideological taint of knowledge" described by Marx is the insight that knowledge can be shaped by interest to advance interests. What human beings apprehend is not *the truth* but *someone's truth*. Truth is shaped often by what someone wants, not what is so. The legitimation of slavery for the economic interests of slaveholders by an ideology of superior/inferior human nature would be one historical example of Marx's insight into knowledge.[45]

In Niebuhr's judgment, the Catholic "undue confidence in reason" neglected to consider the way individual and collective egotism color the human apprehension of justice. Human beings suffer from a root blind spot. They are oblivious to the way their interests affect their apprehensions of truth and justice.

On the other hand, Luther's theory of corruption went too far in the other direction for Niebuhr. By eliminating the scholastic distinction between the natural and supernatural, Luther identified *original right-eousness* with the *image of God*. In contrast to the scholastic theologians who held that Adam lost original righteousness but retained the image of God, Luther maintained that the loss of original righteousness was the loss of the image of God. Self-love (egotism), Luther thought, was natural.[46] Niebuhr broke with this aspect of the Reform tradition. Against Luther, Niebuhr argued that the image of God remains after sin. He identified the image of God in human nature with mutuality, the inner normative orientation of the law of love. The orientation is not destroyed by sin. The image of God remains in nature the transcendent criterion of all human thinking and doing. On this basis, Niebuhr argued that egotism is unnatural. It is a contradiction to essential nature.

Niebuhr also thought Luther's emphasis on corruption led to defeatism. This has consequences for social ethics. If human reason is completely corrupted, achieving the human good is an impossibility. In political terms, there would be no point of working for justice. Pelagius had put the same question to Augustine's theory of moral impotence: *Why try?* Niebuhr turned Luther's theology around, arguing that it is total corruption that is the impossibility:

> Mankind does not destroy the law of life by violating it....Nor is mankind totally depraved. Total depravity is an impossibility, since man can be a sinner only because he is a child of God. He can do evil only because he has freedom; and freedom is the mark of his divine sonship....The pattern of life is not corrupted by historic existence but in historic existence.[47]

Niebuhr also rejected Augustine's theory that original sin is transmitted through sexual intercourse. The explanation that sin is inherited through procreation seemed to Niebuhr to make sin a natural necessity. While sin is inevitable, Niebuhr thought, it is not necessary.[48] By rejecting the biological theory of inheritance, Niebuhr dismissed what for Augustine had functioned as an explanatory principle for sin's universality. In accord with his own method of analysis, Niebuhr turned to psychological experience for an explanatory principle. He found it in the universal lack of compliance with the law of love. The human failure to meet the criterion of mutuality is a permanent feature of freedom. But unlike Augustine's, this principle is empirically verifiable in one's own experience. The fact of evil is evidence enough that groups as well as individuals fail to meet the criterion imposed on human action by the inner law of love.

3. Sources for the Truth of Original Sin

Niebuhr believed the symbol of original sin pointed to a fundamental truth about human existence.[49] He found this truth grounded in two sources: (1) the transcendent perspective of the Christian gospel, and (2) a phenomenology of selfhood, a method of psychological introspection.

What is the perspective of the gospel? What does it reveal? Niebuhr argued that the gospel discloses the norm of human self-realization as well as the basic contradiction in human nature.

For Niebuhr, Jesus' teaching reflected his grasp of the dynamics of social existence. He captured the norm of self-realization in the paradox, "For those who want to save their life will lose it, and those who lose their life for my sake, and for the sake of the gospel, will save it" (Mark 8:35). Self-determination takes place in and through social relations. Self-giving conditions the possibility for self-realization.[50] Forgetting one's own concerns and interests creates the space to discover the essential requirement for self-realization, as Niebuhr suggests: "Individuals may on occasion forget themselves and discover that self-realization is the consequence of such forgetfulness; and that it is most surely its consequence if not its designated and desired end."[51] Undue self-concern is ultimately defeating.

Scripture expresses the inner orientation toward the other normative to the human spirit as an external word, the great command to love God and love neighbor. What Niebuhr describes in psychological terms as an other-regarding orientation, the biblical writers call "the image of God." In his theological anthropology, Niebuhr describes this other-regarding tendency—the law of love—as essential nature and the law of being. It is the origin of the moral life. The law of love demands, as an inner dynamism and criterion of moral action, that human beings not only be in relation but respond to one another's needs.[52] It is this norm that the gospel reveals as integral to self-realization. The gospel exposes egotism as a betrayal of the law of love and the fundamental contradiction in human nature. As a denial of the human other, egotism is sin against the divine other.

Niebuhr argued that a genuine Christian anthropology is neither overly pessimistic nor unduly optimistic. A pessimistic anthropology depicts human beings as egotists by nature. An optimistic one portrays human beings as capable of transcending egotism by intelligence, moral virtue, religious piety—or something. In Niebuhr's view, the psychological reality lies in between. The normative orientation of the law of love embedded in the human spirit signals capability—an optimistic feature. But the law of love is routinely contradicted by egotism—a pessimistic feature. Egotism is the inevitable sin. But an anthropology adequate to the Christian vision grasps that human beings are egotists in contradiction to their essential nature. "This is the doctrine of original sin," Niebuhr wrote, "stripped of literalistic illusions."[53]

Niebuhr found the tendency to live at the expense of others the root sin disclosed by scriptural revelation. But human experience itself yields the same insight. A common feature among moral systems is the judgment that mutuality (other-regarding acts) is the source of the human good and egotism (self-regarding acts) is the source of human evil.[54]

In Niebuhr's judgment, self-reflection uncovers the "precondition of egotism" as an anxiety about existence built into freedom itself.[55] Anxiety itself is not sin. But it issues forth in sin as insecurity generates a desire to become secure at any cost. The false security to which all are tempted—and many labor to establish—is the security of power. The driving interest that seeks power over others leads, inevitably, to a blindness to the needs and well-being of others.[56] By default, security through power for those who gain it entails insecurity for those who lack it.[57]

Niebuhr, echoing Friedrich Nietzsche, names this driving interest in establishing security the will to power. In religious terms, he calls it "sin as assertion."[58] Assertion is not the only form of sin, but it is a fundamental kind. By his two psychological terms—mutuality and egotism—Niebuhr contrasts genuine self-realization with sinful self-realization. Both individual and social self-realization occur through adherence to the inner criterion of mutuality embedded in the human spirit as the ideal and norm of human living. This orientation intrinsic to human being demands that human living not be restricted to the interests of the self or the group but be open to the well-being of others.

Human existence is imbued with insecurity. The will to power deals with insecurity without acknowledging that mutuality is normative for created nature or that created nature has a transcendent term.

Niebuhr saw his analysis of the will to power as an empirical and psychological understanding of Augustine's sin of pride and the Protestant tradition's notion of sin as unbelief. The concept of the will to power is a central feature of Niebuhr's reinterpretation of original sin.

Sinful self-realization occurs through the will to power. In both individuals and groups, the will to power violates the orientation toward mutuality. Niebuhr saw it as the key feature of the isms that divide human beings—nationalism, racism, classism. Pushing aside the legitimate interests of others, the will to power creates an unjust accumulation of advantages. Reason serves the ends of the will to power by justifying the inequality of privilege. In social and ethical terms, the effect of sinful self-realization is injustice.[59]

4. Redemption and Society

Niebuhr's two basic categories in his social ethics are collective egotism and collective mutuality. They offer a foundation from which he distinguishes schemes of injustice from schemes of justice in the social order. The very idea of justice presupposes sin:

> Every definition of justice actually presupposes sin as a given reality. It is only because life is in conflict with life, because of sinful self-interest, that we are required carefully to define schemes of justice which prevent one life from taking advantage of another. Yet no scheme of justice can do full justice to all the variable factors which the freedom of man introduces into human history.[60]

Sin is the "consequence of man's self-centeredness and egotism by which he destroys the harmony of existence."[61] Collective egotism generates social sin. Social inequalities deepen as the needs of some are advanced and those of others ignored. The disparity of security and power fosters social conflict. As conflict escalates, social discord and disintegration follow. Schemes of injustice are social policies, laws, and customs into which advantage, privilege, and unequal distributions of power—class, race, gender—are embedded. Niebuhr calls these privileges "false absolutes."

Collective mutuality promotes harmony in social relations. In contrast to legal, political, and economic structures that protect privileges of some, schemes of justice are social policies, laws, and customs that balance needs and interests. They prevent persons from taking advantage of one another. By reducing social conflict, development of a healthy social order is furthered. But Niebuhr rejected the simplistic Christian view that conflict is to be avoided. He argued that it is bad politics and bad religion to judge an individual or a nation "good" on the basis of its avoidance of conflict.[62] Conflict is a permanent dimension of historical existence. Privilege and advantage are always unbalanced, and self- or group interest always an interfering factor in human decisions and actions. It is the primary function of politics to negotiate conflict—eliminating conflict is a pipe dream, in Niebuhr's view—by balancing competing interests, claims, and power.

In bringing the human good about in concrete policies, programs, and structures, schemes of justice foster the well-being of the social order. They are redemptive. Schemes of justice transform the evil of injustice that the sin of egotism creates. Sin destroys the harmony of existence in personal relations and the social order. Redemption rebuilds and promotes harmony. In eschatological terms, schemes of justice realize the reign of God. In contrast to the disintegration collective egotism creates, collective mutuality collaborates with God in the realization of a just social order.

Niebuhr rejected the characterization that redemption is from sin. Because individual and group egotism are permanent factors in the dynamics of history, sin is permanent. Redemption does not eliminate sin. The interference of sin calls for grace. The power of interest is too great to obey the inner law of love, Niebuhr says, by a "simple act of the will."[63] Christ reveals the mercy of God, he writes, "and the gospel declares that everyone is in need of that mercy, that without it we are undone."[64] As mercy, God's grace forgives the contradiction wrought in human nature by egotism. As healing, divine grace restores to human beings the capacity to do what the normative orientation of the law of love commands.[65] Divine grace does not remove egotism or its effects but enables human beings to attend to the welfare of the other.[66] The vicious circle of sin created by individual and collective self-interest is broken by the pull of divine love reorienting human freedom to meet the demands of mutuality.[67] In this reorientation, at once individual and social, divine redemption is at work.[68]

Niebuhr believed the symbol of original sin pointed directly to the persistence and universality of individual and collective egotism. He was surprised that contemporary social theorists missed the radical nature of his reinterpretation presented in *The Nature and Destiny of Man.* By even talking about original sin they pictured him, he said, "as a regressive religious authoritarian caught in the toils of an ancient legend."[69] Niebuhr believed the roots of their misunderstanding lay in their identification of the meaning of the symbol of original sin with the doctrine's premodern assumptions—an historical time of original perfection, a first couple and first sin, a fall, a change in human nature. Niebuhr thought that he had severed the untenable historical and metaphysical assumptions from the meaning of original sin and replaced them with verifiable psychological and social experience. When misunderstood by contemporary social thinkers, Niebuhr's disappointment was acute.

Niebuhr brought a uniquely modern interpretation of original sin to the Reformation tradition while remaining in continuity with it. Martin Luther had eschewed the metaphysical definition of original sin as the privation of supernatural gifts. He reemphasized Augustine's description of original sin as something in nature—a willful tendency toward evil, pride, concupiscence, unbelief. Niebuhr shared Luther's orientation. His own exploration of the meaning of original sin as egotism, the will to power, and the ideological taint of knowledge was consistent with the Reformation tradition while bringing its understanding into a thoroughly modern idiom.

Starting from Liberation

Social theologies emerging in the 1960s were marked by new kinds of questions guiding theological method. The works of Johannes Baptist Metz and Jürgen Moltmann made significant contributions to political theology in Europe.[70] In Latin America, the foundational articulation of liberation theology and the meaning of the gospel from a new social perspective was the 1968 work of Gustavo Gutiérrez, *A Theology of Liberation.*[71]

Liberation theologians criticized the metaphysical theology of the Catholic scholastic tradition as incapable of addressing the redemptive message of the gospel to a social situation characterized by oppression, poverty, and injustice. Like Reinhold Niebuhr, they found new intellectual resources for theology in theories of history and culture in the social sciences and Marxist thought.

While the Vatican chastened some Catholic theologians for their integration of Marxist perspectives into theology, gradually papal documents themselves began to reflect a theological milieu permeated with the sharpness of liberation critique. Pope John Paul II's 1984 *Reconciliation and Penance* and 1987 encyclical, *On Social Concern,* for example, speak to the problems of "social sin" and the "structures of sin," both of which were theological ideas made prominent by liberation theologians. Official statements by the Latin American Bishops in the 1970s and 1980s clearly draw from Gutiérrez and others.[72]

Picking up on the critique initiated by moral theologians a decade earlier, liberation theologians depicted the Catholic tradition's theology of sin as individualistic and legalistic. By focusing so intently on the individual, it misses the larger social context within which decisions and actions take place. As legalistic, it ends up supporting the status quo by equating sin with disobedience of law. Even though divine law and social law are distinguished, the values of obedience and acquiescence carry over from one to the other.

For the oppressed, however, the disparities of power and social inequities from which they suffer are embedded in social, political, and legal structures. If disobedience of authority and law is sinful, unjust authorities and laws remain entrenched. The social order as it is becomes what must be. An individualistic and juridical theology of sin does not have a standpoint from which to expose social injustice as sinful. At most it attributes evil to the problem of original sin, but without insight into the way in which social systems and structures perpetuate evil. Such a theology promotes conformity and stifles legitimate critique of the social order.

A basic question for liberation theologians was whether a theology of sin that worked with only two basic categories—personal or actual sin and original sin—could accommodate social analysis. In the tradition, personal sin has been conceived as an act that violated positive, natural, or divine law. Actual sin is sin in the moral sense. Original sin has been understood as analogous to personal sin. It is not actual sin in the sense of a wrong act individually committed, but through inheritance, a sin for which each human being is guilty. Original sin is sin in the ontological sense, a defect in human nature. Liberation theologians argued that each category privatizes sin. Even the universality of evil is understood in terms of the individual inheritance of Adam's sin.

But with the tradition, liberation theologians acknowledged that sinfulness is rooted in personal acts. To grasp the dimensions of human evil, however, requires moving beyond individual categories—actual or inherited sin—to uncover the way in which human beings create social systems and structures that institutionalize oppression, domination, and privilege. Without denying personal or original sin, liberation theologians advocated the inclusion of a third category, *social sin*.[73] Social sin is a consequence of individual sinful acts, yet it goes beyond the individual. Social sin becomes embodied in customs, personal relations, and social structures. What has been socially constructed distorts personal consciousness, leading both oppressor and oppressed into believing that the social order reflects what is natural.

Liberation theologians grounded their expansion of the tradition's understanding of sin in revelation. Both the Johannine "sin of the world" (John 1:29) and the Pauline "evil age" (Gal 1:4) symbolize the penetration of evil into every dimension of human living. The Hebrew prophets see sin as social, not simply individual. The prophet Amos condemns those "that trample on the needy, and bring to ruin the poor of the land" (Amos 8:4). Isaiah correlates good with justice, a social remedy to evil: "Cease to do evil, learn to do good; seek justice, rescue the oppressed, defend the orphan, plead for the widow" (Isa 1:17).

Since original sin has been the Christian tradition's explanation for the universal sin, the obvious question asked of liberation theologians regarded the relation between social sin and original sin. Are they the same? Is social sin *original sin?* Some theologians equated them. Others differentiated between them. The Roman Catholic magisterium specifically denied an equivalence. The widely popular Dutch *Catechism,* commissioned by the Bishops of the Netherlands and published in the United States in 1967, offers an example of the divide between these views.[74]

The Dutch *Catechism* characterized itself as offering a fresh and innovative reinterpretation of Christian beliefs for a new age framed by a dynamic evolutionary and historically conscious worldview. Its section on "The Power of Sin" includes questions about historical beginnings, Genesis 3, and the origin of sin (259–69). The authors candidly present contemporary difficulties with the traditional doctrine of original sin resulting from modern scientific and historical inquiry.

The writers acknowledge the symbolic genre of Genesis 3. Adam and Eve's sin, they write, "is closer than we imagine. It is our own selves" (263). About the beginning of human sinfulness they conclude that "its origin in world history remains incomprehensible" (264). They bridge theological and historical views of the story by writing that Genesis 3 "can never be replaced as a summary of how man stands before God. But it can and must be replaced as a description of the beginning of mankind" (262).

Sin is not just imperfection, the *Catechism* insists. Yet in a world of ascending evolution, "sin is often nothing but the refusal to grow in the direction which conscience reveals" (264). This description of sin, reminiscent of the early church theologian Irenaeus, reflects the *Catechism*'s effort to break away from legal descriptions of sin.[75] The collective character of evil reveals "degrees of contagiousness which attach to our sins" (265). This contagion of sin subverts the apprehension of authentic values. "In a covetous family, children find it natural to be grasping, in a selfish society, individuals are easily selfish, colonialism produces exploiters and racism produces racists" (265).

The biblical indictment that "sin reigns in the world" means that the "whole of humanity is in a condition in which its values are obscured" (265). The writers identify this condition with original sin. It belongs to each person as his or her own. Prior to acts and coloring all of them, this condition is "an unwillingness to respond to God, a refusal in the face of real love" (266). This condition creates an impotence and a solidarity in guilt that are not caused by propagation or descent from one man and woman but by the refusal of human beings to heed God's call. The sin that stains others, the *Catechism* insists, "was not only committed by an Adam at the beginning of man's story, but by 'Adam,' man, every man. It is 'the sin of the world.' It includes my sins. I am not an innocent lamb which is corrupted by others. I help in the work of corruption" (266).

The Dutch *Catechism*'s theology of sin was enormously successful on the popular level but raised concerns on the magisterial level. The Roman Catholic College of Cardinals explicitly countered its interpretation of original sin. The cardinals issued a response to the *Catechism* reinforcing the church's traditional teaching on original sin. The cardinals specifically rejected an equivalence between the biblical sin of the world and the doctrine of original sin. In the cardinals' judgment, the *Catechism*'s discussion of historical beginnings, solidarity in sin, and the contagion of sin portrayed the transmission of original sin sociologically (the influence of evil persons and acts on others) rather than biologically, through physical generation, as the Tridentine dogma maintained. Recalling the fifth-century debate between Augustine and Pelagius, the cardinals criticized the *Catechism*'s understanding of original sin as too Pelagian.[76]

Conclusion

The work of theologians such as Piet Schoonenberg and Reinhold Niebuhr has been influential in bringing a basic theological question out into the open. Is the meaning of humankind's alienation from God inexorably tied—for Christian doctrine—to Genesis 3, the classical formulation shaped by Augustine, and the metaphysical categories of the medieval theologians? For Catholic theologians, the question must be extended slightly. Is the dogmatic formulation of the sixteenth-century Council of Trent the only way that humankind's root sin may be conceptualized?

Both Schoonenberg and Niebuhr drew upon modern insights and categories to rethink the reality early church writers named in their theological anthropology a condition in human beings of original sin, *peccatum originale originatum.* Each appealed to different biblical texts in a different way from the theological tradition for different insights into human sinfulness. Each sought to understand the reality of human alienation from God and evil within the context of a dynamic, evolutionary world and a modern critical apprehension of history and human origins. Each drew from modern thinkers such as Karl Marx to integrate into their theology of original sin modern insights into ideology and the social construction of knowledge. Finally, both Schoonenberg and Niebuhr left the abstract anthropology of the Christian theological tradition behind, moving into a concrete method of self-reflection and social analysis to understand the dynamics of sin in the human person and in history.

7. ORIGINAL SIN IN FEMINIST THEOLOGY

CHRISTIAN FEMINIST THEOLOGIES of sin and redemption commonly derive insight from two historical vantage points: (1) an analysis of the origin and development of male domination, and (2) a recovery of the redemptive vision embedded in Jesus' preaching and activity and the praxis of the early Jesus communities.

The Meaning and Effect of Doctrines

In their interpretation of the Christian doctrine of original sin, feminist theologians introduce gender as a specific category of analysis. How is gender construed within the religious worldview created by the doctrine? What effect has this doctrine had on the personal, social, and religious worlds in which women and men live?

For the feminist evaluation of the doctrine and understanding of original sin, we draw especially from the work of *Rosemary Radford Ruether*[1] and *Elisabeth Schüssler Fiorenza.*[2] The theological analysis of sin, and the reinterpretation of original sin, is a central topic in the work of many feminist theologians.[3]

Religious traditions arise from particular human beings, perspectives, and settings. This human particularity generates distinctive religious beliefs, practices, institutional structures, texts, and theological reflection. Until recent decades, these public dimensions of Christianity were influenced largely by males.[4] For feminist theologians, this fact begs explanation. How does gender influence the appropriation and understanding of religious realities? Does the theological interpretation

153

of these realities—God, grace, sin, Christ, redemption, faith, church—reflect male *interests* as well as male experience?

The Christian theology of original sin was developed by individual theologians in the early church. Understanding these theologians requires locating them in relation to their historical time, cultural setting, ethnic group, class, ecclesial status, and gender. The historical question "How did early church theologians think of the origin of evil?" uncovers even further data for insight when gender is included: "How did male theologians in the early church think of the origin of evil?" Raising gender explicitly as a category of analysis highlights aspects of theological reflection that otherwise go unnoticed:

- What—or whom—did male theologians blame for evil?
  Would women have thought of themselves as the cause of evil?
- How did men conceive of redemption for women?
  Would women have made acquiescence to motherhood the condition for their salvation?
- What did male theologians assume about women in their anthropology?
  Would women have defined themselves as defective males?
- In whom did men locate the image of God?
  Would women have denied they possessed the image of God in themselves?
- How did men limit preaching the gospel?
  Would women have excluded themselves from preaching the good news of Christ's redemption?
- How did male theologians conceive of woman's place in the social order, in marriage, and in the church?
  Would women have restricted themselves to the domestic realm without the social, political, legal, and religious privileges of persons?

What has been the *effect* of the classical doctrine of original sin? To answer this question requires evaluation. Has the doctrine been beneficial or detrimental to the well-being of women? Did the doctrine developed by male theologians promote or diminish the full humanity of women? Did the doctrine men formulated validate equality between women and men or reinforce inequality? Did the doctrine advanced by males in the early church challenge cultural views of female inferiority and female evil as sinful or sanction these cultural views as divine revelation?

For many Christians today, the doctrine of original sin refers to the story of Adam and Eve. Their rejection of the historicity of the story often results in a subsequent dismissal of the doctrine itself as myth.[5] In Rosemary Radford Ruether's judgment, however, original sin has a real meaning apart from its traditional connection to the Genesis story. There is a fundamental sin that distorts personal relations and social structures. There is a root sin—a basic original sin—that alienates humankind from divine mystery. Naming this sin, Ruether argues, is central to theological analysis today.

1. Explaining Sin by Gender

Early church theologians appealed to the story of Adam and Eve as divine revelation. In their writings, reference to Genesis 2–3 often includes specific concern with gender. The history they found revealed was threefold: (1) woman's creation as an inferior human being, (2) woman's sin as the cause for the fall of humankind from divine friendship, and (3) male rule as a divinely willed feature of the created order.

The earliest example is the New Testament text 1 Timothy 2:8–15. This letter is the work of an anonymous author writing in Paul's name near the end of the first century or early in the second century C.E.[6] The writer prescribes a subordinate place for women in the *ekklesia* on the basis of Eve's derivative creation and her primary role in sin:

> Let a woman learn in silence with full submission. I permit no woman to teach or to have authority over a man; she is to keep silent. For Adam was formed first, then Eve; and Adam was not deceived, but the woman was deceived and became a transgressor. (2:12–14)[7]

For this writer, the subordinate place of women in the "household of God" (3:15) corresponds with their subordinate place in the patriarchal household in the social order.[8] His prerequisite for women's salvation—acquiescence in childbearing—follows the cultural definition of women in relation to procreative capacities. Further, he makes her children part of the condition for salvation: "Yet she will be saved through childbearing, provided they continue in faith and love and holiness, with modesty" (2:15). "This is a truly shocking statement," Linda Maloney writes, "since it seems to say that Christ's redemptive work does not extend to women; rather they must save themselves by a particular mode of conduct."[9] Subsequent patristic writers, citing this 1 Timothy, reinforced the bond between woman's procreative purpose and her salvation. Ambrose of Milan wrote, citing 1 Timothy, "Yet woman, we are told, 'will be saved through childbearing,' in the course of which she generated Christ."[10]

Early church theologians picked up on 1 Timothy's perspective and broadened its scope, blaming women not only for the origin of sin but regarding them as sin. Tertullian's invective against women exposes a not-so-latent misogynism in his interpretation of Genesis 3. Addressing women, he writes:

> *You* are the devil's gateway: *you* are the unsealer of that (forbidden) tree: *you* are the first deserter of the divine law: *you* are she who persuaded him whom the devil was not valiant enough to attack. *You* destroyed so easily God's image, man. On account of *your* desert—that is, death—even the Son of Man had to die.[11]

This explanation of the origin of sin depicts the root sin by which human beings distort the created order. Androcentric or male-centered ideologies of female inferiority and evil distort the relations of mutuality that should exist between women and men. Theologians have pointed to the sin of Eve to ground the subjugation of all women to male rule. Domination extends beyond gender, but the form of the root sin remains the same. The natural superiority of some (by class, ethnicity, religion) is elevated as the legitimation of their rightful domination over others in the personal, social, and religious realms of human living.

From the vantage point of gender, the theology of original sin in the Christian tradition has not been beneficial for women. Embedded in the doctrine's conceptual world is a gender dualism of male superiority and female inferiority, a denial that women possess the image of God fully as persons, and the assumption that male privilege and rule is the divinely guaranteed order of creation. An example is John Chrysostom's retelling of Genesis 3. Speaking in God's voice, he writes:

> Because you abandoned your equal, who was sharer with you in the same nature and for whom you were created, and you chose to enter into conversation with the evil creature the serpent, and to take the advice he had to give, accordingly I subject you to him in

future and designate him as your master for you to recognize his lordship, and since you do not know how to rule, learn well how to be ruled.[12]

2. The Purpose of Feminist Theology

Rosemary Radford Ruether places the critique of the classical doctrine of original sin at the heart of feminist theology. The very purpose of feminist theology is to name evil rightly. Ruether writes that the essential core of feminist theology "lies in the unmasking of this victim-blaming ideology of sin. *Patriarchalism* is named as evil, as a system that both produced and justifies aggressive power and domination of women and all subjugated people."[13]

Human beings are molded by the human world they have created. Walter Wink writes that "we come into a world already institutionally organized, often for injustice."[14] To confine gender relations to the private realm of the authority of individual males over individual females misses the systemic and structural dimension of evil. Ruether describes patriarchy as a massive historical system of victimization of women. Patriarchalism is a social construction rather than "nature." In its expression as male domination, patriarchalism is the "original sin of sexism."[15] Describing the comprehensiveness of sexism as a structural sin, and linking it with the metaphorical language of Paul, Elisabeth Schüssler Fiorenza writes that sexism encompasses

> the dehumanizing trends, injustices, and discriminations of institutions, the theology and symbol system that legitimate these institutions, and the collective and personal "false consciousness" created by sexist institutions and ideologies and internalized in socialization and education. This "false consciousness" permits oppressed people and groups to accept their oppression and to internalize the values of the oppressor. This understanding of patriarchal sexism as structural sin and evil power institutionalized in societal and ecclesial oppressive structures is akin to Paul's understanding of sin as transpersonal, destructive power whose ultimate expression is the life-destroying power of death.[16]

In this light, one of the doctrine's central judgments—that no one can avoid sin—takes on a critical and distinctively modern meaning. What cannot be avoided, Ruether argues, are the distortions of the social order created and sustained by male domination. "We are all products of the original sin of sexism."[17] Sexism embeds male privilege and female marginalization into all aspects of human living. Feminist theology unmasks this sin:

> The classical justifications of women's subordination as due to natural inferiority, subordination in the order of creation, and punishment for sin are assumed to be false ideologies constructed to justify injustice. The domination of men over women is sinful, and patriarchy is a sinful social system. Far from reflecting the true will of God and the nature of women, such theological constructions subvert God's creation and distort human nature. Feminist theology is about the deconstruction of these ideological justifications of male domination and the vindication of women's equality as the true will of God, human nature, and Christ's redemptive intention.[18]

For Ruether, the critical principal of feminist theology is the full humanity of women. She utilizes this principle to evaluate scripture as revelatory. Are scriptural texts that marginalize women revelatory? Do patriarchal texts speak the word of God? Are texts that privilege men divine revelation?[19] Until recent decades, Christian men easily answered Yes. Some continue to do so. Beginning from the judgments that patriarchalism is humankind's original sin and sexism a primary expression of original sin, Ruether rejects patriarchal texts as mediators of revelation: "Whatever denies, diminishes, or distorts the full humanity of women is, therefore, appraised as not redemptive."[20] Biblical scholar Schüssler Fiorenza argues that *the* litmus test for invoking scripture as the Word of God "must be whether or not biblical texts and traditions seek to end relations of domination and exploitation."[21]

As Schüssler Fiorenza points out, nineteenth-century feminist biblical interpretation was initiated by the insight that those who opposed the emancipation of slaves and women used the Bible to do so. The problem was not that they misused the texts. Scripture could be used against women's struggle for liberation, Schüssler Fiorenza writes, because "they are patriarchal texts and therefore can serve to legitimate women's subordinate role and secondary status in patriarchal society and church."[22] She characterizes the feminist dimension of biblical interpretation in this way:

> Biblical interpretation as theological interpretation is concerned with the divine presence dwelling among the people of God in the

past and present. Feminist biblical interpretation makes explicit that divine truth and revelatory presence are found among women, who are the invisible members of the people of God. It makes explicit that the receivers and proclaimers of revelation are not solely men but also women.[23]

Feminist biblical interpretation brings to light the way androcentric texts marginalize the role of women in the history of salvation. The visibility of men as speakers and actors and the corresponding invisibility of women in the *written text* does not correspond with *historical reality* as lived. The text reflects the androcentric lens through which the male writer filtered reality.[24] This remains a feature of androcentric writings in the present, too.

The Emergence of Patriarchy

For feminist theologians, the historical question about original sin is entwined with that of the origin of male privilege in the ancient world. Patriarchal society has an historical origin, even if the details of its emergence and development remain obscure. Over a long period of time, through complex processes of socialization and violence, it became a particular means of structuring human relations.

Ruether writes that patriarchal societies developed gradually "with the change from food gathering and gardening to plow agriculture, private landholding, urbanization, and class stratification. In the ancient Near East this happened between the seventh and the fourth millennia B.C.E."[25] The development of pre-industrial agrarian cultures created the conditions for rise of kingship, standing armies, conquest states, and empires. New Testament scholar Walter Wink describes these societies as domination systems. They are characterized "by unjust economic relations, oppressive political relations, biased race relations, patriarchal gender relations, hierarchical power relations, and the use of violence to maintain them all."[26]

The emergence of private property generated the historical conditions for economic disparities and class stratification. Within elite and non-elite classes, hierarchical relations were extended by the gradual development of a gender ideology that privileged males.[27]

1. Social Order

The smallest social and economic unit in pre-industrial agrarian societies is the patriarchal household or family. The household refers to that over which the *paterfamilias,* the father or male head of household, has authority. The household is property—human beings (wives, children, servants, slaves), animals, land, and equipment. In the patriarchal household, relations among persons are hierarchically structured according to multiple and interwoven factors of gender, birth, and class status.

Of the many kinds of human subordination to the rule of another, gender is the most basic form. In contrast to children and slaves, who are "temporarily or situationally in a status of dependency," Ruether writes, "women are generically in this status."[28] Political, legal, and religious laws of the ancient world fixed the superior and inferior status of men and women as normative. Socialization embedded gender hierarchy in personal and cultural consciousness as the way the human world must be.[29] Walter Wink writes that people become "mired in a counternarrative that they endow with indubitable historicity: the belief that domination by males, by the powerful, and by the rich is given in the nature of things, from time immemorial, from the mind of God."[30] The supremacy of males and rule by elites, he says, is uncritically assumed to be normative, natural, and inevitable.

The fourth-century B.C.E. Greek philosopher Aristotle took the hierarchical divisions of class and gender for granted. His political paradigm for the state was the patriarchal household—the natural subjection of populace to king was analogous to the natural subjection of the female to male in marriage. In contrast to the Sophists, Schüssler Fiorenza writes, Aristotle

> stressed that the patriarchal relationships in the household and city, as well as their concomitant social differences, are based not on social convention but on "nature." He therefore insisted that the discussion of political ethics and household management begin with marriage, defined as the union of natural ruler and natural subject (*Politeia* I. 1252a. 24–28).[31]

It is well known that Aristotle defined the female fetus as a misbegotten male. His idea made its way into the anthropology assumed by medieval theologians. Thomas Aquinas accepted and cited it.[32]

But what was Aristotle's interest in defining female nature? In the view of classics scholar Marilyn Arthur, Aristotle's biological theory was occasioned by the desire to resolve the contradiction between the Athenian political ideals and the actual political structures created by Athenian ruling males.[33] His biological theory legitimated the status quo.

The Athenian political ideal espoused democratic equality for all persons. Yet actual rights and privileges of the social order—represented by full citizenship—were restricted to a few, namely, free propertied male heads of households. If the democratic ideal was to be coherently maintained, the denial of rights to some required justification. Aristotle's biological theory of female nature as defective legitimated the political exclusion of women as well as their subordinate place in the patriarchal household. *Person* applied to *male nature,* that is, complete nature. In a parallel way, Aristotle appealed to class stratification to justify the exclusion of non-elite males from political participation in the social order. *Person* applied to *propertied elite males.* In two swift strokes, both dependent on hierarchical relations as natural, Aristotle resolved the contradiction between the political ideal of democracy *(inclusion of all)* and the actual political order *(exclusion of most).*

2. Anthropology

Patriarchal anthropologies divide human beings into two basic groups: those whose nature entitles them to rule and those whose nature it is to be ruled. Humanness is imagined hierarchically on a continuum of "more or less." Those who name their own nature as superior or complete grant themselves rights and privileges of persons. Others, as nonpersons, are denied full participation in the economic, political, legal, and religious dimensions of the social order. This difference between human beings structures the social order. Distinctions between elite/non-elite, free/slave, and male/female are depicted—and internalized—as natural to the social order, or in the religious terms of some traditions, intrinsic to the created order. Adherence to one's place is a primary value in domination systems and the chief obligation of all members of the social order.

The inequities expressed in cultural ways of living, ethical and religious precepts, and legal systems in the ancient world reflect developments reaching over long periods of time. Gender subordination, along with slaveholding, is an aspect of the economics of private property. As property became concentrated in the hands of a few, the means of subsistence as well as wealth were also limited to a few. Studies suggest that the elite were only 1–5 percent of the population.[34]

Patriarchal conceptions of human nature and the social order reflect the perspectives of elite males. The projection of a gender dualism parallels a similar class dualism. In both cases, one "nature" (male/elite) is defined as fully human and the other (female/non-elite female) is defined as less than fully human. Already-existing privilege is sustained by defining the other as incomplete, defective, or flawed in some way.[35] Ideologies of superiority codify these differences through stories, theories, and laws. Aristotle's biological theory and 1 Timothy's appeal to Genesis 2–3 offer two examples of patriarchal gender ideologies. Projections of male superiority and female inferiority become actual differences by restriction of females from participation in the public dimensions of the social order—education, politics, economic life, and religious cult.

Androcentric anthropologies differentiate male and female nature by their possession of distinctively human capacities. Male nature is identified with the most valued of human capacities, reason. While not denying females some share of intelligence and rationality, males link female nature with body—procreative capacities, emotions, and instincts. The author of 1 Timothy, for example, is most concerned that women not teach or have authority over a man—roles identified with reason, thus with males. He seeks to realign women with their proper, bodily role of procreation, even at the price of losing the equality of salvation in Christ and the meaning of salvation as gift.[36]

A gendered conception of good and evil is completed by the identification of (1) the *good* with *reason* and *reason* with *male* nature, and (2) *evil* with *body* and *body* with *female* nature. Women are depicted as more prone to evil, or worse, as evil.[37]

In Ruether's terms, patriarchy names evil as physical and social otherness.[38] The other is not-male. Males attempt to secure themselves against evil by separating themselves from females. Ruether calls this identification of women with the lower half of the gender dualism *a false naming of evil*. It misses the real evil—*patriarchalism*.

3. Religion
In the ancient world, the modern separation of "church and state" does not exist. Religion is embedded in social life. It is integrated with

the social, political, legal, and economic dimensions of the social order. Religious beliefs, structures, and rituals mirror basic features of the wider culture.

In patriarchal societies, religion is patriarchal. Religion reinforces the status quo of male rule. Ruether writes that "women are systematically subordinated, treated as quasi-property of fathers and husbands, denied autonomous public status and confined to domestic service roles as well as marginalized and denigrated in the religious cult."[39] Patriarchal religion

> models religious law and symbols, including the symbols for God, after a patriarchal, hierarchical, ethnocentric and slave-holding society. It uses the religious symbols to validate this society, to make it appear normative, to make God appear to be the creator and sanctioner of this society and adherence to it to be the divine will and the means of salvation. The existing human order and the divine order are seen as coherent and unified. God as creator, lawgiver and redeemer spreads "his" sacred canopy over things as they are. The rulers in the present social hierarchy are God's agents in rule; those who are subject to them are admonished to obey. To disobey one's king, priest, father or husband is to disobey God. This is the religion of the sacred canopy which stabilizes and sanctifies the present patterns of society.[40]

In ancient Israel, Torah commands were gender-specific.[41] The sign of circumcision marked Israelite males as full members of the covenant community. Their obligation was observance of the whole law. Women were members of Israel through the man to whom a primary relation of dependence existed—father, husband, son. Their place in the covenant community was subordinate to men.[42] Religious privileges given to men were denied to women. They were not allowed to observe the whole law but were limited to the negative commandments and laws specifically designed for women. This difference created "separate and unequal spheres for women and men," Jewish historian Ross Kraemer writes.[43]

The same must be said for the New Testament. Androcentric texts structure and sanction male domination. Cultural "household codes" are integrated into several New Testament texts to prescribe proper behavior and roles within the *ekklesia*. These codes mandate relations of domination and subordination as normative between husband and wife, master and slave, and parents and children.[44]

This is the obvious interest of the writer of 1 Timothy. He desires an *ekklesia* in conformity with the cultural paradigm, not one opposed to its norms. The place of women and men in the Christian community should be, in his view, the same as in the patriarchal world around them. He makes this explicit by describing the *ekklesia* as the household of God (3:15). Class and gender domination are not evils that redemption overcomes—as they are in Galatians 3:28—but normative for human living. He directs his counsel about slavery not to the Christian owner of slaves but to the slave. The chief virtue of the slave is obedience to the master. For the slave, the prerequisite for being a good Christian is acquiescence to slavery:

> Let all who are under the yoke of slavery regard their masters as worthy, so that the name of God and the teaching may not be blasphemed. Those who have believing masters must not be disrespectful to them on the ground they are members of the church; rather they must serve them all the more since those who benefit by their service are believers and beloved. (6:1–2)

The author secures the privileged place of male Christians by appeal to Eve's derivative creation and her initiative in sin.[45] In doing so, the writer laid the foundation for a distinctively Christian pattern of scriptural interpretation and religious construction of gender relations. Subsequent Christian theologians embraced 1 Timothy as a divinely revealed starting point for their reflections on the historical origin, cause, and punishment for sin.[46]

The World Transformed in Jesus' Preaching

Recovery of a more liberating, women-friendly strand in Christian origins has been fueled by contemporary New Testament scholarship. Studies have gradually transformed two prior dominant assumptions about Jesus: (1) that the object of Jesus' message was the disclosure of his divine identity, and (2) that Jesus' understanding of salvation was other-worldly. These insights generate a different understanding of what Jesus meant by sin, the social order, and redemption.

The presumption that Jesus' message was about himself developed naturally in the early church. This is clearly the portrayal of Jesus in the Gospel of John, for example. Early Christians read the post-resurrection Gospel narratives as descriptions of the historical life of Jesus. As proclamations of faith in the risen Jesus, however, the Gospels are not histories. The Jesus followers' experience of the risen Jesus shapes the portrayal of Jesus' words and activity.[47] Their experience is projected backward into the depiction of Jesus' life.

The object of Jesus' preaching was not himself but the familiar eschatological symbol of Jewish hope and expectation of *basileia,* the "reign of God."[48] Jesus took this symbol as a means of social critique. It mediated a vision of an alternative kind of rule to that experienced under elites.

1. God's Empire

New Testament scholar Stephen Patterson translates *basileia* as "empire" rather than the more common choices of "reign," "rule," or "kingdom."[49] By doing so, he highlights the meaning this symbol would evoke for Jesus' Jewish hearers. The marginalized, oppressed, and exploited persons who heard Jesus' preaching would hear God's empire as a contrast to the empire of their experience—Rome. Everyone knew what Rome's rule was like. It was not pretty. Indiscriminate violence against innocent people was routine, as was exhaustive tribute, wide-scale peasant indebtedness and loss of land, ever-growing estates of the wealthy and powerful elite, subsistence level existence for most, and desperation for virtually all.[50]

A common theme marked Jesus' words and actions. What would *God*'s empire be like? What would life be like if *God*'s *interests* shaped the social order rather than the interests of the elites? Jesus' befriending of expendables, outsiders, the subordinate, and exploitable announced God's empire as inclusive, accepting, and compassionate. He prayed for God to meet the basic problems experienced by the oppressed: bread, forgiveness of debt, relief of unnecessary suffering.

Rome's empire was a domination system. Jesus directed his preaching toward a social world radically divided between the few for whom the means of life were assured and the many for whom the means of life were unavailable. His teaching, parables, and relations with the non-persons of this social order exposed what was evil about the world in which they were immersed. As Walter Wink writes, Jesus' words and deeds were not those of a "minor reformer, but of an egalitarian prophet who repudiates the very premises on which domination is based: the right of some to lord it over others by means of power, wealth, shaming, or titles."[51]

2. Jesus and Patriarchy

Biblical scholar and theologian Elisabeth Schüssler Fiorenza has been at the forefront of feminist exegetical and historical studies of the New Testament and Christian origins.[52] She brings new questions to the data. What did women find attractive in Jesus' words and actions? Why were women drawn to the movements before and after Jesus' death? What would Jesus' appeal to the *basileia* of God have meant to them? How did they find his message redemptive? What was the liberating power of the *basileia* for them? Pursuing these kinds of questions has resulted in a fuller apprehension of Jesus' preaching and the religious movement that followed his death.

Walter Wink reinforces the significance of feminist questions. The unusual nature of Jesus' treatment of women in the first century went unnoticed, Wink notes, until the rise of contemporary feminist studies. It is now clear, Wink writes, "that Jesus treated women as he did, not because he was 'gallant' or 'nice,' but because the restoration of women to their full humanity in partnership with men is integral to the coming of God's egalitarian order."[53]

Rosemary Radford Ruether begins her historical work on women and redemption on a similar note. "The story necessarily begins with Jesus," she writes, "because 'something happened' in his ministry that suggested to some early Christians that gender relations had been changed by redemption."[54]

Jesus' portrayal of his new family offers a clue into Jesus' vision of redemptive change. In Mark 3:34–35,[55] Jesus disparages identification with his biological family to signal a new kinship group.[56] This group consists of those who do the will of God. Notably absent in Jesus' new family is the *paterfamilias,* the male head of household. His kinship group is not the patriarchal family. Only God is father in this reconstituted family. God's compassionate acceptance and inclusion of all members as persons replaces the sovereignty of the *paterfamilias* and the far-reaching prerogatives accorded him by patriarchal laws and customs.

Without insight into historical patriarchy, this memory of Jesus' words is unintelligible to modern readers. Jesus' exclusion of the *paterfamilias* is a rejection of patriarchy. Patriarchal structures generate and fix disparities in power. They promote the dignity of a few at the expense and dehumanization of the many. Inequalities are sustained as well as internalized by ideologies of superiority. A social system in which the ownership of human beings by others is taken for granted is a primary expression of sin.[57] Jesus' affirmation of those rendered non-persons in the patriarchal social order embodies redemption.

Women were part of the groups described in gender-neutral terms as the expendable, oppressed, and exploited. They heard Jesus preach and engaged with him in personal encounters and open table fellowship. Gender is explicitly visible, however, in the historical memories of Jesus' words. Jesus calls a woman "daughter of Abraham" when he heals her of a spinal disease. Walter Wink writes that this designation "was to make her a full-fledged member of the covenant and of equal standing before God" with men.[58] Jesus' refused to acknowledge the value of women simply as bearers of male children in his response to the woman who called from the crowd, "Blessed is the womb that bore you and the breasts that nursed you!" His words reinforce again the liberating condition for membership in this new family: "Blessed rather are those who hear the word of God and obey it."

Gender is also explicit in Jesus' actions.[59] Jesus transgressed cultural gender norms and boundaries by speaking with women in public and private, sharing table fellowship with Jewish and Gentile women, recognizing them as disciples, having his mind changed by at least one, and ignoring the androcentric labeling of economically destitute women forced into prostitution as unclean and sinful. He healed women and responded to their needs as legitimate. The patriarchal presumption of male privilege is absent in Jesus' words and actions. He did not exploit his status as male at the expense of women, as a patriarchal culture assured even a non-elite male.

In his teaching and parables, Jesus appeals numerous times to feminine images to depict divine reality. He compares the empire of God not only to leaven, considered in the ancient world a corrupt and unclean substance and within Israel as a symbol of unholy Israel, but even further to the actions of a woman—who as female also symbolizes impurity—working with the leaven.[60]

3. Following Jesus

In his words and actions—parables, stories, healings, exorcisms, friendships, and encounters—Jesus signaled domination as *sin* and freedom from subordinate status as *redemption*. Redemption restores creation to its divinely intended order. Continuity between Jesus' insight into redemption and the redemptive reality lived by the Jesus communities is suggested by the baptismal fragment cited by Paul in his letter to the Galatians: "There is no longer Jew or Greek, there is no longer slave or free, there is no longer male and female; for all of you are one in Christ Jesus" (3:28). In each of the three contrasts, relations of mutuality transform hierarchical and sinful relations of domination and subordination. In the judgment of historical theologian Sheila Briggs, "The words of Gal. 3:28 are the clearest statement of women's equality to be found in the Christian scriptures."[61]

Equality among Jesus followers is a constant refrain in Paul's letters. In Galatians, for example, he grounds equality in the gift of God's Spirit. By proclaiming "freedom from the law," Paul argued that inclusion in Israel's covenant no longer required that Gentile women and men become Jewish women and men by doing the works of the law, that is, by living as Jews.[62] Paul located the sufficient condition for Gentile inclusion in each believer's response to the resurrection preaching. In his view, God had already validated this condition: "The only thing I want to learn from you is this: Did you receive the Spirit by doing the works of the law or by believing what you heard?" (3:2).

In the exegetical tradition, Pauline interpreters focused exclusively on the equality established by Christ between Jew and Gentile. But the experience of redemptive equality was also between women and men. Those who believe in the risen Christ, Paul writes, are equally "descendants of Abraham" (3:6), "children of God" (3:26), "heirs according to the promise" (3:29). Descendents, children, and heirs are "brothers and sisters in Christ" (1:11; 3:15). Like the woman Jesus called "daughter of Abraham," women are now full-fledged members of Israel's covenant and of equal standing with men before God.[63]

Paul's language is striking. By rejecting circumcision as the sign of full membership in Israel, Paul implicitly renounces what Jewish theologian Ross Kraemer describes as the "separate and unequal spheres" mandated by the Torah.[64] Paul did not eliminate gender roles and norms entirely, but neither did he substitute a new norm for the Torah that would sustain gender hierarchy.[65] This absence of substitution is significant. Paul appealed to the Galatians: "For freedom Christ has set us free. Stand firm therefore, and do not submit again to the yoke of slavery" (5:1).[66] This appeal bears as much relevance for gender relations as for ethnic relations—perhaps even more. Gentiles had not been under the yoke of the Torah to which they were not to submit again, as had women under the yoke of male domination.

Paul calls upon the Galatians to live the redemptive equality that had begun with the Christ event. His proclamation "For neither circumcision nor uncircumcision is anything; but a new creation is everything!" (6:15) transposes Jesus' vision and preaching of the *basileia*. The new creation is a community, a new kinship group—the new family constituted by those who do the will of God, as Jesus envisioned it. Paul's vision was a radical one. The Torah was no longer a "fence" around Israel, separating Jew from Gentile. Circumcision would no longer mark Jewish privilege over Gentiles. No longer would class privilege sustain slavery or male privilege sustain female subjugation. The baptism fragment renounces *privilege* as sin. It signals the Jesus followers' apprehension of the *root* sin by which human beings alienate themselves from God and from one another.

Schüssler Fiorenza pinpoints the similarity between Jesus' insight into redemption preserved in Mark's Gospel and Paul's theology of the Spirit:

> According to Mark's Gospel, the discipleship of equals is the community of brothers and sisters who do not have a "father." It is the "new family" that has replaced all the natural, social kinship ties of the patriarchal family. It does not consist of rulers and subjects, of relationships of superordination and subordination. According to Paul it is the *ekklesia,* the "assembly of saints" who have equal access to God in the Spirit and are therefore coequal members in the body of Christ. Social roles in this *ekklesia* are not based on natural or social differences but on charismatic giftedness.[67]

In the Pauline communities, membership and roles were linked to the Spirit. Paul's description of the gifts of the Spirit and different roles in the body of Christ—apostles, prophets, teachers—in 1 Corinthians 12 is gender-neutral. Romans 16 specifically identifies a number of women leaders in the Jesus movement, including Paul's fellow evangelist,

Prisca, and Junia, "prominent among the apostles."[68] To the implicit question, "Does redemption in Christ dissolve gender hierarchy?" these texts assert "Yes."

Not all New Testament writings will make such an assertion about redemption. The author of 1 Timothy offers an unambiguous "No" to this implicit question.[69] Subjection to male rule is God's enduring punishment of woman for Eve's sin. The writer's designation of the *ekklesia* as the "household of God" (3:15) explicitly reappropriates patriarchal norms of the broader culture. The letter stratifies both religious participation and leadership according to the divisions structuring the patriarchal social order. In contrast to the charismatic giftedness that generates roles in the Pauline communities, roles in 1 Timothy reflect prerequisites of class and gender (3:4, 8). At least prescriptively, church order mirrors the social order. Ruether describes 1 Timothy as the cornerstone text for a Christian gender ideology of male domination.[70]

The deutero-Pauline letters reflect conflicts about gender in the first-century Jesus movement.[71] They provide evidence for the patriarchalization of the church in the late first and early second century C.E. In particular, the writers appeal to "household codes," brief summaries of the proper relation of persons in the patriarchal household. Elisabeth Schüssler Fiorenza proposes that a more accurate designation is "patriarchal submission texts" because they seek to bring the communal structure of the *ekklesia* into line with the structure of the patriarchal household."[72] Schüssler Fiorenza notes that the complete form of the patriarchal submission text is found only in Colossians 3:18–4:1and Ephesians 5:22–6:9, although elements of it are found elsewhere in New Testament and early Christian writings. As in the patriarchal household, relations in the *ekklesia* are to be hierarchical:

> Wives, be subject to your husbands, as is fitting in the Lord. Husbands, love your wives and never treat them harshly. Children, obey your parents in everything, for this is your acceptable duty in the Lord. Fathers, do not provoke your children, or they may lose heart. Slaves, obey your earthly masters in everything, not only while being watched and in order to please them, but wholeheartedly, fearing the Lord. (Col 3:18–22)
>
> Wives, be subject to your husbands as you are to the Lord. For the husband is the head of the wife just as Christ is the head of the church, the body of which he is the Savior. Just as the church is subject to Christ, so also wives ought to be, in everything, to their

husbands....Children, obey your parents in the Lord, for this is right....Slaves, obey your earthly masters with fear and trembling, in singleness of heart, as you obey Christ; not only to please them, but as slaves of Christ, doing the will of God from the heart. (Eph 5:22–6:6)

The appropriation of patriarchal submission texts submerged the redemptive meaning of Jesus' discipleship family as a specific rejection of patriarchal structures. Overshadowed, too, was the communal experience reflected in Galatians 3:27–29. Jesus' vision of the *basileia* as an alternative kind of social order gradually shifted from an exigence to transform the present to a distant and future destiny. The import of the *basileia* for gender relations was submerged. The Christian church created its own separate and unequal spheres for women and men.[73] The doctrine of original sin mediated a theological anthropology that justified inequality on the basis of woman's responsibility for the origin of sin and her subordination to male rule as punishment.

The Theological Tradition

As we have seen, a theology of original sin developed in the writings of early church theologians as a way of explaining the necessity of Christ's forgiveness, the universality of human sinfulness, and the role of the church in God's plan of salvation. In taking Genesis 2–3 and 1 Timothy as primary sources for reflection, theologians transposed the cultural sexism of the patriarchal world around them into a theology of gender inequality. Following 1 Timothy, male theologians assumed Eve's disobedience to be the origin of evil. In this case, androcentric language accurately depicts a commonly shared theological judgment: *Woman* caused the fall of *man* from *his* paradise. The fall was not all bad. While man lost paradise, he gained privilege.

Irenaeus writes, "Having become disobedient, [Eve] was made the cause of death, both to herself and to the entire human race."[74] For Origen, "What is seen with the eyes of the creator is masculine, and not feminine, for God does not stoop to look upon what is feminine and of the flesh." Ambrose writes, "[Eve] was first to be deceived and was responsible for deceiving the man." John Chrysostom put the matter bluntly: "The woman taught once, and ruined all." Augustine made women responsible not only for the fall but for the flood: "The calamity [the Flood], as well as the first [the Fall], was occasioned by woman, though not in the same way." He placed female subordination in creation *prior* to the fall: "For we must believe that even before her sin woman *had been made* to be ruled by her husband and to be submissive and subject to him."[75] Augustine noted the parallel between slavery and gender subjugation, grounding both in punishment for sin: "The servitude meant in these words [that woman is to be ruled] is that in which there is a condition similar to slavery rather than a bond of love (so that the servitude by which men later began to be slaves to other men obviously has its origin in punishment for sin)." The power of androcentricism in Christian theologians overshadowed the redemptive insight of Jesus and the early Jesus followers that slaveholding and male domination are sin.

The Genesis story of Eve was not unique in the ancient world in blaming women for evil. Hesiod's story of Pandora offers a parallel in Greek literature. Blaming someone for evil is common in the history of human conceptions of evil, as Elaine Pagels demonstrates in her historical study *The Origin of Satan.*[76] The other is demonized as evil. It may be an external enemy—a hostile tribe or a threatening empire. In some cases, a group's word for itself may be equivalent to the word *human,* reducing outside groups to the nonhuman. The other may also be an internal. Social groups in conflict within a culture may demonize one another as evil. The other may be a racially or religiously distinct group such as Jews. In patriarchal cultures, women are the enduring other demonized as evil.

Androcentric stories like those of Eve and Pandora portray women as the cause of evil. As myths of female evil, they establish male privilege on the basis of female fault. Unlike the Pandora story, and with greater consequence, Christian theologians advanced the myth of Eve as divinely revealed history. The story became pivotal in the thought of the early patristic theologians as an explanation for the universality of human sinfulness. They proposed a reason for the universality of evil not found among the ancient Israelites, namely, the inheritance of Adam and Eve's sin by all humankind.

The structure of the Yahwist's story of Eve's creation in Genesis 2 points to the writer's fundamental affirmation that human beings are fulfilled only when there are two who enter into a relation of love and community with one another. Biblical scholar Phyllis Trible notes that

in the original Hebrew the first human Yahweh creates is an earth creature, *hā'ādām* (2:7).[77] Only with the creation of two human beings does
the Hebrew denote sexual differentiation, *'iššâ* (woman) and *'îš* (man).
The nuances of the Hebrew, however, are not carried over in translation.
In the NRSV Oxford Bible, for example, the English text is masculine-
specific. The bracketed words inserted illustrate the original gender-
neutral character of the text:

> The LORD God formed man [*hā'ādām,* the earth creature] from the
> dust of the ground.... (2:7)
>
> And the rib that the LORD God had taken from the man
> [*hā'ādām,* earth creature] he made into a woman [*'iššâ*] and
> brought her to the man [*hā'ādām,* earth creature]. Then the man
> [*hā'ādām,* earth creature] said, "This at last is bone of my bones
> and flesh of my flesh; this one shall be called *woman* [*'iššâ*] for out
> of *man* [*'îš*] this one was taken." (2:22–23)

Without insight into the nuances of the Hebrew, male theologians
of the early Christian centuries read the story of Adam and Eve as confirmation of gender hierarchy. Man was created first, thus superior, and
woman created second, thus inferior. The fact that man was created after
the animals was not a bothersome discrepancy in the assertion of superiority. The myth was rationalized into a set of ontological principles. The
female, Ruether writes, came to represent the "qualities of materiality,
irrationality, carnality, and finitude, which debase the 'manly' spirit and
drag it down into sin and death."[78]

Ruether describes the myth of Eve as a victim-blaming ideology
that mislabels evil. Real evil exists "precisely in this false naming, projection, and exploitation."[79] The real fall was into patriarchy. Woman
was not the cause of evil but the victim of it. Patriarchal cultures promote gender ideology of superiority and inferiority. Male nature is portrayed as fully human and possessing all the valued capacities of
humanness. The other, female, is portrayed as less than fully human and
lacking those capacities prized as distinctly human.

In the development of early Christianity, the patriarchalization
of Christian theology and structures reversed the egalitarian *praxis* of
Jesus and the early Jesus communities. The image of a discipleship
community of equals in Galatians 3:28 and the image of the *ekklesia*
as the household of God in 1 Timothy 3:15 are contradictory images of

redemptive reality. The former renounces privilege and subordinate place as evils. The latter sanctions both as divinely willed.

Like the contradiction between the Athenian democratic ideal of equality for all and the reality of political restriction of social rights and privileges to free elite males, the disparity between the redemptive proclamation of gender equality in Christ and the historical exclusion of women from full participation in the life of the Christian community required theological resolution. In Athens, Aristotle's biological theory resolved the contradiction. In Christianity, the fall overcame the contradiction between the Christian proclamation of equality in Christ and the personal and social reality of gender inequality. Appeal to original sin became the primary means of explanation for women's subjection to male rule subordination. So Eve, so all women. The gender ideology embedded in patriarchal societies of the female as incomplete or defective finished the resolution. Not-male, women are not persons to whom the privilege of ecclesial rights and full participation are accorded.[80]

As a Christian theology of sin gradually appropriated the myth of Eve as its paradigmatic story of sin, the existential import of Paul's language of freedom in the Spirit and oneness in Christ was spiritualized. It no longer evoked the emancipatory *praxis* characteristic of Jesus or the transformed social reality experienced by those attracted to the first Jesus communities. In the household of God, everyone has their place. In Schüssler Fiorenza's view:

> Hand in hand with the repression and elimination of the emancipatory elements within the church went a theological justification for such an oppression. The androcentric statements of the Fathers and later church theologians are not so much due to a faulty anthropology as they are an ideological justification for the inequality of women in the Christian community.[81]

In recent ecclesial statements, the patristic argument for the exclusion of women has been reversed.[82] The patristics argued for the natural inequality of women with men while affirming their spiritual equality in Christ. Their inferiority was reason for women's subordinate status in personal relations, the social order, and church structures. In the nineteenth and twentieth centuries, however, emancipatory movements were successful in many cultures in gaining acknowledgment of the equality of women and men. Following cultural insights into sexism and gender exclusion, Roman Catholic documents gradually came to affirm gender equality.[83] Present-day official statements affirm the natural equality of women and men but maintain their spiritual inequality because women do not resemble Christ as a male.[84]

Naming Sin Rightly

Feminist theologians raise many questions about the traditional doctrine of original sin. They have identified aspects of its assumptions and use in the theological tradition. They also point to genuine insights in the church's doctrine.

Rosemary Ruether affirms the judgment of Christian theologians that sin is to be distinguished from finitude. Matter is not evil, as some religious traditions assert. Human sinfulness does not arise out of our materiality or finite existence but out of the misuse of human freedom. In freedom lies the possibilities for enhancing life or stifling it. Sin stifles life. Ruether writes that sin is "the misuse of freedom to exploit other humans and the earth and thus to violate the basic relations that sustain life."[85] While sin is personal, it is never individual. "There is no evil that is not relational."[86]

The theological tradition was right, too, Ruether writes, to emphasize that "humanity has become *radically alienated* from its true relationship to itself, to nature, and to God."[87] Paul's lament expresses an existential dilemma experienced by each person: "I can will what is right, but I cannot do it. For I do not do the good I want, but the evil I do not want is what I do" (Rom 7:18–19). From the Pauline-Augustinian tradition, Ruether says, "we derive a profound existential recognition of the divided self, acting against its own interests and desires."[88]

Further, the theological tradition was right that human beings live in an *atmosphere of evil* that predisposes individuals to choose evil over good. Ruether agrees that sin is inherited. But she deepens the biological image of inheritance utilized by Augustine:

> In the concept of inherited sin, we also recognize that evil is not simply the sum of individual decisions. We do not start with a clean slate, but we inherit historical systems of culture and social organization that bias our minds and wills negatively. Our freedom to choose good is not only limited by the fluid boundaries of finitude,

but also distorted by a heritage of deception and injustice mas-
querading as good.[89]

Ruether's understanding of sin as inherited in biased and unjust social
systems and structures complements Piet Schoonenberg's notion of
being-situated. Cultures in both their insights and oversights are prior to
individuals. The biases and blind spots embedded in social orders shape
the personal horizon within which individuals think and act. Systemic
social evils—classism, sexism, racism, religious exclusivism, colonialism—condition "our personal choices before we choose and prevent us
from fully understanding our own choices and actions."[90]

Finally, in Ruether's judgment, the Christian theological tradition
was right that humanity is *fallen.* The patristic and medieval theologians
took for granted the historicity of Adam and Eve, a time of innocence,
and single act of disobedience within edenic existence. This historical
worldview has been displaced by a conception of history shaped by
modern intellectual and scientific discoveries and insights. While the
pre-critical naïveté—to use Paul Ricoeur's term—of the early church
theologians cannot be sustained by Christians today, their theological
judgment can be shared: history is not as divine goodness desires.
Human beings distort personal relations and social structures by various
kinds of self- and group biases.

But the Christian doctrine of original sin sustained the patriarchal
distortion of gender relations by portraying female subordination as
God's punishment for Eve's sin. In reading Genesis 3 as divine revelation of woman's inferior nature and responsibility for the fall, male theologians sanctified a social order distorted by patriarchy as the order of
creation. Feminist theologians broke through the androcentrism of the
fall, as Schüssler Fiorenza notes:

> Feminist theology has shown that our societal oppression and
> ecclesial exclusion is not women's "fault," it is not the result of
> Eve's sin nor is it the will of God or the intention of Jesus Christ.
> Rather it is engendered by societal and ecclesiastical patriarchy
> and legitimised by androcentric world-construction in language
> and symbol systems.[91]

The fall is not due to woman, Ruether argues, but to patriarchy. Patriarchal societies reinforce what should not be—hierarchy, domination,
privilege—and make every effort to eliminate what should be—relations

of mutuality. Walter Wink describes the fall as a structural aspect of all personal and social existence, not just a temporal myth of the past. It affirms the radicality of evil. The Christian doctrine of the fall points to "the sedimentation of thousands of years of human choices for evil," not *wrong* choices merely, he says, but actual choices *for* evil.[92]

Ruether locates the meaning of the fall in relation to psychological realities. She begins with the interior relations that constitute community. The relation between *self* and *other* is the basic form of community. This relation should be one of mutuality and interdependence. Patriarchal gender dualism, however, identifies self with male and other with female. Further, patriarchal dualism concepts of the relation between the self (male) and other (female) are hierarchical. This fundamental distortion is the ground of evil. "Evil comes about precisely by the distortion of the self-other relationship into the good-evil, superior-inferior dualism."[93] This distortion generates sexism, racism, colonialism, homophobia, and a host of other social ideologies. The fall is into distorted relationality.[94]

For Ruether, personal and social exploitation express distorted relationality. The "perception of the other as inferior rationalizes exploitation of them."[95] Subjugated peoples are denied possibilities for their full human self-determination and self-realization. Humankind's original sin is patriarchalism—the creation of social systems that protect and advance the power and privilege of some by reducing others to subordinate status, property, powerlessness, and ultimately, to meaninglessness. Such a system alienates itself and its members from the transcendent. Everything the alienated person does, Walter Wink writes, "is infected by alienation, even the quest for God." This is why, he says, "God has taken the initiative and come searching for us."[96]

In their interpretation of original sin, feminist theologians Rita Nakashima Brock and Marjorie Hewitt Suchocki join Ruether in identifying the fall with distorted relationality and naming patriarchalism as the root sin that imposes violence and suffering on its victims.[97] As Brock emphasizes, the social realities of male privilege and female marginalization are not built into the order of nature. They reflect human choices and decisions for evil. Patriarchalism creates gender inequalities. In her work on original sin, Suchocki emphasizes the dimension of violence inherent in the distortion of relationality. She describes sin as a "a violation of well-being entailing violence against creation and

God."[98] Suchocki views original sin as this primordial tendency toward violence, a tendency that harms possibilities for mutual well-being and human solidarity. The fall is a fall to violence.

Conclusion

The historical analysis of patriarchy and biblical recovery of Jesus' preaching are core features of feminist Christian theologies of sin and redemption. They offer a historical framework within which the theological meaning of original sin unfolds in a distinctively modern voice.

Understanding patriarchal culture opens up the social import of Jesus' preaching of the reign of God. Jesus' affirmation of women, rejection of patriarchal structures, and vision of a new discipleship family spoke to a world arbitrarily divided by power and privilege. The early Jesus followers complemented their proclamation of Jesus by their embodiment of his vision of the reign of God as an inclusive communal reality. The baptismal fragment in Galatians 3:28 signals their apprehension of the structural dimension of sin. Basic forms of privilege—religious, class, gender—are rejected as sin. The redemptive reality announced by Jesus and embraced by the early *ekklesia* transforms privilege by inclusion and acknowledgment of the full humanness of each. Ruether writes that "redemption is about the transformation of self and society into good, life-giving relations, rather than an escape from the body and the world into eternal life."

Male theologians have used the doctrine of original sin to denigrate women, blame them for evil, and prohibit them from full participation in the life of the church. By deeming female subordination a divine punishment, instead of exposing it as human bias, the doctrine reinforced a cultural ideology of male superiority. Feminist theologians insist that this use of the doctrine be faced for its reinterpretation to speak an authentic revelatory word for women and for men.

A feminist reconstruction of the doctrine of original sin calls for anthropology expunged of gender hierarchy and privilege, a critical theory of history, and a social analysis of the dynamics of power and ideology.

8. SUSTAINED UNAUTHENTICITY

TODAY'S INTELLECTUAL CONTEXT of the Christian doctrine of original sin differs dramatically from that of its first centuries. The evolutionary world discovered by scientific and historical inquiry over the last three centuries has succeeded the static world imagined by premodern Christians. An existential apprehension of human subjectivity and development brought forward by modern psychology, sociology, and philosophy has displaced the metaphysical anthropology and ahistorical view of culture characteristic of the patristic and medieval tradition.

Recognition of this changed situation for theology sin is not new. As we have seen, Reinhold Niebuhr, Piet Schoonenberg, and Rosemary Ruether, among others, have addressed the meaning of original sin in light of this new vision of the world and human existence. Increasingly evident to theologians is that a genuine appropriation of this doctrine in a transformed intellectual context requires more than an exchange of old words for new ones. The doctrine must be reunderstood within a different historical framework and in relation to a different apprehension of the human person.

In this chapter we turn to a valuable resource for rethinking the theoretical basis for this endeavor, the noted Jesuit theologian and philosopher *Bernard J. F. Lonergan, S.J.* (d. 1984).[1] In particular, Lonergan offers a theory of history and an empirical anthropology within which original sin and redemption may be reconceived. His work complements and deepens the contribution of the theologians reviewed in the last two chapters. The import of Lonergan's work for the doctrine of original sin will be drawn out in the following four sections: (1) a methodical theology, (2) the conditions for human development, (3) the problem of development, and (4) sustaining human development.

179

A Methodical Theology

A major dimension of Lonergan's work was devoted to negotiating the shift from what he called a metaphysical theology to a methodical theology. Medieval theology is metaphysical. Its style of thinking was influenced by classical Greek philosophy and law. As new questions arose among patristic and medieval theologians about the meaning of Christian beliefs, technical concepts and distinctions gradually replaced the symbolic and ordinary language of the biblical writers. While the appropriation of theory facilitated a systematic understanding of religious realities such as sin and grace, a theoretical theology also disconnected them from lived human experience. Metaphysical terms and categories—*soul, intellect* and *will, habit, sanctifying grace, original justice, original perfection, original sin*—are abstract rather than empirical and concrete.

The medieval theology of original sin in Anselm of Canterbury and Thomas Aquinas is characteristic of a theoretical theology. The reality they sought to explain—human alienation from God, sin—is experiential and empirical. Sin is manifest in the personal and systemic evils caused by human beings. But medieval theology described the experience of sin and alienation—as well as religious conversion that of—abstractly. Anselm's definition of original sin was derived from his metaphysical anthropology. Original sin is the privation of original justice. Neither the gift of original justice nor the privation of original sin are empirical realities verifiable in interior human experience.

In a metaphysical theology, then, the technical explanation of religious realities is abstract. To what psychological or existential experience, for example, does the infusion of sanctifying grace or sanctifying grace as a supernatural habit refer? The metaphysical terms of medieval theology do not disclose the lived spiritual experience they attempt to explain. In an evolutionary worldview, further problems arise with the theological categories such as the state of original perfection.

In contrast to a metaphysical theology, a methodical theology, though equally systematic, grounds the meaning of theological categories in the dynamism of human consciousness. Consciousness is the empirical base from which concrete meanings of theological terms may be derived. A brief remark Lonergan makes about Thomas Aquinas's concept of sanctifying grace suggests a transposition of meaning from a metaphysical to methodical framework relevant for our topic:

> Where he conceived the grace of justification as a *supernatural habit,* we can note his doctrine that that grace makes us choose what is right where before we chose what was wrong, and so can give it the more familiar name of *conversion.*[2]

Lonergan uses the term *conversion* to denote an inner reorientation of existential development. It is a change from one basis for thinking or acting to another. Lonergan distinguishes three distinct but interrelated types of reorientation.

Intellectual conversion refers to the discovery that knowing is not just seeing but understanding correctly.[3] It is a discovery of the self-transcendence proper to the human process of coming to know. Truth is not what individuals or groups wish were the case or promote in the service of their own interests but what may be affirmed on the basis of sufficient evidence. *Moral conversion* is the discovery of the self-transcendence proper to genuine moral agency. It shifts the criteria for moral decisions from the immediacy of satisfactions and vested interests to values. The fruit of moral conversion is regular intelligent and responsible actions that meet human needs and desires.

In addition to intellectual and moral conversion, there is also *religious conversion.* It is this reorientation that Lonergan intends in his remark regarding Thomas's conception of sanctifying grace. In the theology of the tradition, the existential dimension of spirituality is described statically as the "spiritual life" or a little more dynamically as the "spiritual journey." Lonergan grounds spirituality in the reorientation motivated, effected, and sustained by the indwelling presence of divine love. He correlates it with existential activities of deliberation and commitment. It is generated by questions: Whom are we to love? Will I love? Who will save us? For Lonergan, religious conversion is being-in-love with divine mystery. This love may be experienced as a dramatic event or remain a subtle undertow of one's living. Either way, however, in a methodical theology the *meaning* of sanctifying grace—as well as spirituality—is correlated empirically with activities actually experienced in conscious intentionality. The theological category is no longer abstract but concrete.

In contrasting the dynamics of love and those of hate, Lonergan points to the difference between an orientation shaped by religious conversion and one in which conversion is absent. In traditional terms his contrast is between holiness and sin, where sin denotes the condition of original sin, *peccatum originale originatum:*

> At once [love] commands commitment and joyfully carries it out, no matter what the sacrifice involved. Where hatred reinforces bias, love dissolves it, whether it be the bias of unconscious motivation, the bias of individual or group egoism, or the bias of omnicompetent, shortsighted common sense. Where hatred plods around in ever narrower vicious circles, love breaks the bonds of psychological and social determinisms with the conviction of faith and the power of hope.[4]

Lonergan makes the transposition of the meaning of sanctifying grace from a metaphysical to a methodical theology more explicit in another context. He describes religious conversion as an "other worldly love" and as a "dynamic state whence proceed the acts, that constitutes in a methodical theology what in a theoretical theology was named sanctifying grace."[5]

For Christian faith, God's gift of God's love has significance for history as well as for individual spirituality. God's remedy for the problem of human sinfulness is God's own self-communication to humankind. A methodical theology derives a concrete meaning for each category from the dynamics of conscious intentionality.

In consciousness, the experiential correlate for the metaphysical concept of sanctifying grace as a supernatural habit is religious conversion. We may then infer a corresponding empirical meaning for the privation of sanctifying grace, the medieval metaphysical definition of original sin. *The absence of religious conversion* is the experiential reality to which the abstract metaphysical term referred. The human situation into which all are born is permeated and distorted by the refusal of individuals and groups to seek God and to accept the divine gift of love that bears fruit in faith and compassionate relations with others. The early church theologians conceived of this universal situation of alienation by way of a theory of human nature. Alienation is a condition in nature that should not be, *peccatum originale originatum.* Empirically, the absence of being-in-love with divine mystery is manifest in the incalculable expressions of disregard of human well-being found in interpersonal relations and social structures—neglect, abuse, violence, domination, genocide.

Without using the term, in *Insight: A Study of Human Understanding,* Lonergan locates the meaning of *peccatum originale originatum* in relation to a specific feature of personal and social development: "Essentially the problem lies in an incapacity for sustained development."[6] The problem, he says, is radical, permanent, and real. This is the meaning of original sin in an historically conscious theology.

Human development requires the reorientations effected by religious, moral, and intellectual conversion.[7] Each reorientation is a dimension of the divine remedy for the problem of universal sinfulness. The absence of a desire and commitment to understand correctly, to realize the human good, and to be in love is of great and unfortunate consequence for the authenticity of personal development as well as the authenticity of cultures, traditions, and human history. Their absence breeds the evil of patriarchalism in its profusion of forms, its justification in ideologies of superiority, and consequent disparities in political, economic, and religious power. The presence of religious, moral, and intellectual conversion fosters human progress and offsets decline.

Conditions for Human Development

In comparing an older metaphysical account of human nature and the more recent apprehension of human subjectivity, Lonergan noted that by abstracting from all the "accidentals" the older account overlooked the existential realities that make a person who she or he actually is. He described its account of nature this way:

> There is the older, highly logical, and so abstract, static, and minimal apprehension of being human. It holds that being human is something independent of the merely accidental, and so one is pronounced human whether or not one is awake or asleep, a genius or a moron, a saint or a sinner, young or old, sober or drunk, well or ill, sane or crazy.[8]

The roots of the theological anthropology of the tradition lie in Platonism, Stoicism, and other philosophical influences of the ancient world. The anthropology of the medievals was further influenced through Thomas's appropriation of Aristotle's metaphysical faculty psychology. For Aristotle, the soul is the first act of an organic body. Plants have souls, animals have souls, human beings have souls. Differences among souls are determined by the particular potencies, habits, acts, and objects proper to each. *Soul* is an abstract metaphysical category. It is not a psychological reality empirically verifiable in human consciousness.

In contrast to an abstract anthropology, Lonergan writes, there is a contemporary, concrete, dynamic, maximal view of the human person

> that endeavors to envisage the range of human potentiality and to distinguish authentic from unauthentic realization of that potentiality. On this approach, being human is ambivalent: one can be human authentically, genuinely, and one can be human unauthentically.[9]

Contemporary anthropologies are empirical. They highlight human becoming, process, development, self-transcendence, and subjectivity. Aristotle's static definition of human being as the rational animal has been replaced by symbolic or historic animal and self-transcending subject. A metaphysical anthropology presents humanness as a given nature. In contrast, a methodical anthropology of the subject presents humanness as a precarious achievement. Human beings are more or less authentically human. Unauthenticity results from the failure to meet the intrinsic exigences of intentionality.

A methodical anthropology "prescinds from the soul, its essence, its potencies, its habits," Lonergan says, "for none of these is given in consciousness."[10] What is given in consciousness are intentional activities of knowing and doing. Lonergan develops an explanatory account of intentionality in his magisterial work, *Insight: A Study of Human Understanding*. His later work, *Method in Theology*, deepens the existential and religious dimensions of the analysis of human consciousness.[11]

Human knowing and doing are constituted by an interrelated set of conscious activities.[12] Cognitional and moral operations coalesce into groups Lonergan designates by the shorthand terms *experience, understanding, judging,* and *deciding.*

Consciousness is a dynamic structure that puts itself together through the occurrence and interrelation of intentional operations. What is *experienced* is data for questioning and understanding. What is *understood* is data for judging true or false, probable or certain. What is

Cognitional and Moral Activities

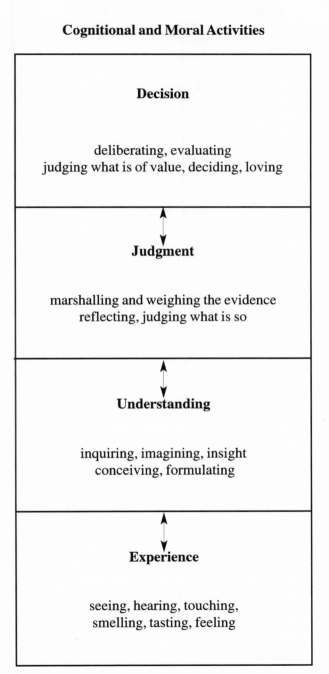

Decision

deliberating, evaluating
judging what is of value, deciding, loving

Judgment

marshalling and weighing the evidence
reflecting, judging what is so

Understanding

inquiring, imagining, insight
conceiving, formulating

Experience

seeing, hearing, touching,
smelling, tasting, feeling

known becomes data for deliberation and action. Lonergan uses the metaphor of *levels* to denote different dimensions of this ongoing and creative process. There is "the consciousness of the dream, of the waking subject, of the intelligently inquiring subject, of the rationally reflecting subject, of the responsibly deliberating subject."[13] On each level, Lonergan says, we are aware of ourselves, but "as we mount from level to level, it is a fuller self of which we are aware and the awareness itself is different."[14]

Questions generate the emergence of higher operations that take over from the lower. Questions for understanding make sense of experience. What is this? Why? How? Questions for judgment manifest the incompleteness of understanding and the ground of truth in the sufficiency of evidence. Is this so? Is my understanding correct? Questions for decision shift intentional concerns from knowing to doing. What should we do? What is responsible? Is this worthwhile? Deliberative questions transform the desire to know into the desire for the good. On this existential level, Lonergan writes, human beings are responsible "individually, for the lives they lead and, collectively, for the world in which they lead them."[15]

A metaphysical anthropology started with nature and identified what is substantial and common to human nature. An empirical anthropology begins with subjects. But the latter approach does not forfeit something "substantial and common" in subjects. Lonergan locates what is common in exigences intrinsic to empirical, intelligent, reasonable, and responsible consciousness. These demands generate the dynamism of interiority and serve as the criteria for the achievement of goals proper to cognitional and moral operations. Because these exigences are common to human beings as human, Lonergan calls them "transcendental norms." They are prior to and the source of categorical norms—culturally and historically determined precepts, laws, and customs.

The exigence to *be attentive* is normative to sensible operations. The exigence to *be intelligent* is normative in questioning and inquiry. The exigence to *be reasonable* is normative in judging. The exigence to *be responsible* is normative to the activities of deliberation, evaluation, and choice.

Questions for decision shift the cognitional orientation of intentionality to an existential one. They initiate the moral and religious dimensions of consciousness. Both dimensions have to do with deliberation,

Transcendental Norms

Moral and Religious Subjectivity

Be holy
Be loving
Be responsible

Rational Subjectivity

Be reasonable

Intelligent Subjectivity

Be intelligent

Empirical Subjectivity

Be attentive

evaluation, commitment, and love. The exigency of this level—*be responsible*—is actually threefold. In judgments of value is experienced the demand that knowing and doing *be consistent.* Because moral decisions open persons to interpersonal relations, there arises a further exigence to *be loving.* And because the human desire for truth and value is not restricted to the natural order but open to transcendent mystery, the indwelling of the divine is experienced in interiority as the summons to *be holy.*

Conscious intentionality is open and creative. The desire to know generates the upward and cumulative results of the activities of experiencing, understanding, and judging. Knowing is a compound of the operations. The process generated by questions for understanding is brought to an initial closure through insight and formulation of understanding. But insights can be wrong, so further questions generate a checking: Is this so? Am I right? Full closure is brought to the process of questioning in affirmations based on sufficient evidence: "Yes, this is correct." Cognitional self-transcendence occurs in judgments of fact. Judgments are inner events, but through them human beings reach what is independent of them—the real, being.[16]

Deliberation, evaluation, deciding, and doing follow upon and depend upon cognitional operations. The broader an understanding of reality, the more solid the foundation for moral reflection and insight. Moral self-transcendence occurs in deciding and acting responsibly. The human project is moral self-transcendence:

> We experience and understand and judge to become moral: to become moral practically, for our decisions affect things; to become moral interpersonally, for our decisions affect other persons; to become moral existentially, for by our decisions we constitute what we are to be.[17]

The transcendental exigences of intentionality provide the source as well as the criteria for genuine moral decisions. For both individual conscience and the ethics of the social order, right decisions result from the cumulative attentiveness to situations, intelligence in thinking about possible courses of action, reasonableness in judgments of fact, and responsibility in carrying out actions appropriate to and beneficial for the situation. Inadequate, wrong, or evil decisions result from a mixture of inattentiveness, oversight, irrationality, and irresponsibility.[18]

Lonergan's appeal to the existence of intrinsic norms does not predict or mandate what decisions will be morally right or wrong. Ethical questions and decisions arise from engagement with concrete situations. A methodical anthropology confirms that the dynamism of human knowing and doing is guided by exigences built into the structure of human intentionality. This grounds the judgment that morality is not arbitrary or accidental.

In concern with courses of action, moral knowing moves beyond strictly cognitional concerns. Questions shift from understanding a situation—"What is going on?"—to the personal or social response to its needs—"What should be done?" Answers to questions for deliberation are judgments of value. This—rather than that—should be done. Judgments of value grasp intelligent and reasonable courses of action that would be truly worthwhile and responsible. Like judgments of fact, judgments of value are inner events in the subject. Like judgments of fact, through judgments of value human beings reach what is independent of them. Here what is independent of the subject is the good. But neither judgments of fact nor those of value are automatically correct or responsible. Given the interference of vested interests in knowing and doing, they can easily be false and irresponsible, too.

Judgments of value are critical events in both individual and social development.[19] What is judged worthwhile and acted upon shapes the person. In the social sphere, the character and direction of a people or a nation result from judgments of value as they are actualized in common agreements, policies, and programs. In both the individual conscience and the ethics of the social order, the moral exigence for consistency between what is known to be responsible and what is done is both the source of moral obligation as well as the standard against which moral failure may be measured. Moral self-transcendence is achieved only by the full closure of the process—by *doing* what intelligent, reasonable, and responsible consciousness has grasped as a worthwhile course of action.[20]

For moral action to occur, there must develop in interiority a willingness that transforms decision into action. Sustained moral development requires the acquisition of a habitual willingness to do what is worthwhile. Fidelity to the moral exigence for consistency between knowing and doing results in responsibleness coming easily and with regularity.

The conditions generating historical progress and decline have the same source as those of personal development. While operations of consciousness are individual, they become cooperation as individuals develop customs, ways of living, and social structures to meet recurring needs and desires.[21] Historical progress is the achievement of the human good in the social sphere. Just as individual growth depends on expanding the range and depth of conscious operations, social development depends on expanding cooperation. In both spheres, the presence or absence of the willingness to carry through responsible decisions is crucial. The wheel of insights, ideas, judgments, decisions, and actions will actualize the human good only if decisions are transformed from their initial emergence as inner events to their completion as external actions.

Human self-transcendence is also affective. Affective self-transcendence occurs in falling in love. Being in love operates as a principle of human actions in the self-giving that occurs in interpersonal relations. Lonergan points to three manifestations of affective self-transcendence in the love of family, loyalty in community, and faith in God.

Religious subjectivity is affective. It is a further and deeper dimension of moral self-consciousness. The dynamism of human intentionality is the desire not for restricted but for ultimate and unrestricted meaning, truth, goodness, and love. The openness of intentionality is openness for God. Just as persons in love desire to give themselves to the other, so the person in love with God desires to give herself or himself over fully to the divine Other.[22]

In interiority the basic awareness of God and the inner pull experienced toward transcendent mystery are given by God. The *inner word* of God is religious experience. Religion is the social and historical manifestation of religious experience, the *outer word*. Religions are culturally and historically distinct in their apprehension, interpretation, and naming of the experience of divine mystery.

Religious self-transcendence occurs in relation to questions for deliberation and commitment. Lonergan describes religious subjectivity as that type of consciousness

> that deliberates, makes judgments of value, decides, acts responsibly and freely. But it is this consciousness as brought to a fulfilment, as having undergone a conversion, as possessing a basis that may be broadened and deepened and heightened and enriched but not superseded, as ready to deliberate and judge and decide

and act with the easy freedom of those that do all good because they are in love.[23]

The gift of God's love, Lonergan writes, occupies the ground and root of the fourth and highest level of intentional consciousness. Religious conversion is the human response to this abiding presence of divine love. Faith is its acceptance. God's gift of God's love reorients human development toward transcendent meaning and love. It does not diminish the significance of the intellectual and moral dimensions of consciousness. But now "all human pursuit of the true and the good is included within and furthered by a cosmic context and purpose," Lonergan writes, and there is given to human beings the power of love that enables them "to accept the suffering involved in undoing the effects of decline."[24]

Lonergan grounds the meaning of both holiness and sinfulness in relation to conscious intentionality, specifically, the presence and absence of self-transcendence. Human beings exist authentically, he writes, in the measure that each "succeeds in self-transcendence"; and "I have found that self-transcendence has both its fulfilment and its enduring ground in holiness, in God's gift of his love to us."[25] We know about this gift when we notice its fruits in our lives. The gift overflows in love of neighbor.

Lonergan's understanding of sin retains the category of privation. Derived from consciousness, however, the meaning of privation is empirical and concrete rather than metaphysical and abstract. Sinfulness, Lonergan writes, "is distinct from moral evil; it is the privation of total loving; it is a radical dimension of lovelessness."[26]

The facts of unauthenticity and radical lovelessness raise a question. If normative exigences built into the dynamism of human intentionality itself ground the possibility of authentic development, why do persons diverge from them? The human predicament would not be so dire, if the exigences for intelligence, reasonableness, responsibleness, and love were not routinely left unmet.

Failure to meet the demands of intellectual, moral, and religious self-transcendence constitutes the fundamental problem of human living. In both the personal and social realms there is a permanent tension between aspiration and performance. What we want to do or know we should do is not automatically done.[27] A technical grasp of this tension is not a prerequisite for acknowledging its presence. Paul's insight into this psychological tension—and the failure to negotiate it adequately—

is clear in his remark: "For I do not do the good I want, but the evil I do not want is what I do."[28]

The self-contradiction to which Paul points does not reflect the absence of intrinsic norms. It points rather to an infidelity to them. A methodical anthropology and theory of history takes into account the presence as well as the absence of fidelity to the exigences of consciousness. One must account not only for the achievements and progress resulting from fidelity to these normative exigences but also the breakdowns and decline resulting from infidelity to them.[29] In the personal as well as the social realm, fidelity and infidelity are critical factors in the matter of genuine human development. Human living is an ambiguous mixture of each. In the next section we turn to the problem of infidelity and what derails human self-transcendence from its intended goals.

The Problem of Development

Authentic human development occurs in and through cumulative instances of understanding correctly, deciding and living responsibly, and loving fully. The absence of cognitional, moral, and affective self-transcendence creates situations ripe for tensions, conflicts, and disparities in human living. The human achievement of authenticity is more arduous than that of unauthenticity. As Lonergan points out:

> Unauthenticity is realized by any single act of inattention, obtuseness, unreasonableness, irresponsibility. But authenticity is reached only by long and sustained fidelity to the transcendental precepts. It exists only as a cumulative product. Moreover, authenticity in man or woman is ever precarious: our attentiveness is ever apt to be a withdrawal from inattention; our acts of understanding a correction of oversights; our reasonableness a victory over silliness; our responsibility a repentance for our sins.[30]

Authenticity in both the personal and social realms comes as the fruit of sustained fidelity to the transcendental exigences of interiority:

> For authenticity results from a long-sustained exercise of attentiveness, intelligence, reasonableness, responsibility. But long-sustained attentiveness notes just what is going on. Intelligence repeatedly grasps how things can be better. Reasonableness is open to change. Responsibility weighs in the balance short- and

long-term advantages and disadvantages, benefits and defects. The longer these four are exercised, the more certain and the greater will be the progress made.[31]

Inasmuch as human intentionality is the source of meanings and values, authentic meanings and values require such sustained fidelity. Distorted meanings and false values derive from inattentiveness, oversight, bias, unreasonableness, irresponsibleness, and hatred. They engender social and historical decline, not progress. The rationalization of infidelity to the exigences of consciousness lower the probabilities that human living will be intelligent and responsible.

The creative and positive capacities of human intentionality thus have their dark sides. While the human desire for insight is natural, just as natural is resistance to insight.[32] Meeting the inner demand for consistency between knowing and doing issues forth genuine judgments of value, but the demand may be ignored and left unmet in an individual conscience as well as the ethics of the social order. Intelligent moral action occurs regularly, but just as regularly the habitual unwillingness of individuals and groups to transcend self- or group interests and narrow visions frustrates the possibility that what needs be done will be done.

Human development thus depends on the regular occurrence of practical insights and judgments of value. But such occurrence is neither automatic nor easy. Lonergan locates two basic interferences with authentic development in tensions operative in individual and group consciousness.

In individual consciousness, a permanent tension exists between *practical intelligence* and *spontaneity*. Practical intelligence is the capacity for and achievement of genuine insights that hit the nail on the head, decisions that meet the demands of a situation, and actions that responsibly bring decisions from thought to reality. By spontaneity Lonergan denotes the experiential correlate to what the theological tradition defined abstractly as concupiscence. Spontaneity is the tendency experienced in cognitional and moral deliberation to think or choose what is immediately beneficial, satisfying, or desirable.[33] In the tradition, concupiscence results from the fall. For Lonergan, spontaneity is a dimension of created nature.

A form of this immediacy exists in the social realm as well. In groups the tension is between *practical intelligence* and *intersubjectivity*. On the social level, practical intelligence is the ongoing cooperation that meets recurring needs and desires. Intersubjectivity is the egoism that puts group needs and concerns first, whether or not these interests are detrimental to the social order and common good.

An ideal line of human development would occur as a continuous intelligent and responsible process. But development has conditions. Primary among the conditions for personal and social development are the openness to letting questions arise, desire for genuine insights, receptivity to new ideas, and willingness to find and try solutions that would meet problems adequately. The dominant interference of interest frustrates the realization of these conditions.

Interest creates three forms of bias—individual egoism, group egoism, and a general bias of common sense thinking. Lonergan describes the last as "the illusory omnicompetence of common sense."[34] "Evaluation may be biased," he writes, "by an egoistic disregard to others, by a loyalty to one's own group matched by hostility to other groups, by concentrating on short-term benefits and overlooking long-term costs."[35]

The interference of bias in cognitional and moral intentionality reduces probabilities that persons and groups will conceive of intelligent and responsible courses of action, or if they do, will actually carry them out. The roots of wrongdoing and moral evil lie in the distortions created by bias. Evil is by omission or commission—failing to do what is responsible or doing what is irresponsible.[36] Development is further derailed by justifying ideas and actions skewed by bias. "Corrupt minds have a flair for picking the mistaken solution," Lonergan writes, "and insisting that it alone is intelligent, reasonable, good."[37] The rationalization of irrationality and irresponsibility embeds false meanings and inauthentic values into the fabric of the social world. Ways of living, legal systems, political orders, religious structures, and economic patterns can all reflect the privileges of those whose interests are backed by power. The Johannine author referred symbolically to the distortions caused by bias, its effects, and justification as the "darkness of the world." The Johannine metaphor became conceptualized as *peccatum originale originatum,* the condition of original sin, in the theological anthropology of Augustine.

Augustine also gave a name in his theory of human nature to the cumulative effect of bias: "moral impotence." Lonergan correlated Augustine's term with conscious operations. The failure to make knowing responsible and to make doing consistent with responsible knowing becomes so habitual that rising above self- or group interests and short-term concerns to choose and do what is genuinely worthwhile becomes a virtual if not a real impossibility.

Moral impotence generates a characteristic of social and historical reality Lonergan calls the "social surd." The social order does not correspond to any one set of genuine insights. It is rather an ambiguous mixture of rationality and irrationality. The social situation is all fact "but partly it is the product of intelligence and reasonableness and partly it is the product of aberration from them."[38] The social surd is a "false fact," "the actual existence of what should not be."[39] The facts in the situation "more and more are the absurdities that proceed from inattention, oversight, unreasonableness and irresponsibility."[40]

Moral failure is the consequence of the inconsistency between responsible knowing and doing. In a religious horizon open to divine mystery this "contraction of consciousness," as Lonergan calls it, is basic sin.[41] Two difficulties in human development bring about the cumulative result that the biblical writers metaphorically called the reign of sin.[42]

Lonergan argues that in part the reign of sin results because human beings have to become fully engaged in living before they have learned how to live, before they have acquired the habitual willingness to live rightly, and before they have developed skills that would make right living habitual.[43] It results, too, because human beings surrender to this incompleteness in their development. Persons could avoid the inconsistency between knowing and doing by stopping to reflect on each particular occasion, but they "cannot bear the burden of perpetual reflection; and long before that burden has mounted to the limit of physical impossibility," Lonergan notes, they choose the easy way out. The social surd is the cumulative effect of basic sin and its justification.

The social surd is not a transitory problem. It is not limited to particular cultures or historical periods. It is not eliminated by new political structures, technical advances, scientific specializations, or spiritualities. Its roots are permanent and lie in the contingency of human freedom. It is a radical problem of human living, and no one is born outside it. It is what Augustine named the condition of original sin.

The predominantly cognitional language of Lonergan's *Insight* gave way in his later writings to a richer existential language of self-transcendence and authenticity. Basic sin in *Insight* is the failure to make one's doing consistent with the grasp of a rational (thus moral) course of action. Basic sin is a failure of rational self-consciousness.[44] But in *Method in Theology,* Lonergan grounded the meaning of sin in the self-contradiction produced by the refusal or absence of self-transcendence. Sin is alienation from one's authentic being, Lonergan writes, "which is self-transcendence, and sin justifies itself by ideology."[45]

Lonergan derives the meaning of alienation and ideology from the infidelity to the normative exigences of human intentionality. They explain historical decline:

> The term, alienation, is used in many different senses. But on the present analysis the *basic form of alienation* is man's disregard of the transcendental precepts, Be attentive, Be intelligent, Be reasonable, Be responsible. Again, the *basic form of ideology* is any doctrine that justifies such alienation. From these basic forms, all others can be derived. For the basic forms corrupt the social good. As self-transcendence promotes progress, so the refusal of self-transcendence turns progress into cumulative decline.[46]

The *incapacity to sustain development* became in Lonergan's post-*Insight* writings the problem of *sustained unauthenticity:*

> Just as sustained authenticity results in increasing responsibility and order, increasing reasonableness and cohesion, increasing intelligence and objective intelligibility, increasing knowledge and mastery of the situation, so sustained unauthenticity has the opposite effects.[47]

Sustained unauthenticity brings its own punishment. "A civilization in decline," Lonergan writes, "digs its own grave with relentless consistency."[48]

In the classical theology of original sin, the gift of original justice sustained the right relation between the lower powers of the body and the higher powers of the soul, the intellect, and the will. With the loss of this gift, theologians argued, lower passions ruled over the higher powers of the soul. Christian theologians assumed that what God intended in divine creation was the proper subjection of body to mind and mind to God. If human nature exhibited the *lack* of proper subjection, it must be due to an original change in human nature, for God was not to blame. Human nature was described as wounded, or in stronger theological views, as corrupted. The classical theology of original sin often appeared to locate the problem of original sin in the body, with its unruly passions, impulses gone astray, and paucity of self-control.

In a methodical anthropology, the dualism of mind and body is replaced by an apprehension of human reality as organic, chemical, biological, neurological, psychic, and conscious.[49] Distinctive kinds of events and relations among events constitute these different levels of humanness. Human reality is a unity of these schemes of recurrence. Each set of recurrent schemes is "higher" or "lower" in relation to other schemes in terms of its function of integration. Neurological events are dependent on "lower" chemical events, for example, but their function establishes a "higher" set of recurrent events, and so on. A methodical anthropology is free from gender dualism as well as the dualism of mind and body.

Conscious schemes of recurrence are empirical, intelligent, rational, and responsible events. Integrating and moving beyond lower physical and psychic events, conscious intentionality initiates a new dimension of reality. The activities of interiority have their own structured and ascending dynamism. Questions go beyond experiencing to generate further events of intelligence. Reflection goes beyond experiencing and understanding to generate further events of judgment and affirmation. Moral deliberation moves beyond knowing reality to bring into being what does not yet exist. Human intentionality is self-transcending. In an empirical anthropology, the disorder of human experience is not created by the body nor by a change in nature itself. The potentialities of the levels of schemes of recurrence constituting humanness, both positive and negative, are created. What early theologians named concupiscence derives from the absence of cognitional, moral, or affective self-transcendence.[50]

The trajectory of personal and social development given in the created order is thus ambiguous. Human beings are free. Their development is open to genuine achievement but subject to failure. The ambiguity of development is rooted in permanent dialectical tensions within human consciousness.

Sustaining Development

In the theological tradition, a theology of sin is preliminary to a theology of redemption. So, too, in the work of Lonergan does the identification of the problem of human development turn to a consideration of its solution. In making this turn, we broaden the framework of a methodical theology of original sin to include features of a methodical theology of grace and redemption.

The means of human development—the activities of intentionality—are intrinsic to the created order. But the created order is open rather than fixed, and responsible knowing and doing do not occur with automatic regularity. Sustained development in both the personal and social realms is thwarted by the interferences of individual egoism, group bias, and the general bias of common sense. Development has conditions, and primary among them is fidelity to the normative exigences of consciousness. Infidelity to built-in demands that human beings be attentive, intelligent, reasonable, responsible, and loving fosters unauthenticity. Lonergan describes the historical situation created by the sustained unauthenticity of individuals, groups, and traditions as an "objective surd."

Because the problem of development has its source in human consciousness, its resolution cannot be generated from within human beings by themselves. Lonergan argues that the remedy lies beyond any normal human procedure:

> There is no use appealing to the sense of responsibility of irresponsible people, to the reasonableness of people that are unreasonable, to the intelligence of people that have chosen to be obtuse, to the attention of people that attend only to their grievances. Again, the objective situation brought about by sustained unauthenticity is not an intelligible situation. It is the product of inattention, obtuseness, unreasonableness, irresponsibility. It is an objective surd, the realization of the irrational.[51]

In the technical language of the theological tradition, the divine remedy for original sin is sanctifying grace as a supernatural habit. The remedy is supernatural, not natural. In the language of a methodical theology, the divine remedy for sustained unauthenticity is the reorientation of development effected by a threefold conversion that promotes the intellectual, moral, and religious self-transcendence necessary for sustained development. The technical distinction of the tradition remains. As divine, the remedy is supernatural, not natural.

Religion announces the problem of human alienation and its divine remedy. The world's religions are culturally diverse in their conceptions of both the problem and solution. But they also share fundamental features. In their common call for repentance and affirmation of the openness of the human spirit for the divine, religions signal human unauthenticity as the problem and the reorientation of human development effected by the shift in values and horizon grounded in religious conversion as its solution. Through engagement with religion, individuals grow in their awareness of personal and social unauthenticity and appropriate the meanings and values that promote and sustain authenticity.

The biblical writers often cast the problem of human sinfulness in the metaphorical language of the "hardened heart." It is clear that they believe the heart closed against God is closed against the human good. The hardened heart becomes fixed in its infidelity and cannot transform itself. Opening the closed heart and softening the hardened heart is the work of divine initiative and action.

The Deuteronomist portrays the divine remedy as a command to do what God wants. What God desires is human authenticity—a heart turned to God. Love of God fosters the right orientation of human living and assures human well-being:

> So now, O Israel, what does the LORD your God require of you? Only to fear the LORD your God, to walk in all his ways, to love him, to serve the LORD your God with all your heart and with all your soul, and to keep the commandments of the LORD your God and his decrees that I am commanding you today, for your own well-being.[52]

The prophet Ezekiel describes the interior process of transformation and conversion as the promise of a new heart and a new spirit. Human authenticity will result from the indwelling of divine mystery:

> A new heart I will give you, and a new spirit I will put within you; and I will remove from your body the heart of stone and give you a heart of flesh. I will put my spirit within you and make you follow my statutes and be careful to observe my ordinances.[53]

The apostle Paul continues the metaphorical description of authenticity as the transformed heart. He saw Ezekiel's promise fulfilled in the reoriented hearts of persons drawn to the risen Jesus: "God's love has been poured into our hearts through the Holy Spirit that has been given to us."[54] The power of the Spirit offsets the power of sin.[55] "Live by the Spirit," Paul instructs his followers. His appeal is not a proposition to be believed but a way of living that promotes human well-being. The fruit of the Spirit is "love, joy, peace, patience kindness, generosity, faithfulness, gentleness and self-control."[56] The divine indwelling effects a shift from one set of values to another. The Spirit opens the heart to seek what is good and sustains moral transformation. The authenticity engendered by the Spirit counters the unauthenticity generated by alienation.

In their developing theologies of grace and redemption, early Christian writers also signaled the authenticity engendered by religious conversion to be the divine remedy to the problem of sin. Augustine utilized the technical distinction between operative and cooperative grace to explain the biblical metaphors of the transformed heart and power of the Spirit. Operative grace is religious conversion itself. God alone opens the closed heart and effects its reorientation toward the good. Cooperative grace sustains the moral transformation of the reoriented life. By operative and cooperative grace, the intentions and actions of the human will are joined with the desires of the divine will. Augustine's self-reflection in his *Confessions* captures his experience of religious conversion, the reorientation of his development, and his struggle to live authentically in the horizon of divine love.

Medieval theologians expanded the technical portrayal of religious conversion and development begun by the patristic writers. Their theology of grace described religious experience and the reorientation of development abstractly in terms such as supernatural habits, infusion of theological virtues, and the spiritual life. Theoretical explanations of grace and human nature masked the dynamic reality of personal transformation they sought to explain.[57]

A methodical theology of grace correlates the metaphorical and technical terms of the biblical and theological tradition with the experiential and psychological realities they denote. We have already suggested Lonergan's methodical correlate in interiority for Augustine's twofold distinction of grace:

Operative grace is religious conversion. Cooperative grace is the effectiveness of religious conversion, the gradual movement towards a full and complete transformation of the whole of one's living and feeling, one's thoughts, words, deeds, and omissions.[58]

Lonergan identifies religious conversion with being-in-love and loving as a higher integration of the cognitional and moral dimensions of consciousness:

To fall in love is to go beyond attention, intelligence, reasonableness, responsibility. It is to set up a new principle that has, indeed, its causes, conditions, occasions, but, as long as it lasts, provides the mainspring of one's desire and fear, hope and despair, joy and sorrow. In the measure that the community becomes a community of love and so capable of making real and great sacrifices, in that measure it can wipe out grievances and correct the objective absurdities that its unauthenticity has brought about.[59]

Genuine religious conversion engenders an ongoing willingness to do the good. It motivates the self-sacrificing love crucial for countering evil and nurturing human development. For Christians, Christ is the model of self-sacrificing love of others.[60] Lonergan identifies Christian authenticity with self-sacrificing love. It is relevant for history and human development: "As human authenticity promotes progress, and human unauthenticity generates decline, so Christian authenticity—which is a love of others that does not shrink from self-sacrifice and suffering—is the sovereign means for overcoming evil."[61] Self-sacrificing love is the principle of redemption. Such love is not self-abnegation but a creative response of the whole of conscious intentionality to human living.

The historical situation in which human beings find themselves is permeated with unauthenticity. Each absorbs it as well as contributes to it. While not individually responsible for the social surd, still each shares in a common guilt for it. Through its symbols and rituals, religion provides a context within which an understanding of the problem and a grasp of the solution is mediated. Human beings are sinners, Lonergan writes:

If human progress is not to be ever distorted and destroyed by the inattention, oversights, irrationality, irresponsibility of decline, men have to be reminded of their sinfulness. They have to acknowledge their real guilt and amend their ways. They have to

learn with humility that religious development is dialectical, that
the task of repentance and conversion is life-long.[62]

Lonergan locates the criterion of authentic religion in whether the
word it announces as divine assists in overcoming the interference of
biases in human living and fosters the attentiveness, intelligence, reasonableness, responsibleness, and self-sacrificing love that will sustain
development. He writes that "a religion that promotes self-transcendence to the point not merely of justice, but of self-sacrificing love, will
have a redemptive role in human society inasmuch as such love can
undo the mischief of decline and restore the cumulative process of
progress."[63] The problem of sin is religion's own, too. Like other religions, Christianity is open to development and progress, but "so too
there is decline; and as there is decline, there also is the problem of
undoing it, of overcoming evil with good not only in the world but also
in the church."[64]

Religious faith broadens the framework for human knowing and
doing by recognizing the universe as a product of divine choice. Without faith, Lonergan says, the origins of value are human beings and the
terminal value is the human good persons bring about. "But in light of
faith, originating value is divine light and love, while terminal value is
the whole universe."[65] A theology grounded in reflection on interiority
and self-transcendence effects an important shift from a static to
dynamic concept of divine reality:

> To conceive God as originating value and the world as terminal
> value implies that God too is self-transcending and that the world
> is the fruit of his self-transcendence, the expression and manifesta-
> tion of his benevolence and beneficence, his glory....To say that
> God created the world for his glory is to say that he created it not
> for his sake but for ours. He made us in his image, for our authen-
> ticity consists in being like him, in self-transcending, in being ori-
> gins of value, in true love.[66]

If human authenticity consists in being self-transcending like
God, human self-transcendence—cognitional, moral, and affective—
has cosmic significance. In light of divine mystery, Lonergan writes in
Insight, true knowledge is not simply true but an apprehension of the
divinely ordained order of the universe. Error is deviation not only
from truth but also from God.[67] Wrongdoing and evil are not just

morally reprehensible but sin against God. And making doing consistent with responsible knowing is not merely moral achievement but also the origin of the human good and cooperation with God in the realization of the universe. By their sustained authenticity human beings participate with God in the realization of the universe. It is through this ordinary and universal means, human authenticity, that the divine remedy to evil works.

Lonergan's understanding of the order of the universe is neither determinist nor naive. The universe that religious faith affirms as divinely created is the same dynamic and evolutionary universe understood theoretically by the insights and judgments of scientific specializations. Its actualization is characterized by emergent probability—statistically emergent schemes of recurrence, open to development and change, always in process, ever subject to breakdown.[68]

Humanness is constituted by emergent schemes of recurrence, too. In addition to levels of chemical, biological, neurological events, human freedom emerges with the structured and recurrent events of conscious intentionality—sensing, questioning, insight, formulating, affirming, deliberating, choosing, loving. No less than other recurrent schemes in the universe, those of conscious intentionality are capable of successful completion and subject to failure and breakdown. Success and failure of these schemes have causes, too. Successful completion requires fidelity to the exigences for intellectual, moral, and affective self-transcendence. Human development and authenticity are the fruit of such fidelity. In history, authenticity promotes progress. Unauthenticity generates decline. This unauthenticity—manifest in ever more violence, conflict, economic disparity, and despair—is the Johannine darkness that early Christian theologians named *peccatum originale originatum*.

Conclusion

If the Christian doctrine of original sin is to speak meaningfully about human existence and radical evil, it must do so with a theological anthropology congruent with modern insights into the human person. Lonergan's analysis of the dynamism of human consciousness provides an empirical base from which we can understand in ourselves what the biblical writers spoke of metaphorically as a heart closed to God, the patristics signified as an ontological state of nature, *peccatum originale originatum,* and the medievals described in metaphysical terms as the privation of original justice. Lonergan derives his understanding of the condition of original sin from a concrete analysis of the conditions for personal and social development, the interference of biases with human development, and historical consequences of the presence or absence of intellectual, moral, and affective self-transcendence.

In his earlier work, Lonergan understood the reality to which *peccatum originale originatum* referred as the incapacity of human beings to sustain development. Given many factors, especially the interference of biases, human beings cannot sustain being thoroughly intelligent, reasonable, and rational for long. In his later work, Lonergan understood the problem of development in more existential terms. Humanness is not given but potential. There can be authentic and unauthentic realizations of its potentiality. In the social and historical realm, *peccatum originale originatum* is humankind's sustained unauthenticity.

A further contribution of Lonergan's analysis of subjectivity is reconnecting the meaning of the theological categories of sin and redemption with existential experience. Lonergan's conception of human subjectivity has the added benefit of being free from the explicit gender bias of patriarchal anthropologies and those advanced more subtly by various contemporary anthropologies.[69]

The early Christians could appeal to the stories of Genesis 1–3 as divinely revealed history. They believed them to be the source of historical knowledge of the past. Such an appeal is neither possible nor desirable in the contemporary context. The way we understand the origin of evil must be congruent with modern sciences and history. Lonergan's theory of history and notion of emergent probability offer such a basis. His analysis of personal and systemic evil and the need for redemption is accomplished without appeal to a primeval event or an ontological change in human nature. Sustained unauthenticity is an empirical fact. It has causes and its consequences are significant. It affects all persons, all social institutions, all realms of meaning, even that of religion. Sustained unauthenticity is a structural aspect of historical existence that the tradition named original sin.[70]

9. ORIGINAL SIN AND ITS MEANING

FROM ITS EARLY CONCEPTION, the doctrine of original sin provided the central organizing principle for the relation among Christian doctrines. It illuminated the purpose of the incarnation and the reason for Christ's redemption. Original sin accounted for why human beings do not seek and love God and the source of their inhumanity to one another. It explained why human beings face the tragedy of death. The doctrine disclosed why women do not share the equality with men that was given to them in creation. It resolved why human beings, not God, are responsible for evil. And for some, the doctrine underscored the indispensability of the church, the sole mediator of Christ's grace of forgiveness.

At its most basic level, the Christian doctrine of original sin answered a cardinal question about human existence: Why are we not good? Behind the question of human evil lay a long and rich history of biblical reflection on this question. The psalmist imagines a pensive God looking down on humankind asking, "Is there anyone who seeks me?" In an acutely pessimistic moment of his own, the psalmist finds none. "They have all gone astray, they are all alike perverse; there is no one who does good, no not one."[1] Amos the prophet laments his time as so evil. He castigates the elite who "sell the righteous for silver, and the needy for a pair of sandals—they who trample the head of the poor into the dust of the earth and push the afflicted out of the way."[2] The apostle Paul turned reflection inward to the experience of contradiction: "I do not understand my own actions. For I do not do what I want, but I do the very thing I hate....For I do not do the good I want, but the evil I do not want is what I do."[3] He objectified the experience as a power within him. "Now if I do what I do not want, it is no longer I that do it, but sin that dwells within me."[4]

205

Early Christians contributed their own ponderings about humankind's alienation from divine goodness and the evil that ensues from it. To the biblical metaphors of a "closed heart" and "heart of stone," they fused psychological ones of the "bondage of the will" and "moral impotence." In the gradual but inevitable move into systematic reflection, the Johannine metaphors of "darkness" and "sin of the world" became in Augustine's theological anthropology and theory of salvation history *peccatum originale originatum,* a distortion of created nature and history caused by Adam's sin. The medieval theologians completed the shift from metaphor to metaphysics. Augustine's idea of a change in human nature brought about by the fall became in Anselm's metaphysical anthropology the loss of something nature once possessed, the "privation of original justice." Even the medieval language of religious conversion was abstract. Thomas Aquinas described the experience of religious conversion and its effects in authentic living by the metaphysical notion of sanctifying grace as a supernatural habit. Contemporary theologians moved from metaphysics into interiority, searching our psychological depths for what incites humanity's inhumanity. Bernard Lonergan brought the abstract scholastic anthropology back to its experiential basis through an analysis of the dynamics of human consciousness and development. From this base, he reconceived the meaning of Augustine's *peccatum originale originatum* and Anselm's *privation of original justice* as the empirically verifiable problem of sustained unauthenticity.

The early Christian explanation of alienation gave Genesis 3 a privileged place. In the first couple's disobedience, early Christian writers found the origin and nature of human sin. The disharmony, suffering, and death that humans experience were revealed to be the consequence of sin, not the action of a capricious creator. Through Genesis 3, Christian theologians balanced the goodness of creation with the experience of evil. From it they also derived an explanation for the universality of sin. All are sinful because all share Adam's sin; thus the reason for redemption and for the mediation of Christ's grace through the church. The doctrine of original sin unified the tradition's theologies of redemption, Christ, and church.

Explanations, as well as their breakdowns, have reasons and dates. The breakdown of the patristic and medieval account of the origin of sin has been in process since at least the eighteenth century. The reasons are numerous. In the modern world, scientific and evolutionary understand-ings of history and human origins displaced the premodern view of his-tory in which the idea of original sin was shaped. Literary studies established the symbolic genre of the Genesis creation and expulsion stories, leaving only fundamentalists to argue for their historicity. Empirical apprehensions of human subjectivity by modern psychology and philosophy replaced the abstract metaphysical anthropology of the medieval scholastics. Moral theologians abandoned the juridical lan-guage of commands and disobedience in favor of thinking about sin in terms of relationship, commitment, and orientation. The question of becoming became primary. Humanness was understood as a fragile process, not a given, and the matter of authenticity and unauthenticity relevant to both the personal and social spheres.

Modern challenges to the Christian doctrine of original sin remain. The doctrine's defenders are as dangerous to the credibility of Christian belief as its detractors when the meaning of original sin is reduced to a literal reading of Genesis 3. Christians themselves rou-tinely raise a disturbing question. Does the doctrine correspond with what is so? If the reality to which the doctrine refers is an historical Adam and Eve, the answer must be No. But if the reality is understood as the sustained unauthenticity of human beings, their alienation from the divine source of their existence, and the personal and systemic evils that issue forth from individual and collective unauthenticity, then, Yes, the doctrine does correspond with what is so.

But this Yes is contingent. Rethinking the reality of human alien-ation and sin—its origin, root—requires a theological anthropology that attends to actual psychological and social experience. It demands a crit-ical theory of history congruent with the dynamic evolutionary universe apprehended by modern science and history. It involves rethinking the redemptive reason for communities of faith, conceiving them not as the solution to an ancient sin but as mediators of the values captured in Jesus' preaching of the reign of God.

Rethinking original sin also entails rooting out oversights and biases from religious meaning itself. Augustine's theory of biological inheritance gave Christian theology an explanatory principle for the universality of sin. But by linking the transmission of sin with sexual relations, it devalued human sexuality. Augustine's views that marital sexual relations were expressions of concupiscence became embedded in the tradition.[5] Further, the doctrine of original sin located salvation exclusively in Christ and the church, fostering a dismissal of salvific possibilities in other religious traditions.[6] Religious denigrating of non-Christians, when allied with political power, becomes religious imperialism.[7] Lastly, the systemic bias of sexism accompanied the idea of original sin in the writings of early church theologians. The doctrine legitimated male privilege and the exclusion of women from full participation in the richness of religious and cultural life.

Reinhold Niebuhr once cited a remark quoted in the *London Times* that "the doctrine of original sin is the only empirically verifiable doctrine of the Christian faith."[8] He agreed wholeheartedly that original sin–demythologized and correctly understood—was verifiable. What the early Christian theologians meant by "original sin," Niebuhr thought, was that human beings have a blindness to their own involvement in sin.

Sustained unauthenticity is empirical. It is the root of what frustrates human development and the possibilities for fulfillment in both the personal and social spheres. It is the source of domination systems, the violence that supports them, and the massive dehumanization they engender. It is the cause of major and minor ways in which we sabotage our personal relationships and fail those who would love us without reserve. It is the reason for God's searching us out in redemptive love. Sustained unauthenticity is that which the indwelling presence of divine compassion transforms in us and, through us, the social structures and history we create.

NOTES

INTRODUCTION

1. Ernest Evans, ed., *Tertullian's Homily on Baptism* (London: SPCK, 1964).

2. Cf. Piet Fransen, "Augustine, Pelagius and the Controversy on the Doctrine of Grace," *Louvain Studies* 12 (1987), 172–81; 175.

3. Quoted in R. W. Southern, *Saint Anselm: A Portrait in a Landscape* (Cambridge: Cambridge University Press, 1990), 209.

4. Piet Schoonenberg, S.J., "Sin and Guilt," in *Encyclopedia of Theology: The Concise Sacramentum Mundi,* ed. Karl Rahner (New York: Seabury Press, 1975), 1579–86; 1584.

CHAPTER 1

1. For the history of this development, see Jacob Neusner, *Foundations of Judaism* (Philadelphia: Fortress Press, 1989), esp. 51–83. Rabbinic Judaism, also called Formative Judaism, is a second-century development. Neusner dates its development from the second through the seventh centuries C.E.

2. James D. G. Dunn traces this historical development in *The Partings of the Ways: Between Christianity and Judaism and Their Significance for the Character of Christianity* (Philadelphia: Trinity Press International, 1991).

3. On Israel and Jewish life, see E. P. Sanders, *Judaism: Practice and Belief, 63 BCE–66 CE* (Philadelphia: Trinity Press, 1992).

4. Exod 6:7. Biblical texts are cited from *The New Oxford Annotated Bible: New Revised Standard Version* (New York: Oxford University Press, 1991).

5. The reference to God's liberating act runs throughout the Hebrew scriptures; cf. Exod 6:6, 19:4; Deut 4:37, 6:10,20, 7:7; Ps 81:10; Jer 2:4; Mic 6:4.

6. Deut 26:17.

7. For a succinct summary of the composition of the Pentateuch, commonly referred to as the source or documentary hypothesis, see Lawrence Boadt, *Reading the Old Testament: An Introduction* (New York: Paulist Press, 1984), 89–108. The documentary hypothesis will be explained more fully in a later section. No precise differentiation will be made here between Priestly and Deuteronomistic writers. Texts cited from Deuteronomy illustrate the "priestly voice."

8. Deut 10:12–13.

9. Deut 26:19.

10. Deut 30:6.

11. Amos 5:14.

12. Exod 24:12.

13. Our concern here does not lie with unpacking the insights or blind spots of the law. The purpose is to suggest the way in which it fits into the biblical conception of the divine remedy to the problem of human sinfulness.

14. The socio-religious order of ancient Israel is described as a "purity system." Sin has a cultic as well as a moral meaning. L. William Countryman discusses the general features of a purity system in *Dirt, Greed, and Sex* (Philadelphia: Fortress Press, 1988), 11–65. Individual purity rules are found throughout the Torah, but the most substantial codes are in Leviticus 11–16 and 17–26 (22). For the relation between purity and Jesus' preaching, cf. Marcus J. Borg, *Conflict, Holiness, and Politics in the Teachings of Jesus,* 2nd ed. (Harrisburg, PA: Trinity Press, 1998), 8–16, 247–56.

15. While sacrifice may appear strange and repugnant, as E. P. Sanders points out, in antiquity, religion *was* sacrifice. This aspect of Jewish worship was not unique in the ancient world. Sanders, *Judaism,* 49.

16. Amos 5:21,23–24.

17. Mic 6:8.

18. Mic 2:2.

19. A helpful study of Israel's religious diversity and the way in which the symbols of Temple, Torah, land, and racial identity are emphasized is N. T. Wright, *The New Testament and the People of God* (Minneapolis: Fortress Press, 1992), 145–243. Cf. Sanders's discussion of parties in *Judaism,* 13–34. Sanders's interest lies with what he calls "common Judaism," that of the ordinary priests and ordinary people. He cautions that the special views of the famous parties (e.g., Sadducees, Pharisees) belong to groups that were actually quite small (11).

20. A comprehensive study of the sacrificial interpretation of Jesus' death, from New Testament texts to the modern era, is found in Gerard S. Sloyan, *The Crucifixion of Jesus: History, Myth, Faith* (Minneapolis: Fortress Press, 1995). In Sloyan's judgment, temple sacrifice is the paradigm for the earliest conviction that Jesus' death had a beneficent effect on Israel (70).

21. Gal 5:10.

22. Sloyan, *The Crucifixion of Jesus,* 101. As we will see in chap. 2, early church writers will ground the origin of the sinfulness of the entire human race (a theme of Paul's) in the disobedience of Adam and its remedy in the obedience of Christ.

23. Heb 9:26.

24. Heb 9:13–14.

25. Heb 10:15.

26. Jer 31:33.

27. A comprehensive analysis of the origin of the resurrection tradition, its development, and meaning is given in Pheme Perkins, *Resurrection: New Testament Witness and Contemporary Reflection* (Garden City, NY: Doubleday, 1984). Debate about what the resurrection was and its meaning today is ongoing. Cf. two views offered in Marcus J. Borg and N. T. Wright, *The Meaning of Jesus: Two Visions* (San Francisco: HarperSanFrancisco, 1999), 111–44.

28. Cf. Acts 2:24,32; 3:15. The contrast between theological and christological is drawn by Stephen Patterson, *The God of Jesus: The Historical Jesus and the Search for Meaning* (Harrisburg, PA: Trinity Press International, 1998). We draw here from pp. 218–20.

29. Ibid., 237.

30. The symbol of the reign of God was central to Jesus' preaching. The Greek term, *basileia tou theou,* may be translated *kingdom of God* or, as in Matthew (because he wants to avoid the divine name), the *kingdom of heaven.* Jesus' vision of the *basileia* is found in a range of material. For example: (1) reign of God parables and similitudes; (2) parables reflecting what the world could be like with a radical transformation of values and others that simply reflect the world as it is; (3) preaching that describes the reign of God as here, in one's midst, as beginning, as to be found, as potential, as not-yet; (4) reversal sayings and beatitudes that subvert conventional values and offer alternative ones; (5) Jesus' healings and exorcisms reestablishing wholeness and health; (6) Jesus' open tableship with sinners, the shamed, outsiders, and expendables; and (7) Jesus' rejection of the patriarchal household and alternative formation of a discipleship group. The data of Jesus' vision of the reign of God should also include *him.* Who and what he was as a person, his relationships, and his activity as a whole were performative expressions of the living God's reign.

31. See E. P. Sanders, *Jesus and Judaism* (Philadelphia: Fortress Press, 1985), 77–90. Also Sanders, *Judaism,* esp. 279–303.

32. For example, 1 Cor 15:3 ff. and Rom 1:4; 4:25.

33. Mark 1:15.

34. Luke 4:18–19.

35. On the Jewish symbol of the reign of God and Jesus' preaching and activity, see Patterson, *The God of Jesus.* A useful analysis of the first-century

Roman social and political order to which Jesus directed his critique is Walter Wink, *Engaging the Powers* (Minneapolis: Fortress Press, 1992), esp. chap. 6, 109–38.

36. Cf. Gal 6:16.

37. Isa 49:6; cf. 60:3.

38. Isa 43:1.

39. Ps 10:13. The psalmist is not above calling for God to take strong measures. "Break the arm of the wicked and evildoers," he continues (v. 15). On Judaism as an entire way of life, cf. Sanders, *Judaism,* 50.

40. "As for me, this is my covenant with you: You shall be the ancestor of a multitude of nations" (Gen 17:4). Cf. Gen 9; God's covenant with Noah includes all humans. Texts that relate the covenantal obligations and promises reflect liturgical settings where the making of the covenant is recalled and renewed.

41. On Gentile conversion, see Shaye J. D. Cohen, "Conversion to Judaism in Historical Perspective: From Biblical Israel to Postbiblical Judaism," *Conservative Judaism* 36 (1983), 31–45; "Proselyte," in R. J. Zwi Werblowsky and Geoffrey Widoger, eds., *The Oxford Dictionary of the Jewish Religion* (New York: Oxford University Press, 1997), 550–51.

42. H. H. Rowley, "Jewish Proselyte Baptism and the Baptism of John," *From Moses to Qumran: Studies in the Old Testament* (London: Lutterworth Press, 1963), 211–35. On baptism in Judaism and early Christianity, see "Baptism," in Colin Brown, ed., *The New International Dictionary of New Testament Theology* (Grand Rapids, MI: Zondervan Publishing House, 1986), 143–61.

43. Gen 17:1–14; Deut 10:16. On conversion and circumcision, see Cohen, "Conversion to Judaism," 31–45; James D. G. Dunn, *The Epistle to the Galatians* (Peabody, MA: Hendrickson Publishers, 1993), 265–67; and John M. G. Barclay, *Obeying the Truth: Paul's Ethics in Galatians* (Minneapolis: Fortress Press, 1988), 45.

44. Gen 17:10,14.

45. Acts 2:27. Cf. Gal 3:27.

46. The original meaning of Paul's often polemical contrast between faith and law is a prominent issue in contemporary Pauline studies. A useful entry to the problem and scholarly literature is Barclay, *Obeying the Truth.* The work of Krister Stendahl has been influential. See Krister Stendahl, *Paul among Jews and Gentiles* (Philadelphia: Fortress Press, 1976). This stage of Pauline studies reflects the post–World War II insight into the contribution of Christian religious views to widespread anti-Semitism. The work of Stendahl, Sanders, Dunn, and others has recovered the social context of the Paul's letters, leading to a reinterpretation of his theological worldview. See also Veronica Koperski, *What Are They Saying about Paul and the Law?* (New York: Paulist Press 2001); and D. A. Carson, Peter T. O'Brien, and Mark A. Seifrid, *Justification*

and Variegated Nomism: A Fresh Appraisal of Paul and Second Temple Judaism, vol. 1, *The Complexities of Second Temple Judaism* (Grand Rapids: Baker Academic, 2001).

47. Dunn, *The Parting of the Ways.*

48. In the Christian tradition, Paul's contrast between faith in Christ and works of the law became a contrast between two *religions* rather than two *conditions* for Gentile entry into Israel. The relation between Christianity (faith) and Judaism (works) was conceived hierarchically. This became a major piece in the supersessionism found in Christian theology. See John T. Pawlikowski, O.S.M., "Christology, Anti-Semitism, and Christian-Jewish Bonding," in Rebecca S. Chopp and Mark Lewis Taylor, eds., *Reconstructing Christian Theology* (Minneapolis: Fortress Press, 1994), 245–68. For a broader historical overview, see Sidney G. Hall III, *Christian Anti-Semitism and Paul's Theology* (Minneapolis: Fortress Press, 1993).

49. Gal 3:2.

50. Cf. Deut 21:22–23. We will return to this more explicitly.

51. Living in the Spirit is the theme of Galatians 5.

52. Paul presumably thought this was also the case for Jewish followers who confessed Jesus as Lord. God's gift of God's Spirit is the eschatological reality of the new covenant.

53. Cf. Hans Dieter Betz: "The differences between man and woman in Judaism are the result of their different position in regard to the Torah." Betz, *Galatians,* Hermeneia (Philadelphia: Fortress Press, 1979), 197. In *Her Share of the Blessings: Women's Religions among Pagans, Jews, and Christians in the Greco-Roman World* (New York: Oxford University Press, 1992), Ross Shepard Kraemer explains that exemptions from Torah obligations circumscribe "separate and unequal spheres for women and men" (105). See also Tal Ilan, *Jewish Women in Greco-Roman Palestine* (Peabody, MA: Hendrickson Publishers, 1996); and idem, *Integrating Women into Second Temple History* (Peabody, MA: Hendrickson Publishers, 1999); Judith Romney Wegner, *Chattel or Person? The Status of Women in the Mishnah* (New York: Oxford University Press, 1988); and Bernadette Brooten, *Women Leaders in the Ancient Synagogue,* Brown Judaic Studies 36 (Atlanta, GA: Scholars Press, 1982).

54. Gal 3:28. As a baptismal fragment, see Betz, *Galatians,* 183–84.

55. Rom 16:1–16. Among the many names Paul mentions, Phoebe is a deacon, Prisca works [evangelizes] with Paul, Mary works among them [evangelizes], Junia is prominent among the apostles. For a fuller account of women in the Christian tradition, see Mary T. Malone, *Women and Christianity,* vol. 1, *The First Thousand Years* (Maryknoll, NY: Orbis Books, 2001).

56. Cf. Shaye J. D. Cohen, "Women in the Synagogues of Antiquity," *Conservative Judaism* 34 (1980), 23–29; Kraemer, *Her Share of the Blessings,* 93, 123.

57. On the origin of Paul's opponents, see Dunn, *Galatians,* 14–15. Cf. Sanders, *Jesus and Judaism,* who notes there is no evidence that Jesus rejected the validity of the Mosaic law, contrary to longstanding Christian arguments (55). The hypothesis that the new sect eventually broke with Judaism on this basis has a problem. "The trouble with this thread," Sanders writes, "is that the apostles in Jerusalem apparently did not know that the Torah had been abrogated [because it had not]: that was the contribution of Paul and possibly other apostles *to the Gentiles*" (55–56, emphasis added). In Paul's case, Sanders continues, the issue had to do with Paul's idea that Gentiles must be admitted into Israel on equal footing with Jews and that the basis of their salvation was not living as Jews, keeping the Torah, but their faith in Christ (57). An accurate historical perspective requires us to see Paul's opponents as authentic Jesus followers who did not believe that Jesus' resurrection had changed the way Gentiles came into Israel (cf. Gen 17) or the condition for staying in (cf. Deut 10: 12–13).

58. Speaking generally of rabbinic literature, E. P. Sanders writes that many scholars assume that the literature fits the genre of *law* and that it determined common *practice.* He questions both assumptions, genre and authority. "Besides the fact that the rabbis did not dictate practice, rabbinic legal discussions are sometimes idealistic, referring to the way things should be done, not describing how they are done. This too requires that the material be used with caution." Sanders, *Judaism,* 11. The rabbis' discussion of women is often idealistic or prescriptive, rather than historically realistic or descriptive. This insight into male-authored texts may be extended from rabbinic literature (e.g., the Mishnah) to the scriptures.

59. Shaye Cohen distinguishes between Judaism as legislated and Judaism as practiced. See Cohen, "Women in the Synagogues of Antiquity," 24. He notes the pluralistic character of Judaism on p. 27.

60. Cohen, "Women in the Synagogues of Antiquity," 24–25.

61. Brooten, *Women Leaders in the Synagogue,* 150.

62. Elisabeth Schüssler Fiorenza, *In Memory of Her: A Feminist Theological Reconstruction of Christian Origins* (New York: Crossroad, 1984), 107.

63. Sanders, *Judaism,* 333, 299–300.

64. 1 Cor 1:23.

65. Deut 21:22–23. Emphasis added.

66. James D. G. Dunn, "The Theology of Galatians," in Jouette M. Bassler, ed., *Pauline Theology,* vol. 1 (Minneapolis: Fortress Press, 1991), 125–46; 145.

67. Rom 5:19. Cf. Phil 2:6–8; Heb 4:15.

68. This is the primary example of dogmatic development in the early church. Original sin is a parallel development. Its dogmatic definition, however, did not come so early. For Roman Catholics, the dogma of original sin was defined in the sixteenth century by the Council of Trent (see chap. 4). The

christological and trinitarian development is traced by Bernard Lonergan in *The Way to Nicea: The Dialectical Development of Trinitarian Theology,* trans. Conn O'Donovan (Philadelphia: Westminster Press, 1976).

69. *Soteriology* comes from the Greek words *sozein* (to save) and *logos* (discourse). Christology considers the person of Christ. Who is Christ? Soteriology refers to the work of Christ. Who is Christ for us? By *work* is meant the purpose of Christ's mission, the incarnation, and the nature of redemption.

70. Deut 30:6.

71. Walter Wink, *Engaging the Powers,* 107. Emphasis added. While Jesus was not likely a Zealot or one who engaged in revolutionary activities, his message to the outcast and marginalized still had political meaning. It was a critique of the social order. Wink contrasts the reign of Rome—a domination system—with Jesus' vision of the reign of God as an alternative system, a domination-free order (107–37). This symbol, with its social and political implications, is the framework within which Jesus' preaching and death should be understood.

72. Cf. Acts 24:14.

73. W. H. C. Frend, *The Early Church* (Philadelphia: Fortress Press, 1982 ed.), 38. On the term *ekklesia* and the development of the institution, see Thomas Halton, "Church," in Everett Ferguson, ed., *Encyclopedia of Early Christianity,* 2nd ed. (New York: Garland Publishing, Inc., 1997), 253–56.

74. In the Gospels, Matt 16:18; 18:15,17. In the Pauline letters, for example, Gal 1:2,13,22. In Thess 2:14, the Jesus community is described as the *ekklesia tou theou,* church of God.

75. Elisabeth Schüssler Fiorenza describes the *ekklesia* as a "discipleship community of equals." See *In Memory of Her* esp. 103–50.

76. Philemon 1:16–17.

77. The patriarchal household will be discussed more directly in chap. 7.

78. Wink, *The Powers that Be: Theology for a New Millennium* (New York: Doubleday, 1998), 39.

79. Ibid., 64. See Wink, *Engaging the Powers,* 109–37, for a more extended discussion of the reign of God as a domination-free order.

80. Cf. the baptismal fragment in Gal 3:28. Gradually the norms of the patriarchal household will characterize the *ekklesia,* too. Note 1 Tim 2:8–15; 3:15; 6:1–2.

81. The story related in Mark 3:31–35 shows Jesus' rejection of the patriarchal family. The new family—"my brother and sister and mother"—has no father. Cf. Wink, *Engaging the Powers,* 119.

82. This is true in both the Jewish and Christian traditions as well as the Greco-Roman world of antiquity. The title of a study of Jewish women puts the alternatives starkly. Cf. Judith Romney Wegner, *Chattel or Person?*

83. Cf. reversal sayings in the Gospel of Mark: 9:33–37; 10:42–44.

84. Gal 5:15.

85. The institutional development of the early Christian church shows the reappropriation of patriarchal assumptions and norms, for example, those of gender and class privilege: "Let a woman learn in silence with full submission. I permit no woman to teach or to have authority over a man; she is to keep silent" (1 Tim 2:11–12). "[Slaves] who have believing masters must not be disrespectful to them on the ground that they are members of the church; rather they must serve them all the more, since those who benefit by their service are believers and beloved" (1 Tim 6:2). On gender in the Christian tradition, see Rosemary Radford Ruether, *Woman and Redemption: A Theological History* (Minneapolis: Fortress Press, 1998). An insightful resource relating gender and racial subordination and their religious legitimation in the Christian tradition is James Newton Poling, *Deliver Us from Evil: Resisting Racial and Gender Oppression* (Minneapolis: Fortress Press, 1996).

86. Cf. Mark Allen Powell, *Fortress Introduction to the Gospels* (Minneapolis: Fortress Press, 1998), 64. The hypothesis that Matthew structured the teaching material of Jesus as the "Five Books of Jesus," analogous to the "Five Books of Moses," was introduced by Benjamin Bacon in 1930. It remains influential today.

87. The Galatian conflict provides a glimpse into this diversity of views. The visiting evangelists obviously thought that living the way of the Torah and faith in Christ were compatible. Paul, however, argued that for Gentiles, living as a Jew was not necessary for salvation. The ground of salvation was the same for both Jews and Gentiles: faith in Christ. Paul's forceful rejection of the Jewish way of living (the law) for the Gentiles cannot be legitimately extended to Jews. He was not concerned with Jewish Christians.

88. A valuable introduction to the interpretation of the New Testament is Sandra Schneiders, *The Revelatory Text: Interpreting the New Testament as Sacred Scripture* (Collegeville, MN: Liturgical Press, 1999).

89. On *yetser ha-ra* and *yetser ha-tov,* evil and good inclinations, see the articles in *The Oxford Dictionary of the Jewish Religion,* 742–43, and *Dictionary of Judaism in the Biblical World* (New York: Macmillan, 1997), 312. For a discussion of *yetser ha-ra* in the Hebrew and Christian scriptures and early Christian tradition, see chap. 5 in James Gaffney, *Sin Reconsidered* (New York: Paulist Press, 1983).

90. Gen 6:5; 8:2.

91. Ps 14:3; 51:5.

92. J. N. D. Kelly, *Early Christian Doctrines* (San Francisco: Harper and Row, 1978), 163.

93. Jer 17:9; Ezek 36:26.

94. Jas 1:14.

95. The *early church* refers to the post–New Testament development of

Christianity in the second century and following. The *patristic period* refers to "the age of the Fathers *(patres)* of the church." In the West, the patristic period closes in the seventh century (with Saint Isidore, d. 636) and in the East in the eighth century (with Saint John Damascene, d. 749).

96. Gaffney, *Sin Reconsidered,* 34.

97. Mark 1:4.

98. Acts 2:38.

99. Rom 3:9.

100. Rom 3:23.

101. John 1:29.

102. 1 John 1:8.

103. John 1:29.

104. Matt 9:13; Luke 5:32. *Sin* is both a moral and a cultic category in ancient Israel. On ancient purity systems and the meaning of sin and sinner, cf. Wink, *Engaging the Powers,* 115–17.

105. Matt 9:6; Luke 5:24.

106. Matt 9:12; Luke 5:31.

107. Rom 10:9.

108. Cf. Deut 26:19.

109. Rom 5:12. Pauline scholars describe Paul's idea here as one of *original corruption,* rather than *original sin* in the sense that the latter took on in the second through the fifth centuries. We will return to these exegetical questions in later chapters.

110. Rom 8:2. *Law* in this context does not refer to the Torah (thus equating Torah and sin) but to the power of sin. In Paul's thinking, Adam's sin introduced the "reign of death." The giving of the law to Moses introduced the possibility of breaking God's specific commands (sin), thus initiating the "reign of sin." Sin became an habitual way of living. Christ frees human beings from the reign of sin by reordering their hearts and minds to God.

111. See Boadt, *Reading the Old Testament,* 89–108. An account of the documentary hypothesis and relevant texts is found in Antony F. Campbell and Mark A. O'Brien, *Sources of the Pentateuch: Texts, Introductions, Annotations* (Minneapolis: Fortress Press, 1993).

112. The Yahwist writer is designated by a *J* and not a *Y* because of the transliteration of the Hebrew word (mistakenly) as "*J*ahweh."

113. We will return to use of Genesis 3 in the early church doctrine of original sin in subsequent chapters.

114. Cf. interpretations of Genesis 3, for example: Claus Westermann, *Genesis 1–11: A Commentary* (Minneapolis: Fortress Press, 1984), 276; Elaine Pagels, *Adam, Eve, and the Serpent* (New York: Random House, 1988); and Paul Ricoeur, "The 'Adamic' Myth and the 'Eschatological' Vision of History," in *The Symbolism of Evil* (New York: Harper and Row, 1967), 232–78.

115. The scriptural genre of historical narrative serves the interest of religious proclamation and confession rather than the criterion of verification called for by modern history.

116. Cf. the punishments for sin given in Genesis 3:14–19. The tenth-century writer lives in a world where painful childbirth, gender domination, toil, and death are present realities. The question is *why* are they? The narrative details of myths often serve an etiological function, explaining the origin of behaviors, customs, and rituals. *J*'s story is an etiology of a kind of world, one plagued by suffering and death.

117. Gen 3:16–24.

118. For a translation and introduction, see Marshall D. Johnson, "Life of Adam and Eve," in James H. Charlesworth, ed., *The Old Testament Pseudepigrapha,* vol. 2 (Garden City, NY: Doubleday and Co., 1985), 249–95. The Greek version is titled the "Apocalypse of Moses" and the Latin version "Life of Adam and Eve." The association of Eve, or woman, with evil will be addressed in chap. 7.

119. For a translation and introduction, see A. F. J. Klijn, "2 (Syriac Apocalpyse of) Baruch," in Charlesworth, *The Old Testament Pseudepigrapha,* 640.

120. We will return to 1 Timothy 2:8–15 in chap. 7. The contradictory perspectives in Galatians (c. 55 C.E.) and 1 Timothy (c. 100 C.E.) regarding gender roles in the *ekklesia* reveal developments of institutional structures in the first-century Jesus movement.

121. On the development of the idea of fall, see Westermann, *Genesis,* 276 ff.

122. Cf. Henri Rondet, *Original Sin: The Patristic and Theological Background* (Shannon, Ireland: Ecclesia Press, 1972). Groups called *Gnostic* (Christian and non-Christian) favored this view (39 ff.). The Christian theologian Origen was also attracted to the idea of a transcendent fall (83–84).

CHAPTER 2

1. For a review of this development, see Henri Rondet, *Original Sin: The Patristic and Theological Background* (Shannon, Ireland: Ecclesia Press, 1972). A chief source of texts from the patristic period is Johannes Quasten, *Patrology,* vol. 1, *The Beginnings of Patristic Literature* (Utrecht-Antwerp: Spectrum Publishers, 1950); idem, *Patrology,* vol. 2, *The Ante-Nicene Literature after Irenaeus* (Utrecht-Antwerp: Spectrum Publishers, 1953); and, idem, *Patrology,* vol. 3, *The Golden Age of Greek Patristic Literature: From the Council of Nicaea to the Council of Chalcedon* (Utrecht-Antwerp: Spectrum Publishers, 1960). On individual patristic writers, see Everett Ferguson, ed.,

Encyclopedia of Early Christianity, 2nd ed. (New York: Garland Publishing, Inc., 1997). Major scholarly historical resources are J. N. D. Kelly, *Early Christian Doctrines* (New York: Harper and Row, 1978 ed.); Jean Danielou, S.J., *A History of Early Christian Doctrine before the Council of Nicaea,* vol. 2, *Gospel Message and Hellenistic Culture,* trans. and ed. John Austin Baker (Philadelphia: Westminster Press, 1973); and Jaroslav Pelikan, *The Christian Tradition: A History of the Development of Doctrine,* vol. 1, *The Emergence of the Catholic Tradition, 100–600* (Chicago: University of Chicago Press, 1971).

2. Historians divide the patristic writers into two traditions—Greek and Latin—based either on language or on geographical divisions between Eastern cities (such as Antioch and Alexandria) and Western cities (such as Rome and Carthage). We bracket this division to review writers chronologically according to the relevance of their ideas for the doctrine of original sin.

3. Chap. 7 will address problems created for women by this theological perspective.

4. A helpful review of this development is found in Russell J. DeSimone, "Modern Research on the Sources of Saint Augustine's Doctrine of Original Sin," *Augustinian Studies* 11 (1980), 205–27.

5. The *Didache* is discussed in F. L. Cross, *The Early Church Fathers* (London: Gerald Duckworth & Co., Ltd., 1960), 8–11, and Quasten, *Patrology,* vol. 1, 29–39.

6. Cf. references to the baptism of women in the Acts of the Apostles 8:12 and 10:47–48.

7. In the theological tradition ahead, speculation will posit an inherited sin to account for the universal need for Christ's redemption.

8. Quoted in Kelly, *Early Christian Doctrines,* 163.

9. The term original sin *(peccatum originale originatum)* will designate an inherited *condition* of sinfulness on the part of all humankind due to the first sin. Rondet, *Original Sin,* 26.

10. Ferguson, *Early Christianity,* 571–73.

11. Gnosticism—its origins, nature, and expressions–is a complex topic. See Pheme Perkins, "Gnosticism" in Ferguson, *Encyclopedia of Early Christianity,* 465–70; idem, *Gnosticism and the New Testament* (Minneapolis: Fortress Press, 1993).

12. Rondet, *Original Sin,* 39.

13. Pelikan, *The Christian Tradition,* vol. 1, 280–83. Our discussion draws from Pelikan.

14. Jaroslav Pelikan notes that it is the Gnostics who have an explicit doctrine of original sin in the second century, not the Christian writers *(The Christian Tradition,* vol. 1, 282–83). He writes that it is "misleading to speak of a 'doctrine of original sin' in church fathers such as Irenaeus." Irenaeus's concern was with human responsibility for sin. His recognition of its inevitability

came from apprehending it as part of human development rather than as a consequence of materiality as evil, as the Gnostics held. For Irenaeus and original sin, we draw from Rondet, *Original Sin,* 37 ff. In Kelly, *Early Christian Doctrines,* see 22–28 (Irenaeus and Gnosticism) and 170–74 (Irenaeus and original sin).

15. Rondet, *Original Sin,* 43.

16. Cf. Pelikan, *The Christian Tradition,* vol. 1, 284.

17. Rondet, *Original Sin,* 70.

18. Gradually technical terms will be utilized in a Christian theological anthropology that will distinguish Adam's nature prior to sin, divine gifts possessed by Adam's nature, capacities proper to human nature, and the consequence of the loss of divine gifts to nature after sin. The *temporal* designation, before and after sin, will denote two distinct *ontological* states of human nature: innocent and fallen—the state of original perfection and the state of original sin.

19. On Justin Martyr, see Quasten, *Patrology,* vol. 1, 196–219; Kelly, *Early Christian Doctrines,* 166–68; and Rondet, *Original Sin,* 27–28.

20. Later authors will utilize one of two principles (and sometimes both) to link humankind to Adam in sin: an *ontological* principle (all humankind was in Adam) or a *biological* principle (all humankind inherits Adam's sin).

21. Quoted in Kelly, *Early Christian Doctrines,* 167. For Tatian and Theophilus, see Kelly, 168.

22. Quasten, *Patrology,* vol. 1, 213.

23. Harry A. Wolfson, "Philosophical Implications of the Pelagian Controversy," in *Studies in Early Christianity,* vol. 10, *Doctrines of Human Nature, Sin, and Salvation in the Early Church,* Everett Ferguson, ed. (New York: Garland Publishing, Inc., 1993), 170–78; 170. Our description of the Stoics here relies on Wolfson. See also Kelly, *Early Christian Doctrines,* 166.

24. Wolfson, "Philosophical Implications," 170–71.

25. Kelly, *Early Christian Doctrines,* 166.

26. The later theological tradition will place the root of sin *prior* to personal sin, namely, in the presence of an inborn and inherited sin.

27. On demonology versus a theory of original sin in the early church fathers, see Danielou, *History of Doctrine,* vol. 3, 405 ff.

28. Kelly, *Early Christian Doctrines,* 349.

29. Quoted in Kelly, *Early Christian Doctrines,* 167. Also Rondet, *Original Sin,* 31. "In the second century," Rondet writes, "demonology is very important; it is a kind of answer to the problem of evil or the disorders of paganism."

30. Cf. Mark 1:23 f.; 1:34; 3:11; 5:1 f. In Acts 10:38, Peter describes "how God anointed Jesus of Nazareth with the Holy Spirit and with power; how he went about doing good and healing all who were oppressed by the

devil, for God was with him." For contemporary analyses of the New Testament language of evil (powers, devils), see Elaine Pagels, *The Origin of Satan* (New York: Vintage Books, 1995); and Walter Wink, *Naming the Powers: The Language of Power in the New Testament* (Philadelphia: Fortress Press, 1984); and idem, *Engaging the Powers: Discernment and Resistance in a World of Domination* (Minneapolis: Fortress Press, 1992).

31. Kelly, *Early Christian Doctrines,* 167–68.

32. Tertullian's work *On Baptism* offers insight into his opinion about infant baptism and the question of original sin. See *Tertullian's Homily on Baptism,* Ernest Evans, ed. (London: SPCK, 1964). It is discussed in Quasten, *Patrology,* vol. 2, 278–81; Kelly, *Early Christian Doctrines,* 174–76 and 350–54; Pelikan, *The Christian Tradition,* vol.1, 290; and Rondet, *Original Sin,* 61.

33. Ancient theories of the origin of the soul and their relevance to a theory of original sin will be discussed more fully later in the context of Origen.

34. Quoted in Rondet, *Original Sin,* 61. A century later, Ambrose of Milan (d. 397), an important influence for Augustine, will offer a similar view but state it more directly in terms of the effect of Adam's sin: "Adam existed, and in him we all existed; Adam perished, and in him all perished." Quoted in Kelly, *Early Christian Doctrines*, 354. The combination of (1) an anthropology of original unity and (2) a biological explanation of the transmission of Adam's *sin* through sexual intercourse answered the question why the sin of *one* individual had an effect on *others*. In other words, it provided the patristic theologians with a specific explanatory principle to account for human solidarity in sin with Adam. This transmission element is not present in Tertullian's views.

35. Quasten, *Patrology,* vol. 2, 280. On infant baptism in Christian origins, see "Baptism," in Colin Brown, ed., *The New International Dictionary of New Testament Theology* (Grand Rapids, MI: Zondervan Publishing House, 1986), 143–61; esp. 154ff.

36. Tertullian, *On Baptism,* 15.

37. Ibid., 39.

38. For Origen's correlation between baptism and original sin, see his *On First Principles,* book 3. Maurice Wiles and Mark Santer, *Documents in Early Christian Thought* (London: Cambridge University Press, 1977), 96–101.

39. Cited from Origen's "Homily on Leviticus" in Quasten, *Patrology,* vol. 2, 83. Emphasis added.

40. Quoted in Quasten, *Patrology,* vol. 2, 83.

41. This exclusivist claim is also found in Cyprian (d. 258). There its context was the question of the validity of baptism administered by schismatics. Its later (1302) formal magisterial context is Boniface VIII's *Unam Sanctum.* In that context the claim regarded papal authority: "We believe that there is one

holy catholic church…outside of which there is no salvation….We declare that it is necessary for salvation for every human creature to be subject to the Roman Pontiff." Quoted in Francis Schüssler Fiorenza, "Christian Redemption between Colonialism and Pluralism," in Rebecca S. Chopp and Mark Lewis Taylor, eds., *Reconstructing Christian Theology* (Minneapolis: Fortress Press, 1994), 269–302; 280.

42. Ancient theories of the origin of the soul and their appropriation in Christian circles are discussed in Rondet, *Original Sin,* 135–36.

43. The developed theory of original sin turns on the assertion that all humankind *inherits* Adam's sin.

44. Tertullian, *On the Soul,* in Quasten, *Patrology,* vol. 2, 287–90. Quasten notes that Tertullian's view that the act of generation reproduces the entire human being, body and soul (traducianism), is now considered heretical. It denies the direct creation by God of each individual soul. Augustine leaned toward the traducian theory, too.

45. Cf. Pelikan, *The Christian Tradition,* vol. 1, 285–87. As Pelikan notes, belief in the virgin birth of Christ and the sacramental practice of infant baptism are prior to the doctrine of original sin, not derived from it. Given their "increasingly secure place in cultus and confession," Pelikan writes, "they became the premises from which conclusions could be drawn about the fall and original sin" (286). On the relation between beliefs in the virgin birth and original sin, cf. DeSimone, "Modern Research," 210. The views of Didymus the Blind on Jesus, the virgin birth, and original sin are noted below.

46. Kelly, *Early Christian Doctrines,* 180. Also Rondet, *Original Sin,* 83–84.

47. Origen, *On First Principles* II, 9, 1–6, 100.

48. Kelly, *Early Christian Doctrines,* 181. Emphasis added.

49. Ibid., 182.

50. Cyprian's views on baptism and original sin are found in Quasten, *Patrology,* vol. 2, 378–79; Kelly, *Early Christian Doctrines,* 176–77; and Pelikan, *The Christian Tradition,* vol. 1, 290–92.

51. Quasten, *Patrology,* vol. 2, 379, citing Cyprian's Letter to Fidus (Epist. 64).

52. Pelikan, *The Christian Tradition,* vol. 1, 292. Emphasis added.

53. Rondet, *Original Sin,* 123–24.

54. On Didymus the Blind, baptism, and original sin, see Quasten, *Patrology,* vol. 3, 97–99.

55. Quoted in Quasten, *Patrology,* vol. 3, 98.

56. On the Cappadocian Fathers, see Quasten, *Patrology,* vol. 3, 236–96, and John Chrysostom, 424–82. The latter is discussed in Kelly, *Early Christian Doctrines,* 349.

57. Quasten, *Patrology,* vol. 3, 419.

58. Pelikan, *The Christian Tradition,* vol. 1, 285.

59. According to Quasten, Theodore's views on original sin were presented by others (then and later) in this way, but critical historical studies confirm that the following views (ascribed to Theodore) are not found in Theodore himself: "Man was not created immortal, but mortal; Adam and Eve harmed only themselves by their sin; universal mortality is not a chastisement of Adam's sin; the effects of the sin of Adam—the present condition of man—are not penalties, but a test, an experiment instituted by God." Theodore did oppose the idea of original sin. Quasten, *Patrology,* vol. 3, 419.

60. Kelly, *Early Christian Doctrines,* 354. Medieval theologians attributed these Latin commentaries to Ambrose of Milan. Augustine thought their author was Hilary of Poitiers (d. 367), a leading Latin theologian. He will take the interpretation of Romans 5:12 as divine revelation of original sin. Erasmus (d. 1536) discredited the judgment that Ambrose was the writer of these commentaries. He gave the name Ambrosiaster to the anonymous author.

61. Emphasis added.

62. Kelly, *Early Christian Doctrines,* 354.

63. Quoting Ambrosiaster, Kelly, *Early Christian Doctrines,* 354.

64. On the fall in Irenaeus, see Danielou, *A History of Early Christian Doctrine,* vol. 2, 404–5.

CHAPTER 3

1. The scholarship on Augustine is immense. An excellent summary article is Margaret R. Miles, "Augustine," in Everett Ferguson, ed., *Encyclopedia of Early Christianity,* 2nd ed. (New York: Garland Publishing, Inc., 1997), 148–55. For a more extended treatment, a valuable source is Eugene TeSelle, *Augustine the Theologian* (New York: Herder and Herder, 1970). Among articles relevant to Augustine and original sin are Anthony Meredith, "Augustine on Sin," *Month* 26 (1993), 367–71; Roland J. Teske, S.J., "St. Augustine's View of the Original Human Condition in *De Genesi contra Manichaeos,*" *Augustinian Studies* 22 (1991), 141–55; Piet F. Fransen, "Augustine, Pelagius and the Controversy on the Doctrine of Grace," *Louvain Studies* 12 (1987), 172–81; Russell J. DeSimone, "Modern Research on the Sources of Saint Augustine's Doctrine of Original Sin," *Augustinian Studies* 11 (1980), 205–27; J. Patout Burns, "The Interpretation of Romans in the Pelagian Controversy," *Augustinian Studies* 10 (1979), 43–54; and Robert J. O'Connell, S.J., "Augustine's Rejection of the Fall of the Soul," *Augustinian Studies* 4 (1973), 1– 32. Gerald Bonner discusses Augustine's anthropology in two articles, "Augus-

tine's Doctrine of Man: Image of God and Sinner," in Everett Ferguson, ed., *Doctrines of Human Nature, Sin, and Salvation in the Early Church: Studies in Early Christianity* (New York: Garland Publishing, Inc., 1993), 71–90; and "Augustine's Doctrine of Man," *Louvain Studies* 13 (1988), 41–57. Henri Rondet traces the development of the idea of original sin leading up to Augustine and the creative contribution of Augustine himself in *Original Sin: The Patristic and Theological Background* (Shannon, Ireland: Ecclesia Press, 1972).

2. Augustine was a prolific writer. Primary sources for Augustine's theology of original sin are *The Confessions of St. Augustine,* trans. Henry Chadwick (Oxford: Oxford University Press, 1992); *On the Grace of Christ* and *On Original Sin* in Whitney J. Oates, *Basic Writings of Saint Augustine,* vol. 1 (New York: Random House, 1948), 582–654; *Saint Augustine, The City of God,* books VIII–XVI, Roy Joseph Deferrari, ed. (New York: Fathers of the Church, Inc., 1952), trans. Gerald G. Walsh, S.J., and Grace Monahan, O.S.U., esp. books 12–14; and *Saint Augustine, Four Anti–Pelagian Writings: On Nature and Grace, On the Proceedings of Pelagius, On the Predestination of the Saints, On the Gift of Perserverance,* Thomas P. Halton, ed. (The Fathers of the Church; Washington, DC: Catholic University of America Press, 1992). Other works, such as *On the Baptism of Infants* and *Against Julian,* also address original sin.

Augustine's thinking on the problem of evil was not uniform through his theological career. *On Genesis against the Manichees,* for example, reflects Augustine's early conception of the problem of evil, one shaped by quite different concerns than those that will dominate his conflict with Pelagius.

Augustine interpreted the Adam and Eve story in three works on Genesis: *On Genesis against the Manichees* (387); *Literal Commentary on Genesis, An Incomplete Work* (392); *Literal Commentary on Genesis* (begun in 401; finished in 416).

3. Ecclesial and sacramental effects flow from Augustine's desire to protect the universal necessity of redemption through Christ. In "Augustine's Doctrine of Man," Gerald Bonner highlights Augustine's Christocentricity: "Man's redemption, then, is realized for the individual within the fellowship of Christ's Church, of which he is made a member by the reception of the sacrament of baptism which Christ ordained, and without which no one, save only the martyrs, can be saved. The narrowness of Augustine's view of salvation, which leaves the vast majority of the human race consigned to perdition, has often been deplored; but it must be remembered and emphasized that it springs from his Christocentricity: in Christ alone is salvation; incorporation into the Body of Christ is possible only by the reception of baptism; it must therefore follow that whoever is left outside can only be lost" (53).

4. Stephen Duffy underscores the accuracy of an earlier date: "The decisive indication that the Pelagian polemic was not the origin of Augustine's view is that in the *Ad Simplicianum* of 397, 15 years before the first anti-Pelagian broadside, his definitive formulation of grace and original sin is already in place." See Duffy, "Our Hearts of Darkness: Original Sin Revisited," *Theological Studies* 49 (1988), 597–622; 602–3. Also, Meredith, "Augustine on Sin," 367–68.

5. Augustine, *Confessions*, 82; see n. 13. Emphasis added.

6. TeSelle, *Augustine*, 192–93.

7. The following quotes are from *The Confessions*, 7–10.

8. Robert O'Connell discusses the scholarly opinion on Augustine's position in "Augustine's Rejection of the Fall of the Soul," 1–32. On Augustine's rejection of a transcendent fall, see TeSelle, *Augustine*, 192.

9. TeSelle, *Augustine*, 260–62.

10. Another example is the story of Philip and the Ethiopian eunuch (Acts 8:26–40).

11. Jaroslav Pelikan, *The Christian Tradition: A History of the Development of Doctrine* (Chicago: University of Chicago Press, 1971), vol. 1, 292.

12. See TeSelle, *Augustine*, 265, for Ambrose's remark and Augustine's appeal to Cyprian and Ambrose.

13. Cf. Augustine, *Against Julian*.

14. In *Contra Man.* 8 Didymus says that Adam's sin is inherited by all children of Adam through its transmission in the intercourse of their parents. Cited in Russell DeSimone, "Sources of Saint Augustine's Doctrine of Original Sin," 210.

15. The Latin Vulgate translated Romans 5:12 *in quo omnes peccaverunt,* "*in whom* [Adam] all have sinned." Contemporary exegetes agree that the original Greek terms, *eph ho, pantes,* and *hemarton* should be translated "because all have sinned." See Joseph A. Fitzmyer, S.J., *Romans, The Anchor Bible: A New Translation with Introduction and Commentary* (New York: Doubleday, 1993), 402–20.

16. Fitzmyer, *Romans,* 418.

17. In Romans 5:12 Paul's purpose is christological and soteriological. He makes a similar appeal to Adam's sin in 1 Corinthians 15:21–22: "For since death came through a human being, the resurrection of the dead has also come through a human being; for as all die in Adam, so all will be made alive in Christ." In both texts, Paul contrasts what Adam brought for humankind (death) and what Christ achieved for humankind (life). Adam is a cypher for the human predicament—sin. With Genesis 3, Romans 5:12 became a primary scripture source for a divinely revealed teaching on original sin. Because of the use of this text in the tradition, questions about what Paul said, what he meant, and what he would have assumed have become central in

contemporary biblical and theological debate about original sin. It must be kept in mind that *original sin* took on a technical meaning in the tradition. *Original* means more than "first." As a theological term, original sin refers specifically to the inheritance of sin by all humankind. No doubt Paul attributed the first sin to Adam and conceived of this in historical terms, but he did not understand Adam's sin as inherited. This concept of sin transmitted through physical intercourse as an explanation of human solidarity with Adam in sin is yet to emerge in the theological tradition.

18. Deferrari, ed., *Saint Augustine, The City of God,* 302. Jesus is the one exception. Because of the virgin birth, Jesus' nature was not transmitted through sexual procreation and is without sin. For others, however, physical intercourse generates a human nature received with original sin. In the patristics, confession of the virgin birth begins with Ignatius of Antioch. See DeSimone, "Sources of Saint Augustine's Doctrine of Original Sin," 210.

19. Quoted in George Vandervelde, *Original Sin: Two Major Trends in Contemporary Roman Catholic Reinterpretation* (Amsterdam: Rodopi, N.V., 1975), 16.

20. Pelikan, *The Christian Tradition,* vol. 3, 260.

21. Rondet, *Original Sin,* 120. Also Gerald Bonner, "Augustine's Doctrine of Man," 79. Augustine could appeal to the authority of scripture for this interpretation of sin. Cf. Sirach 10:13: "The beginning of sin is pride."

22. The Catholic theological tradition linked but did not equate original sin and concupiscence. Their identification is by virtue of a metonymy that identifies a cause with its effect. See Stephen Duffy, "Our Hearts of Darkness," 602. Catholic and Protestant views differ on this matter. We will take this up in chap. 4.

23. Augustine, *The Confessions,* 15.

24. Cf. *Confessions,* book 2, and *The City of God,* books 13 and 14.

25. Margaret R. Miles, *Augustine on the Body* (Missoula, MT: The Scholars Press, 1979), 67.

26. Ibid., 71.

27. Augustine, *Confessions,* 22–23.

28. Gerald Bonner distinguishes between Augustine's moral and metaphysical conceptions of the fall in "Augustine's Doctrine of Man," 46–47.

29. Vandervelde, *Original Sin,* 18. Vandervelde writes, "In this condition of original sin, man is actively involved in a necessity of sinning *(necessitas peccandi)*: he is not able not to sin."

30. Augustine, *On Original Sin,* in Oates, *Basic Writings of Saint Augustine,* 653.

31. Quoted in John M. Rist, "Augustine on Free Will and Predestination," in Ferguson, ed., *Doctrines of Human Nature, Sin, and Salvation,* 420–47; 431.

32. Cf. Rom 7:18–19.

33. Rist, "Augustine on Free Will," 424. *Caritas* and *cupiditas* are discussed on p. 428.

34. Miles, *Augustine on the Body,* 67.

35. Augustine, *Confessions,* 3.

36. TeSelle, *Augustine,* 160–61.

37. Fransen, "Augustine, Pelagius and the Controversy on the Doctrine of Grace," 172–81. Miles provides an overview of this controversy in "Augustine," 148–55. See also Kelly, *Early Christian Doctrines,* 357–61. Pelagius's views are indirectly known through Augustine's polemical portrayal of them. See Halton, *Saint Augustine: Four Anti-Pelagian Writings.* Two of Pelagius's writings, *On Nature* and *On the Freedom of the Will,* have the same titles as works of Augustine.

38. Miles, "Augustine," 151–52.

39. Augustine compared his understanding of human nature to that of Pelagius in *On Nature and Grace* and *On the Grace of Christ and On Original Sin.* For Augustine's description of their differences on faculties, see *On the Grace of Christ,* 585 ff.

40. On Stoicism in the ancient world, see Everett Ferguson, ed., *Backgrounds of Early Christianity,* 2nd ed. (Grand Rapids, MI: William B. Eerdmans Publishing Co., 1992), 333–56.

41. Fransen, "Augustine, Pelagius and the Controversy on the Doctrine of Grace," 179–80.

42. TeSelle, *Augustine,* 288. Whether in fact any human being avoids sin is a further question.

43. Alfred Vanneste compares Pelagius's "natural salvation" to Augustine's argument for the necessity of Christ's grace. *The Dogma of Original Sin* (Brussels: Vander, 1975), 57 ff.

44. For the differences between Augustine and Pelagius on Christ and justification, see Vandervelde, *Original Sin,* 14 ff.

45. TeSelle, *Augustine,* 283. In rejecting an inherited sin, Pelagius joined the company of Tertullian and Theodore of Mopsuestia. As we saw in chap. 2, Tertullian was a vigorous opponent in the Latin Church of the idea of an inherited sin. Theodore shared the widespread view of the Greek Fathers that death and sin passed to all mankind because of Adam's transgression, but in the opinion of historian F. L. Cross and others, Theodore was the only Greek Father of the first four centuries to explicitly deny the doctrine of original sin as theory of inheritance. See DeSimone, "Sources of Saint Augustine's Doctrine of Sin," 212.

46. Rondet, *Original Sin,* 121.

47. As Eugene TeSelle notes, original sin is the *loss* of integrity and concupiscence the *sign* of this loss. TeSelle, *Augustine,* 318. The medieval theologian, Anselm of Canterbury, will appeal to the more technical language of original justice or original integrity, as we will see in the next chapter.

48. J. N. D. Kelly compares Augustine and Pelagius on free will and grace in *Early Christian Doctrines,* 358 ff.

49. Augustine notes Pelagius's rejection in *On Original Sin,* 635.

50. Augustine, *On the Grace of Christ,* 592.

51. J. Patout Burns discusses Augustine's understanding of operative and cooperative grace in "The Interpretation of Romans in the Pelagian Controversy," 51. For discussion of operative and cooperative grace, the state of integrity lost through Adam's sin, and the transmission of original sin through procreation, see TeSelle, *Augustine,* 315–16.

52. It should be noted that the term *creationism*—used today for a fundamentalist reading of Genesis 1 and opposition to contemporary scientific theories of evolution—refers to a different matter here. The contemporary use will be addressed later.

53. Kelly, *Early Christian Doctrines,* 345.

54. This is a complex issue. Cf. Rahner's article on "Creationism" in Karl Rahner and Herbert Vorgrimler, *Theological Dictionary* (New York: Herder and Herder, 1965), 107–8: "By contrast with generationism (Traducianism) creationism is the Catholic doctrine that God creates every individual soul out of nothing (Creation), uniting it with the cells of the parents, which have fused in generation to form a single human being (D 738, 1100, 2317). The soul does not exist before its substantial union with the body (D 203, 236, against Preexistentianism and the theory of the transmigration of souls). The majority of Catholic theologians agree that the soul is infused at the moment when the cells of the parents are united (not at birth: D 1185; and not upon the first intellectual act: D 1910)."

55. Augustine's preferred theory of the origin of the soul is sometimes referred to as "spiritual generationism."

56. Fransen discusses the controversy in "Augustine, Pelagius and the Controversy on the Doctrine of Grace," 172–81. Because of political turmoil in the Roman Empire, both Pelagius and Celestius had come to Africa. Pelagius continued on to Palestine.

57. Augustine's work *On Original Sin* discusses Celestius's teachings, the proceedings of the Council of Carthage, and the proceedings of the Synod of Palestine against Pelagius. Oates, *Basic Writings of Saint Augustine,* 620 ff.

58. See J. Neuner and J. Dupius, eds., *The Christian Faith in the Doctrinal Documents of the Catholic Church* (Westminster, MD: Christianity Classics, 1975), 127 (canon 1) and 130 (canon 2). The Council of Trent adopted

with only slight modification the second canon of Carthage. In Neuner, this second canon of Carthage is found as canon 4 in those issued by Trent. The two decrees are quoted in the following two notes. For discussion of Carthage, see Vandervelde, *Original Sin,* 21–22, and Vanneste, *The Dogma of Original Sin,* 57–65.

59. "1. This has been decided by all the bishops…gathered together in the holy Synod of Carthage: Whoever says that Adam, the first man, was made mortal in the sense that he was to die a bodily death whether he sinned or not, which means that to quit the body would not be a punishment for sin but a necessity of nature, *anathema sit.*"

60. "If anyone denies that infants newly born from their mothers' womb are to be baptised, even when born from baptised parents, or says that, though they are baptised for the remission of sins, yet they do not contract from Adam any original sin which must be expiated by the bath of regeneration that leads to eternal life, so that in their case the formula of baptism 'for the forgiveness of sins' would no longer be true but would be false, *anathema sit.* For, what the apostle says: 'sin came into the world through one man and death through sin, and so death spread to all men because all have sinned' (Rom 5.12), should not be understood in another sense than that in which the Catholic Church spread over the whole world has understood it at all times. For, because of this rule of faith, in accordance with apostolic tradition, even children who of themselves cannot have yet committed any sin are truly baptised for the remission of sins, so that by regeneration they may be cleansed from what they contracted through generation. For 'unless one is born of water and the Spirit, he cannot enter the kingdom of God' (John 3.5)."

61. Fransen, "Augustine, Pelagius and the Controversy on the Doctrine of Grace." The historical overview here draws from Fransen.

62. The Council of Orange is discussed in both Vandervelde, *Original Sin,* 26, and Vanneste, *The Dogma of Original Sin,* 95 ff.

63. Neuner and Dupius, *Doctrinal Documents of the Catholic Church,* 128. "If anyone says that through the offence of Adam's sin the whole man, body and soul, was not changed for the worse, but believes that only the body was subjected to corruption while the freedom of the soul remained unharmed, he is misled by the error of Pelagius and goes against Scripture which says: 'the soul that sins shall die' (Ezek 18.20), and: 'do you now know that if you yield yourselves to anyone as obedient slaves you are slaves of the one whom you obey?' (Rom 6.16); and again: 'whatever overcomes a man, to that he is enslaved.' (2 Pet 2:19)."

64. Cited in Vanneste, *The Dogma of Original Sin,* 95.

65. Cited in Rondet, *Original Sin,* 122.

66. Cf. Pelikan, *The Christian Tradition,* vol. 1, 280. See the discussion of determinism in Gnostic and Stoic views and the response of Clement of Alexandria, Justin Martyr, and others in chap. 2.

CHAPTER 4

1. On medieval theology, see G. R. Evans, *Philosophy and Theology in the Middle Ages* (New York: Routledge, 1993).

2. On medieval theology, anthropology, and doctrine of original sin, see Gabriel Daly, "Original Sin," in Joseph Komonchak, Mary Collins, and Dermot A. Lane, eds., *The New Dictionary of Theology* (Wilmington, DE: Michael Glazier, 1987), 726–31; Jaroslav Pelikan, *The Christian Tradition: A History of the Development of Doctrine,* vol. 3, *The Growth of Medieval Theology* (Chicago: University of Chicago Press, 1978); Karl Rahner, S.J., "Original Sin," *Encyclopedia of Theology: The Concise Sacramentum Mundi* (New York: Seabury Press, 1975), 1148–55; Henri Rondet, *Original Sin: The Patristic and Theological Background* (Shannon, Ireland: Ecclesia Press, 1972); idem, *The Grace of Christ: A Brief History of the Theology of Grace,* trans. Tad W. Guzie, S.J. (Westminster, MD: Newman Press, 1966); George Vandervelde, *Original Sin: Two Major Trends in Contemporary Roman Catholic Reinterpretation* (Amsterdam: Rodopi, N.V., 1975); and Alfred Vanneste, *The Dogma of Original Sin* (Brussels: Vander, 1975).

3. The term *supernatural* was in use in theology by the ninth century and was given its full technical sense in the *De bono* of Philip the Chancellor (c. 1225). See Quentin Quesnell, "Supernatural," in Komonchak, et al., *The New Dictionary of Theology,* 995–96. The scholastic hierarchy of nature encompasses levels from mineral to divine nature. On the theological category of the supernatural, Quesnell writes that "anything found in a lower nature which is proper only to some higher nature is relatively supernatural. Anything found in a lower nature which is proper to the divine nature is absolutely supernatural" (995). The distinction between natural and supernatural was of particular importance in the theologies of original sin and grace.

4. On Anselm, see G. R. Evans, *Anselm and a New Generation* (Oxford: Clarendon Press, 1980) and R. W. Southern, *Saint Anselm: A Portrait in a Landscape* (Cambridge: Cambridge University Press, 1990). Anselm's understanding of original sin is discussed by Rondet, *Original Sin,* 145–46; and Vandervelde, *Original Sin: Two Major Trends,* 26–28.

5. Today the term *justice* refers to a social policy, structure, or situation that balances the needs and rights of persons. The theological meaning of *justitia* intended by Anselm refers to a capacity of human nature, one that is bestowed by God on nature rather than being a capacity intrinsic to human nature. *Justitia* is

thus a category in Anselm's metaphysical theological anthropology. He posits it as the opposite of sinful alienation from God—what was in nature prior to sin that created a relation of friendship.

6. On original blessedness and the essence of human nature, see Rondet, *Original Sin,* 148–49; and Evans, *Anselm,* 95–96, 131.

7. Anselm, *De Libertate Arbitrii.* Quoted in Southern, *Saint Anselm,* 173.

8. Rondet, *Original Sin,* 151. Emphasis added.

9. Anselm, *Concept. Virg.* (26–28), quoted in Pelikan, *The Christian Tradition,* vol. 3, 111.

10. See Thomas's discussion of original sin in the *Summa Theologica* (New York: Benziger Brothers, Inc., 1947 ed.), I–II, q. 81–83. (Hereafter, *ST.*) Accounts of his theology of original sin are found in Rondet, *Original Sin,* 160–68; and Vandervelde, *Original Sin: Two Major Trends,* 28–32. Also helpful is William A. Van Roo, S.J., *Grace and Original Justice according to St. Thomas* (Rome: Gregorian University, 1955). Jacques Maritain discusses Thomas's metaphysics of evil in *Saint Thomas and the Problem of Evil* (Milwaukee, WI: Marquette University Press, 1942). A major study of Thomas is Bernard J. F. Lonergan, S.J., *Grace and Freedom: Operative Grace in the Thought of St. Thomas Aquinas,* Patout Burns, S.J., ed. (London: Darton, Longman, and Todd, 1971).

11. See n. 3. In relation to human beings, the natural order refers to potentialities, capacities, operations, acts, habits, and ends proper to human nature. The order of grace refers to potentialities, capacities, operations, acts, habits, and ends proper to divine nature and, if given to human nature, aid in its performance and achievement of its ultimate fulfillment. A theological category introduced by medieval christian theologians, the supernatural is not a category for Aristotle.

12. Rondet, *Theology of Grace,* 208.

13. Cf. Quesnell, "Supernatural," 995–96.

14. On the history of the theology of grace, see Quentin Quesnell, "Grace," in *The New Dictionary of Theology,* 437–50. For Thomas specifically, see 440–41.

15. "Now the universe of creatures, to which man is compared as part to whole, is not the last end, but is ordained to God, as to its last end. Therefore the last end of man is not the good of the universe, but God himself." Thomas, *ST,* I–II, q. 2, art. 8.

16. See Rondet, *Theology of Grace,* 201–3. On Thomas's understanding of grace and the theological virtues, see Quesnell, "Grace," 440.

17. Ibid., "Grace," 440.

18. Rondet, *Theology of Grace,* 247.

19. Van Roo, *Grace and Original Justice,* 15.

20. *ST,* I–II, q. 82, art. 2, ad 3m. On the function of justice in establishing harmony, see Van Roo, *Grace and Original Justice,* 91.

21. Thomas makes Anselm's definition of original sin the "formal element" (essence) of original sin. In *ST,* I–II, qs. 82, art. 3, Thomas writes, "The privation of original justice, whereby the will was made subject to God, is the formal element of original sin...."

22. Thomas, *ST,* I–II, q. 82, art. 2m: "The privation of original justice [removes] the subjection of man's mind to God."

23. On the loss of the internal harmony established by justice, see Van Roo, *Grace and Original Justice,* 73–75.

24. Ibid., 91. See the remarks on sanctifying grace as the cause of original justice. Also Vandervelde, *Original Sin,* 29.

25. Brian M. Nolan, "Nature," in *The New Dictionary of Theology,* 710–713; 712.

26. Cf. George D. Smith, ed., *The Teaching of Catholic Church: A Summary of Catholic Doctrine,* vol. I (New York: Macmillan, 1950), 322 (emphasis added): "Our parents before their fall were endowed with the three qualities of justice, integrity, and immortality....The word justice, as here used, means first and principally the *supernatural gift of sanctifying grace,* which raised Adam to a higher state and nobler dignity, which put him into a relationship of real friendship with God in this life, and gave him the pledge of eternal happiness in the closest union with him in the next....immortality and integrity, are called preternatural gifts."

27. Vandervelde, *Original Sin,* 41.

28. Ibid., 41–42; Gabriel Daly, "Original Sin," 728; Rahner, "Original Sin," in *Sacramentum Mundi,* 329.

29. Thomas brings the two conceptions of original sin together by making Anselm's the *formal element* and Augustine's the *material element.* The complete twofold definition is given in *ST,* I–II, q. 82, art. 3: "Consequently the formal element of original sin must be considered in respect to the cause of original sin. But contraries have contrary causes. Therefore the cause of original sin must be considered with respect to the cause of original justice, which is opposed to it. Now the whole order of original justice consists in man's will being subject to God: which subjection, first and chiefly, was in the will, whose function it is to move all the other parts to the end, as stated above (q. 9, a. 1), so that the will being turned away from God, all the other powers of the soul became inordinate. Accordingly the privation of original justice, whereby the will was made subject to God, is the formal element in original sin; while every other disorder of the soul's powers, is a kind of material element in respect to original sin." In summary, Thomas writes, "Hence original sin is concupisence, materially, but privation of original justice, formally." On Thomas's fusion of

the two approaches, see Vandervelde, *Original Sin: Two Major Trends,* 28–32; and Van Roo, *Grace and Original Justice,* 38.

30. Thomas calls the material element of original sin an inordinate disposition of nature, a "habit *inborn* due to our corrupt origin." *ST,* I–II, q. 82, art. 1, ad 3m. It is a habit, he says, "for it is an inordinate disposition, arising from the destruction of the harmony which was essential to original justice....Original sin is called the *languor of nature.*" *ST,* I–II, q. 82, art. 1. Following the tradition, Thomas places the cause of original sin in physical transmission. See *ST,* I–II, q. 81, art. 1; q. 82, art. 2 and art. 4; q. 83, art. 1 and art. 1, ad 2m. Thomas's characterization of original sin as an *inborn* habit—and not an *infused* one—serves an important purpose. It removes blame from God for the sin of nature. "The corruption of original sin is nowise caused by God, but by the sin alone of our first parent through carnal generation." *ST,* I–II, q. 83, art. 1, ad 4m.

31. Thomas refers to original sin as a "sin of nature" in *ST* q. 82, art. 1, ad 2m and q. 82, art. 4.

32. Thomas says of original sin in *ST,* I–II, q. 82, art. 1, ad 1m, "Consequently, it is not pure privation, but a corrupt habit."

33. For Thomas's metaphysics of evil described here, see Maritain, *The Problem of Evil,* 20–39.

34. Thomas, *ST,* I–II, q. 82, art. 2: "The first sin alone of our first parent was transmitted to his posterity." Thomas refers to the physical transmission of original sin several times in the texts pertaining to original sin, cf. *ST* I–II, q. 82, art. 1, ad 3m; q. 82, art. 2 (cited previously); q. 82, art. 4; q. 83, art. 1; and q. 83, art. 1, ad. 4m. In q. 83, art. 2, ad 2m, Thomas writes that "original sin is caused by the semen as instrumental cause."

35. Brian Kelly, "Redemption and Original Sin," *Irish Theological Quarterly* 60 (1994), 1–16.

36. The decrees of the Council of Trent are found in J. Neuner and J. Dupius, eds., *The Christian Faith in the Doctrinal Documents of the Catholic Church,* 129–32. Helpful resources on Trent are H. J. Schroeder, O.P., *Canons and Decrees of the Council of Trent* (Rockford, IL: Tan Books and Publishers, Inc., 1978), 21–23 (original sin) and 29–45 (justification); Hubert Jedin, *A History of the Council of Trent,* trans. Ernest Graf, O.S.B. (St. Louis, MO: B. Herder Book Co., 1957), 125–65 (original sin) and 166–96 (justification); idem, *Ecumenical Councils of the Catholic Church: An Historical Outline,* trans. Ernest Graf, O.S.B. (New York: Herder and Herder, 1960), 145–86. On Martin Luther and the Council of Trent, see also Rondet, *Original Sin,* 169–75; Vandervelde, *Original Sin,* 32–41; and Karl Rahner, "Original Sin," 1148–55, esp. 1151–52. For original texts, see *Enchiridion Symbolorum Definitionum et Declarationum,* ed. H. Denziger and A. Schönmetzer, 36th ed. (Freiburg im Breisgau: Herder, 1965), §1510–16.

37. A primary source for Luther's understanding of original sin is Hilton C. Oswald, ed., *Luther's Works,* vol. 25, *Lectures on Romans* (St. Louis, MO: Concordia Publishing House, 1972), esp. 299– 307; also 272–75 and 259–63. Helpful resources are Martin Brecht, "Martin Luther," in Hans J. Hillerbrand, ed., *The Oxford Encyclopedia of the Reformation,* vol. 2 (New York: Oxford University Press, 1996), 461–67; and Robert Kolb, "Lutheranism: Overview and Theology," in *The Oxford Encyclopedia of the Reformation,* 467–73.

38. Trent's decree on original sin is the foundation for its decree on justification. See Jedin, *History of the Council of Trent* and idem, *Ecumenical Councils.* Session V (June 1546) affirmed the Catholic understanding of original sin. Session VI (January 1547) asserted the Catholic conception of justification and merit.

39. Justification is religious conversion in Thomas. It is the opening of the person's heart to God and the initiation of a new habitual orientation to God effected by the infusion of grace. See Quesnell, "Grace," 440. On justification in Paul, cf. Rom 5:1 and Gal 2:16. However, medieval theological language of religious conversion was neither biblical nor existential. The terms describing conversion and its effects were abstract and metaphysical—sanctifying grace, supernatural habits, operative and cooperative grace. Luther's teaching of the Pauline letters was formative for his theological perspective and critique of scholastic theology as he knew it. His language for sin and grace shows his rejection of abstract explanations of personal religious experience.

40. Cf. Luther's *Lectures on Romans,* 261–62, and his discussion of whether one can love God and perform the works of the Law without grace.

41. Original sin in Luther's *Lectures on Romans* is "a propensity toward evil," "this universal concupiscence" (299); "the very tinder of sin" (259, 273, 274, 300). Original sin refers to *sin itself,* Luther writes, "the passion, the tinder, and the concupiscence, or the inclination, toward evil and the difficulty of doing good..." (259). The phrase "tinder of sin," unusual today, carried the meaning of concupiscence in its medieval context. See n. 7 (259): "The scholastics used the term *fomes* ('tinder,' 'spark'), especially in the combination *fomes concupiscentiae,* to designate man's natural attraction toward evil."

42. Vanneste, *Original Sin,* 130. See also Bernhard Lohse, *Martin Luther's Theology: Its Historical and Systematic Development,* trans. and ed. Roy A. Harrisville (Minneapolis: Fortress Press, 1999), esp. 70–72 and 248–57.

43. This is called an "imputation" theory of justification. God *regards* human beings as just even though they are not. In its religious use, *just* means being in the right relation with God. Cf. Luther's *Lectures on Romans,* 260: "Now, is he perfectly righteous? No, for he is at the same time both a sinner and a righteous man; a sinner in fact, but a righteous man by the sure imputation and promise of God that he will continue to deliver him from sin until He has

completely cured him." Also 259, 301. See Kolb, "Lutheranism: Overview and Theology," 471, on *simul iustus et peccator* as a theological principle in Luther's theology.

44. Kolb, "Lutheranism: Overview and Theology," 471.
45. Vanneste, *Original Sin,* 125.
46. Luther, *Lectures on Romans,* 299.
47. Ibid.
48. Ibid., 272.
49. Ibid, 299–300. Luther compares scholastic theologians with Paul and Augustine.
50. Ibid., 299.
51. Vanneste, *Original Sin,* 126.
52. Vandervelde, *Original Sin,* 41.
53. Canon 1 in the Decree on Original Sin notes that original sin is a loss of the supernatural gifts of holiness and justice. Neuner and Dupius, *Doctrinal Documents of the Catholic Church,* 129. The canons noted below are found on pp. 129–32.
54. Canon 2.
55. Canons 3, 5.
56. Origen (d. 299) grounded the church's necessity in each person's need for the forgiveness mediated through baptism. "There can be no salvation without this church," Origen wrote. *Extra hanc domum id est ecclesiam, nemo salvatur.* Cited in Quasten, *Patrology,* vol. 2, *The Ante- Nicene Literature after Irenaeus* (Utrecht-Antwerp: Spectrum Publishers, 1953), 83.
57. Cf. "The Decree on the Relationship of the Church to Non-Christian Religions" in *The Documents of Vatican II,* Walter M. Abbot, S.J., ed. (New York: America Press, 1966), 660–68. On the conception and history of Christian religious exclusivism, see Francis Schüssler Fiorenza, "Christian Redemption between Colonialism and Pluralism," in Rebecca S. Chopp and Mark Lewis Taylor, eds., *Reconstructing Christian Theology* (Minneapolis: Fortress Press, 1994), 269–302; and John P. Galvin, "Salvation Outside the Church," in Peter Phan, ed., *The Gift of the Spirit: A Textbook on Ecclesiology in Honor of Patrick Greenfield, O.S.B.* (Collegeville: Liturgical Press, 2000), 249–66.
58. Cf. Augustine, *On Original Sin,* in Whitney J. Oates, ed., *Basic Writings of Saint Augustine,* vol. 1 (New York: Random House, 1948), 653.
59. On exegetical questions regarding Romans 5:12, see Joseph A. Fitzmyer, S.J., *Romans, The Anchor Bible: A New Translation with Introduction and Commentary* (New York: Doubleday, 1993), 405–7.
60. Canons 1, 4.
61. Vandervelde, *Original Sin,* 38.
62. Canon 5.
63. Canon 1.

64. Canon 1.

65. Canon 5.

66. Canon 3.

67. Canons 1, 2, 3, 4.

68. Canon 3. The term *imitation* is a red flag, seeming to connote *Pelagian*. By its insistence that original sin is "transmitted by propagation and not imitation," Trent explicitly grounds the universality of sin by a theory of biological inheritance, rejecting—to put it in modern terms—a sociological interpretation that evil spread through bad example.

69. Canon 4. To associate the transmission of original sin with sexual intercourse reflects a predisposition of patristic theologians (cf. Augustine) to link sex with sin. That association becomes embedded in the sexual ethics of the church's teaching. While sex and marriage are acknowledged as created goods, this concession is clouded by a lingering ambiguity. In *Between the Sexes: Foundations for a Christian Ethics of Sexuality* (Philadelphia: Fortress Press, 1985), Lisa Sowle Cahill writes that "Augustine takes a more negative view of sex in marriage than does Aquinas, seeing it as inescapably tainted by concupiscence. Although he declines to pronounce definitively on whether, if Adam and Eve had retained their original purity, God would have found 'some other way' to continue the race, Augustine does volunteer the judgment that 'freedom from sexual intercourse' is 'an angelic ideal'" (114). To seek sexual pleasure within marriage, for example, is considered by Augustine as a venial sin (121, n. 52). Following sentiments expressed by Paul, Augustine portrays virginity as a higher Christian state than marriage.

70. Canon 1.

71. Canon 3.

72. Canons 4 and 5.

73. Canon 4.

74. Canon 5.

75. Canon 3.

76. Rondet, *Original Sin,* 269.

77. Stephen J. Duffy, "Our Hearts of Darkness: Original Sin Revisited," *Theological Studies* 49 (1988), 597–622; 605.

78. Cf. Luther, *Lectures on Romans,* 259–63.

79. Cf. Canon 5.

80. Luther, *Lectures on Romans,* 261. Luther found Augustine an authority: "But blessed Augustine says very clearly that 'sin, or concupiscence is forgiven in Baptism, not in the sense that it no longer exists, but in the sense that it is not imputed'" *(De nuptiis et concupiscentia).*

81. Ibid. 301; cf. 261, 300.

82. Ibid., 299–300. It is likely that Luther would have taken this contemporary explanation of the Catholic theologian Karl Rahner as a chief example

of what he opposed. Rahner writes, "The essence of original sin is the absence of grace, or of that supernatural elevation which was originally intended for man (D 788f.): this 'state of privation' really separates man from God (D 789) and yet is not a personal sin of the individual (D 236), that is, is only to be called 'sin' in an analogous sense; *it leaves unchanged all that man himself is by nature* (D 1055) although the whole concrete man is 'wounded' by the consequences of original sin and 'weakened' in his natural powers (D 788)..." Karl Rahner, "Original Sin," in Karl Rahner and Herbert Vorgrimler, eds., *Dictionary of Theology* (New York: Herder and Herder, 1965), 330–31. Emphasis added.

83. Ibid., 259–60.

84. Vandervelde, *Original Sin,* 41.

85. Discussing Romans 5:12, Luther writes, "For later on the apostle says, 'For as by one man's disobedience many were made sinners' (v. 19), and this is the same as saying that all have sinned in the sin of the one man...that is, while one man sinned, all men sinned....Therefore, you also are a sinner, because you are the son of a sinner; but a sinner can beget nothing but another sinner like himself." Luther, *Lectures on Romans,* 302, 304.

86. Pope Pius IX convened the First Vatican Council in Rome in 1869.

87. Vandervelde, *Original Sin,* 41–42. Vandervelde notes that the definition of Robert Bellarmine (d. 1621) was key in this development. Cf. Gabriel Daly, "Original Sin," in *The New Dictionary of Theology:* "From the time of Robert Bellarmine onwards original sin was interpreted mainly in terms of the loss and continued privation of sanctifying grace" (728). In George D. Smith, ed., *The Teaching of Catholic Church: A Summary of Catholic Doctrine,* vol. 1 (New York: Macmillan, 1950), justice means "principally the *supernatural gift of sanctifying grace*" (322). Emphasis added.

88. Ludwig Ott, *Fundamentals of Catholic Dogma,* trans. Patrick Lynch (St. Louis, MO: B. Herder Book Company, 1955; 5th edition, 1962), 106.

CHAPTER 5

1. For our topic, useful resources are Ernst Cassirer, *The Philosophy of the Enlightenment;* trans. Fritz C. A. Koelln and James P. Pettegrove (Boston: Beacon Press, 1955; orig. publ. 1932); Philip L. Quinn, "Sin and Original Sin," *A Companion to Philosophy of Religion,* ed. Philip L. Quinn and Charles Taliaferro (Cambridge, MA: Blackwell Publishers, 1997), 541–48, esp. "Modern Philosophical Critiques," 545 ff.; Peter Henrici, "The Philosophers and Original Sin," *Communio* 18 (Winter 1991), 489–501; Henri Rondet, *Original Sin: The Patristic and Theological Background* (Staten Island, NY: Alba House, 1972), esp. 192–217.

2. Cf. Charles C. Hefling, Jr., "Science and Religion," in Joseph A. Komonchak, Mary Collins, and Dermot A. Lane, eds., *The New Dictionary of Theology* (Wilmington, Del: Michael Glazier, Inc., 1987), 938–45.

3. The impact of modernity on the church and theology—and now, developments described as postmodern—remains a much-examined subject. A helpful overview is Mark William Worthing, *God, Creation,* and *Contemporary Physics* (Minneapolis: Fortress Press, 1996), 7–32. Essays of Bernard Lonergan, S.J., discuss the topics of modernity, modern science, theories of knowledge, and method in theology among others. See Frederick E. Crowe, S.J., ed., *Collection: Papers by Bernard J. F. Lonergan, S.J.* (New York: Herder and Herder, 1967); idem, *A Third Collection: Papers by Bernard J. F. Lonergan, S.J.* (New York: Paulist Press, 1985); Bernard J. F. Lonergan, S.J., *A Second Collection,* William F. J. Ryan, S.J., and Bernard J. Tyrrell, S.J., eds. (Philadelphia: Westminster Press, 1974). Helpful, too, are essays by William J. Hill, "Theology," 1011–27, and Wayne L. Fehr, "History of Theology," 1027–35 in Komonchak, et al., *The New Dictionary of Theology.*

4. A helpful introduction to the changed situation of reading scripture in the context of modern critical biblical scholarship is Sandra M. Schneiders, *The Revelatory Text: Interpreting the New Testament as Sacred Scripture* (Collegeville, MN: Liturgical Press, 1999). On the development of method, see Edgar Krentz, *The Historical-Critical Method* (Philadelphia: Fortress Press, 1975).

5. Krentz, *Historical-Critical Method,* 9.

6. On the use of the Bible as a historical source in the doctrine of original sin, see Rondet, *Original Sin,* 220.

7. Krentz, *Historical Critical Method,* 11. Rondet discusses this development and the example of Isaac de la Peyere in *Original Sin,* 219.

8. John Barton, "Reading and Interpreting the Bible," *Harper's Bible Commentary,* ed. James L. Mays (San Francisco: Harper & Row, 1988), 9.

9. Rondet, *Original Sin,* 193.

10. Quoted in Christian Duquoc, "New Approaches to Original Sin," *Cross Currents* 28 (1978), 189–200; 193–94.

11. Paul Ricoeur devoted two volumes of his work to sin. *L'homme faillible* (1960) is a transcendental analysis of the human capacity to sin, and *Symbolique du mal* (1960) is an analysis of the essence of evil. The latter work includes an examination of the myth of the fall, "The 'Adamic' Myth and the 'Eschatological' Vision of History," 232–78. The English title is *The Symbolism of Evil,* trans. Emerson Buchanan (New York: Harper and Row, 1967). See also Ricoeur, "Original Sin: A Study of Meaning," in D. Ihde, ed., *The Conflict of Interpretations: Essays in Hermeneutics* (Evanston: Northwestern University Press, 1974), 272–73.

12. Cited in Roger Hahn, "Laplace and the Mechanistic Universe," in David Lindberg and Ronald Numbers, eds., *God and Nature: Historical Essays*

on the Encounter between Christianity and Science (Berkeley: University of California Press, 1986), 26.

13. An example of a sustained critique of original sin is the turn-of-the-century work of F. R. Tennant, *The Origin and Propagation of Sin* (Cambridge: Cambridge University Press, 1906).

14. Cassirer, *The Philosophy of the Enlightenment,* 141.

15. Stephen J. Duffy, "Our Hearts of Darkness: Original Sin Revisited," *Theological Studies* 49 (1988), 597–622; 605.

16. See, for example, Pascal's *Pensées,* trans. A. J. Krailsheimer (London: Penguin, 1966).

17. On Pascal and original sin, see Cassirer, *The Philosophy of the Enlightenment,* 142–44; and Henrici, "The Philosophers and Original Sin," 490–91.

18. Pascal's remark is quoted by Henrici, "The Philosophers and Original Sin," 490.

19. Cassirer, *The Philosophy of the Enlightenment,* 146.

20. Quoted in Henrici, "The Philosophers and Original Sin," 492.

21. Cassirer, *The Philosophy of the Enlightenment,* 147–48.

22. See Henrici, "The Philosophers and Original Sin," 498–99; and Rondet, *Original Sin,* 192–217. Schelling's work develops that of Immanuel Kant (d. 1804). Kant is discussed below.

23. Ibid.

24. Duquoc, "New Approaches to Original Sin," 193.

25. Cassirer, *The Philosophy of the Enlightenment,* 159.

26. Ibid.

27. Jean-Jacques Rousseau, *The Essential Rousseau,* Lowell Bair, trans. and Matthew Josephson, ed. (New York: New American Library, 1974). On Rousseau, see Cassirer, *The Philosophy of the Enlightenment,* 153–58; Henrici, "The Philosophers and Original Sin," 493.

28. Rousseau, "Discourse on Inequality," *The Essential Rousseau,* 125–201.

29. Cassirer, *The Philosophy of the Enlightenment,* 156.

30. Rousseau, "Discourse on Inequality," *The Essential Rousseau,* 173.

31. Ibid., 186.

32. Ibid, "The Social Contract," 8.

33. Ibid, 7–24.

34. Immanuel Kant, *Religion within the Limits of Reason Alone,* trans. R. Thomte (Princeton: Princeton University Press, 1960). On Kant's interpretation of original sin as the problem of radical evil see the works cited in n. 1.

35. *Yetser ha-ra* and *yetser ha-tov* are discussed in chap.1. See, for example, *The Oxford Dictionary of the Jewish Religion,* 742–43.

36. Rondet, *Original Sin,* 197.

37. Kant was especially strident in the rejection of inherited sin, saying of the origin of moral evil that "surely of all the explanations of the spread and propagation of this evil through all members and generations of our race, the most inept is that which describes it as an inheritance from our first parents." Kant, *Religion within the Limits of Reason Alone,* 35.

38. Ibid., 3; 142.

39. See, for example, Arthur Peacocke, *Theology for a Scientific Age* (Minneapolis: Fortress Press, 1993 ed.); idem, *The Sciences and Theology in the Twentieth Century* (Notre Dame, IN: University of Notre Dame Press, 1981); David Lindberg and Ronald Numbers, eds., *God and Nature*; Harold P. Nebelsick, *Circles of God: Theology and Science from the Greeks to Copernicus* (Edinburgh: Scottish Academic Press, 1985); Thomas F. Torrance, *Reality and Scientific Theology* (Edinburgh: Scottish Academic Press, 1985); Robert Jastrow, *God and the Astronomers* (New York: W. W. Norton, 1978); and Worthing, *God, Creation, and Contemporary Physics.* The influential work of Charles Darwin is *The Origin of Species,* ed. J. W. Burrow (Penguin Books, 1968). On the persons and disciplines discussed following, see topical encyclopedia entries—Cuvier, Darwin, Lamark, Lyell, anthropology, archaeology, biology, culture, Darwinism, evolution, geology, man, paleontology, catastrophism, uniformitarism—in addition to works cited here. For an interpretation of original sin in the context of an evolutionary world, cf. Jerry D. Korsmeyer, *Evolution and Eden: Balancing Original Sin and Contemporary Science* (New York: Paulist Press, 1998).

40. Immanuel Kant reduced religion to morality. But the relegation of religion to the private realm was not effected entirely by those hostile to religion. The German religious thinker Friedrich Schleiermacher (d. 1834), for example, reduced religion to feeling, by which he meant the immediacy of intuition or consciousness of the infinite. An influential work of Schleiermacher is *On Religion: Speeches to Its Cultured Despisers* (1799), trans. J. Oman (New York: Harper and Brothers, 1958). Cf. Quinn, *Philosophy of Religion,* 114–15.

41. William Paley's work, among others, is addressed by Laura L. Garcia, "Teleological and Design Arguments," in Quinn, *Philosophy of Religion,* 338–44.

42. The following section will develop the Roman Catholic reaction to modern theories of evolution. Protestant views will be discussed in chap. 6.

43. See chap. 2 for the discussion of Irenaeus.

44. Modern biblical scholarship would deal with this issue from a literary perspective of genre, i.e., rejecting a literal interpretation of Genesis 3 as history in favor of the view that it is symbolic narrative or myth. The author intends to say something true about human existence and sin but is not concerned with "what happened" in the sense of documenting history.

45. Karl Rahner, "Evolution," in Karl Rahner, ed., *Encylopedia of Theology: The Concise Sacramentum Mundi* (New York: Seabury Press, 1975), 475–88; 486.

46. Walter M. Abbott, S.J., *The Documents of Vatican II* (New York: Guild Press, 1966), 120.

47. Pope Pius XII, *Humani Generis,* in Claudia Carlen, I.H.M., ed., *The Papal Encyclicals 1939–1948* (Raleigh: McGrath Publishing Co., 1981), 175–84.

48. *Humani Generis,* 181.

49. Ibid., 181–82.

50. See, Piet Schoonenberg, S.J., *Man and Sin: A Theological View* (Notre Dame, IN: University of Notre Dame Press, 1965); and idem, "Original Sin and Man's Situation," in *The Mystery of Sin and Forgiveness,* ed. Michael J. Taylor (Staten Island, NY: Alba House, 1971), 243–52. James L. Connor, S.J., discusses Schoonenberg's call for hermeneutical principles in "Original Sin: Contemporary Approaches," *Theological Studies* 29 (1968), 215–40. See also Duffy, "Our Hearts of Darkness."

51. Schoonenberg, *Man and Sin,* 169.

52. Ambrosiaster's interpretation of Romans 5:12 is discussed in chap. 2.

53. United States Catholic Conference, *Catechism of the Catholic Church* (Liguori, MO: Liguori Publications, 1994). The *Catechism* distinguishes two historical states: an original state of holiness and justice constituted by friendship with God and the possession of preternatural gifts and a sinful state constituted by the loss of this friendship with God and supernatural gifts through sin. Adam has transmitted a sin with which all are afflicted, and human nature is wounded by their sin. Original sin is human nature deprived of original holiness and justice (396–421). The quote following is from p. 102.

54. See Paul Turner, "Baptism and Original Sin," in Peter E. Fink, S.J., ed., *The New Dictionary of Sacramental Worship* (Collegeville, MN: Liturgical Press, 1990), 81–83.

CHAPTER 6

1. Cf. Ludwig Ott, *Fundamentals of Catholic Dogma,* James Canon Bastible, ed., Patrick Lynch, trans. (St. Louis, MO: B. Herder Book Company, 1962; originally published in German in 1955); and George D. Smith, ed., *The Teaching of Catholic Church: A Summary of Catholic Doctrine,* vols. 1 and 2 (New York: Macmillan, 1950). Ott notes the biblical source of the doctrine, saying, "Since Adam's sin is the basis of the dogma of Original Sin and Redemption the historical accuracy of the [biblical] account as regards the essential facts may not be impugned. According to a decision of the Biblical

Commission in 1909, the literal historical sense is not to be doubted in regard to the following facts..." (106).

2. The *formulation* of the doctrine has never posed the problem for Protestant theologians that it has for Catholic theologians. See the contrast developed in chap. 4, esp. "Protestant and Catholic Perspectives." One difference lies in institutional structures and authority. For Catholic theologians, the reinterpretation of original sin has been governed by the Roman Catholic magisterium's insistence that the *conceptual formulation* of original sin cannot deviate from the terminology adopted by the Council of Trent in its dogmatic definition of original sin. The theological explanation of the doctrine has tended, until very recently, to be a reflection on what Trent said. Cf. Ott, *Fundamentals of Catholic Dogma,* 106–14. For an insightful reinterpretation of the doctrine, see Roger Haight, "Sin and Grace," in Francis Schüssler Fiorenza and John P. Galvin, eds., *Systematic Theology: Roman Catholic Perspectives,* vol. 2 (Minneapolis: Fortress Press, 1991), 75–142.

3. Cf. the discussion of myth in chap. 1.

4. Two interpretations of Genesis 3 are Elaine Pagels, *Adam, Eve, and the Serpent* (New York: Random House, 1988); and Claus Westermann, *Genesis 1–11: A Commentary* (Minneapolis: Fortress Press, 1984). According to the documentary hypothesis of the Pentateuch, the second creation story and the expulsion story, Genesis 2–3, are the initial pieces of the Yahwist tradition, designated as the *J* narrative. It is thought to originate from the royal court setting of David and Solomon in the tenth century B.C.E. The *J* narrative provides the major strand in the larger unified narrative of the Pentateuch edited by the priestly writers *(P)* during and after the Babylonian Exile in the sixth century B.C.E. Cf. remarks on the source hypothesis in chap. 1. The brief review of the doctrine's foundational biblical texts here highlights exegetical assumptions taken into account by contemporary theologians: (1) the literary genre of Genesis 3 and (2) Paul's understanding of sin in Romans 5:12.

5. Joseph A. Fitzmyer, S.J., *Romans, The Anchor Bible: A New Translation with Introduction and Commentary* (New York: Doubleday, 1993), 405.

6. James L. Conner, "Original Sin: Contemporary Approaches," *Theological Studies* 29 (1968), 215–240; 222. Other Pauline texts suggest a similar perspective. If Christ died for our sins (1 Cor 15:3), *then* all are sinners. If Christ was reconciling the world to God (2 Cor 5:19), *then* the world shares a solidarity in sin.

7. See chap. 1 previous, text at n. 90. In the anthropology characteristic of ancient Jewish thinking, two impulses exist in human persons, the inclination to do good, *yetser ha-tov,* and the inclination to do evil, *yetser ha-ra.* The universality of human sinfulness is a fact due to the power of *yetser ha-ra.* On *yetser ha-ra* in the Hebrew and Christian scriptures and early Christian tradition, see James Gaffney, *Sin Reconsidered* (New York: Paulist Press, 1983), chap. 5.

8. Matthew Fox, *Original Blessing: A Primer in Creation Spirituality* (Santa Fe, NM: Bear and Co., 1983).

9. The phrase is Stephen Duffy's. For evaluations of the status of original sin in contemporary theology, published at ten-year intervals, three articles are helpful: James L. Connor, "Original Sin: Contemporary Approaches" (1968), Brian O. McDermott, "The Theology of Original Sin: Recent Developments," *Theological Studies* 38 (1977): 478–525; and Stephen J. Duffy, "Our Hearts of Darkness: Original Sin Revisited," *Theological Studies* 49 (1988), 597–622. For a recent overview, see Gabriel Daly, "Original Sin," in *The New Dictionary of Theology,* ed. Joseph Komonchak, Mary Collins, and Dermot A. Lane (Wilmington, DE: Michael Glazier, 1987), 726–31. Three book-length studies published in the 1970s are Henri Rondet, *Original Sin: The Patristic and Theological Background* (Shannon, Ireland: Ecclesia Press, 1972); Alfred Vanneste, *The Dogma of Original Sin* (Brussels: Vander, 1975); and George Vandervelde, *Original Sin: Two Major Trends in Contemporary Roman Catholic Reinterpretation* (Amsterdam: Rodopi, N.V., 1975). The biblical exegete Herbert Haag has several articles on the relation between biblical sources and church doctrine, including "The Original Sin Discussion, 1966–1971," *Journal of Ecumenical Studies* 10 (1973), 259–89. See also Christian Duquoc, "New Approaches to Original Sin," *Cross Currents* 28 (1978), 189–200; and Siegfried Wiedenhofer, "The Main Forms of Contemporary Theology of Original Sin," *Communio* 18 (1991), 514–29. A now-classic source for the feminist critique and interpretation of original sin is Rosemary Radford Ruether, *Sexism and God-Talk: Toward a Feminist Theology* (Boston: Beacon Press, 1983). More general discussions of sin also treat original sin. See, for example, Patrick McCormick, *Sin as Addiction;* Timothy O'Connell, "A Theology of Sin," *Chicago Studies* 21:3 (1982), 277–92 (New York: Paulist Press, 1989), and Michael J. Taylor, ed., *The Mystery of Sin and Forgiveness* (Staten Island, NY: Alba House, 1971). A useful overview is William E. May, "Sin," in *The New Dictionary of Theology,* 944–67. See also Gary A. Anderson, *The Genesis of Perfection: Adam and Eve in Jewish and Christian Imagination* (Louisville: Westminster John Knox, 2001) and idem., "Biblical Origins and the Problem of the Fall," *Pro Ecclesia* 10 (Winter 2001), 17–30; and Jean Bottéro, *The Birth of God: The Bible and the Historian,* Hermeneutics: Studies in the History of Religions, trans. by Kees W. Bolle (University Park, PA: Pennsylvania State University Press, 2000), esp. 162–77.

10. Schoonenberg, *Man and Sin: A Theological View* (Notre Dame, IN: University of Notre Dame Press, 1965); idem, "Original Sin and Man's Situation." See also idem, "Sin and Guilt," in Karl Rahner, ed., *Encyclopedia of Theology: The Concise Sacramentum Mundi* (New York: Seabury Press, 1975), 1579–86.

11. Schoonenberg, "Sin and Guilt," 1584.

12. Ibid., 1580.

13. Bernard Häring, C.Ss.R., *Sin in the Secular Age* (Garden City, NY: Doubleday, 1974); Louis Monden, S.J., *Sin, Liberty and Law* (New York: Sheed and Ward, 1965). For a more recent study of the historical development of moral theology, see the thorough study of John Mahoney, *The Making of Moral Theology: A Study of the Roman Catholic Tradition* (Oxford: Clarendon Press, 1987). Patrick McCormick provides a useful overview in *Sin as Addiction.*

14. Schoonenberg, "Sin and Guilt," 1584.

15. Schoonenberg, "Original Sin and Man's Situation," 252.

16. Schoonenberg, "Sin and Guilt," 1584.

17. Schoonenberg, "Original Sin and Man's Situation," 251.

18. Ibid., 248.

19. Cf. Ps 53: "God looks down from heaven on humankind to see if there are any who are wise, who seek after God. They are all fallen away, they are all alike perverse; there is no one who does good, no, not one."

20. Cf. John 1:29.

21. Schoonenberg, "Original Sin and Man's Situation," 248.

22. Schoonenberg, "Sin and Guilt," 1581.

23. Ibid., 1580.

24. Schoonenberg, "Original Sin and Man's Situation," 247.

25. Karl Rahner, "Original Sin," *Sacramentum Mundi: An Encyclopedia of Theology* (New York: Herder and Herder, 1969), 328–34; 330.

26. Larry Rasmussen, ed., *Reinhold Niebuhr: Theologian of Public Life* (Minneapolis: Fortress Press, 1991). Niebuhr demurred at calling himself a theologian, but his work is undoubtedly one of the most significant contributions in twentieth-century American theology.

27. Reinhold Niebuhr, *Moral Man and Immoral Society: A Study in Ethics and Politics* (New York: Charles Scribner's Sons, 1932).

28. Reinhold Niebuhr, *The Nature and Destiny of Man,* vols. 1 and 2 (New York: Charles Scribner's Sons, 1941–1943). In vol. 1, see especially chap. 7, "The Temptation of Sin"; chap. 8, "Man as Sinner"; chap. 9, "Original Sin and Man's Responsibility"; and chap. 10, *"Justitia Originalis."*

29. Reinhold Niebuhr, *Beyond Tragedy: Essays on the Christian Interpretation of History* (New York: Charles Scribner's Sons, 1937); *Christianity and Power Politics* (New York: Charles Scribner's Sons, 1940); *The Self and the Dramas of History* (New York: Charles Scribner's Sons, 1955); *Man's Nature and His Communities* (New York: Charles Scribner's Sons, 1965); and D. B. Robertson, ed., *Love and Justice* (Gloucester: Peter Smith, 1976), a collection of Niebuhr's essays.

30. Niebuhr, *Christianity and Power Politics,* 17–18.

31. Niebuhr, *Beyond Tragedy,* 11.

32. Ibid., 120.

33. Niebuhr, *Beyond Tragedy*, 120. Cf. *Christianity and Power Politics*, 14.

34. Niebuhr, *The Self and the Dramas of History*, 157.

35. Niebuhr, *Man's Nature and His Communities*, 94.

36. Ibid., 84.

37. Niebuhr, *The Self and the Dramas of History*, 18. He quotes Henri Bergson on p. 18.

38. Niebuhr, *Man's Nature and His Communities*, 23–24.

39. Niebuhr, *Beyond Tragedy*, 147–48.

40. Ibid., 11.

41. Ibid., 12.

42. Ibid., 11–12.

43. On the relation of the fall and justice, see Niebuhr, *Love and Justice*, 47. In *Nature and Destiny of Man*, vol. 1, see chap. 10.

44. For example, Niebuhr, *The Self and the Dramas of History*, 17–20, and *Beyond Tragedy*, 281.

45. It is important to see the economic interests that generate ideologies of superiority. As James Newton Poling notes about slavery in America, "By the eighteenth century, the southern colonies were already committed to a slave economy, and the coming of 'King Cotton' by 1793 had strengthened the motive for promoting the slave system. In 1792, the nation raised 6,000 bales of cotton; by 1810, 178,000 bales. Cotton, tobacco, rice, indigo, and other crops raised all over the South with slave labor created wealth for both North and South" (12). Christian ministers, often slave owners themselves such as Cotton Mather, contributed to the elaboration of an ideology of white superiority. Appealing to New Testament texts such as 1 Timothy, they portrayed African Americans as created by God to be servants of whites, and in serving their masters, they were serving Jesus Christ. The natural division between those who rule and those who are subject was portrayed as the order of creation (42). James Newton Poling, *Deliver Us from Evil: Resisting Racial and Gender Oppression* (Minneapolis: Fortress Press, 1996). The ideological arguments for white supremacy and male privilege, as well as the influence of economic interests, are parallel in construction: scripture, nature, creation.

46. Niebuhr, *Christianity and Power Politics*, 50.

47. Niebuhr, *Beyond Tragedy*, 190.

48. Niebuhr, *Nature and Destiny of Man*, vol. 1, chap. 9. Cf. *The Self and the Dramas of History*, 99.

49. Niebuhr, *Man's Nature and His Communities*, 161.

50. Ibid., 106–7.

51. Niebuhr, *Beyond Tragedy*, 106.

52. Niebuhr, *Man's Nature and His Communities*, 107–25. Cf. *The Self and the Dramas of History*, 31–32.

53. Niebuhr, *Christianity and Power Politics*, 38.

54. Niebuhr, *Beyond Tragedy,* 257–58.

55. Niebuhr, *Nature and Destiny of Man,* vol. 1, chap. 7.

56. Niebuhr, *Beyond Tragedy,* 98.

57. Ibid., 102.

58. Larry Rasmussen, *Reinhold Niebuhr,* 7–19. Rasmussen notes that Niebuhr distinguishes between sin as assertion and sin as dissolution. The sin of assertion corresponds to the traditional notion of sin as pride. Sin as dissolution corresponds to sensuality, Rasmussen writes, "following the libidinal impulses and attaching ourselves to that which is less than the self, rather than that which is more" (19). Especially relevant for the next section on redemption are Niebuhr's writings included in Rasmussen, chap. 5, "Grace and Sin," 136–73.

59. Niebuhr, *Beyond Tragedy,* 103.

60. Niebuhr, *Love and Justice,* 49.

61. Niebuhr, *Beyond Tragedy,* 165.

62. Niebuhr, *Christianity and Power Politics,* ix–x. Cf. *The Self and the Dramas of History,* 155– 56.

63. Niebuhr, *Man's Nature and His Communities,* 125.

64. Niebuhr, *Love and Justice,* 276–77.

65. Niebuhr, *Christianity and Power Politics,* 3.

66. Ibid.

67. Niebuhr, *Beyond Tragedy,* 105. Cf. *Man's Nature and His Communities,* 118, 125.

68. Ibid., 20.

69. Niebuhr, *Man's Nature and His Communities,* 24.

70. Jürgen Moltmann, *Theology of Hope: On the Ground and the Implications of a Christian Eschatology* (Minneapolis: Fortress Press, 1993 [1965]); Johannes Baptist Metz, *Theology of the World* (New York: Herder and Herder, 1969).

71. Gustavo Gutiérrez, *A Theology of Liberation: History, Politics and Salvation* (Maryknoll, NY: Orbis, 1973). A helpful background source is Robert McAfee Brown, *Gustavo Gutiérrez: An Introduction to Liberation Theology* (Maryknoll, NY: Orbis, 1990).

72. For the influence of Gutiérrez in particular on the Roman Catholic magisterium, see James B. Nickoloff, ed., *Gustavo Gutiérrez: Essential Writings* (Minneapolis: Fortress Press, 1996), esp. p. 8. Reference to liberation themes such as the "preferential option for the poor" is made, for example, in pastoral letters of Latin American bishops ("Liberation and the Gospel," 1985); and encyclicals of John Paul II (*Laborem Exercens,* 1981; *Sollicitudo Rei Socialis,* 1987; *Centesimus Annus,* 1993).

73. For overviews of this debate, see, for example, Mark O'Keefe, O.S.B., *What Are They Saying about Social Sin?* (New York: Paulist Press,

1990); and Patrick Kerans, *Sinful Social Structures* (New York: Paulist Press, 1974). The relations among personal, original, and social sin have been an ongoing topic of debate. A useful article on social sin is Peter Henriot, "Social Sin: The Recovery of a Christian Tradition," in *Method in Ministry: Theological Reflection and Christian Ministry,* ed. James D. Whitehead and Evelyn Eaton Whitehead (San Francisco: Harper & Row, 1980), 127–44.

74. *A New Catechism: Catholic Faith for Adults* (New York: Herder and Herder, 1967). The parenthetical page numbers in this section following refer directly to the *Catechism.*

75. Irenaeus is discussed in chap. 2.

76. Cf. chap. 3 for the discussion of Augustine and Pelagius.

CHAPTER 7

1. Rosemary Radford Ruether's historical and systematic work has been of considerable importance for Christian feminist theologians. Analysis of the doctrine of original sin is central in Ruether's work. Particularly important is her major systematic work, *Sexism and God-Talk: Toward a Feminist Theology* (Boston: Beacon Press, 1983); and the more recent historical work, *Women and Redemption: A Theological History* (Minneapolis: Fortress Press, 1998). Among other writings, see "Patriarchy" in Letty M. Russell and J. Shannon Clarkson, eds., *Dictionary of Feminist Theology* (Louisville, KY: Westminster John Knox Press, 1996), 205–6; *Gaia and God: An Ecofeminist Theology of Earth Healing* (San Francisco: HarperSanFrancisco, 1992); "Women's Difference and Equal Rights in the Church," in Anne Carr and Elisabeth Schüssler Fiorenza, *The Special Nature of Women? Concilium* (1991), 11–18; "The Future of Feminist Theology in the Academy," *Journal of the American Academy of Religion* 53:3 (December 1985), 703–13; "Feminism and Patriarchal Religion: Principles of Ideological Critique of the Bible," *Journal for the Study of the Old Testament* 22 (1982), 54–66; Rosemary Radford Ruether and Eleanor McLaughlin, eds., *Women of Spirit: Female Leadership in the Jewish and Christian Traditions* (New York: Simon and Schuster, 1979); and *Religion and Sexism: Images of Women in the Jewish and Christian Traditions* (New York: Simon and Schuster, 1974).

2. Elisabeth Schüssler Fiorenza is the leading feminist biblical scholar whose work *In Memory of Her: A Feminist Theological Reconstruction of Christian Origins* (New York: Crossroad, 1987) is pivotal in the historical reconstruction of the early Jesus movement and the role of women within its first-century development. Among her books, see *Discipleship of Equals: A Feminist Ekklesialogy of Liberation* (New York: Crossroad, 1993); *But She Said: Feminist Practices of Biblical Interpretation* (Boston: Beacon Press,

1992); and *Bread Not Stone: The Challenge of Feminist Biblical Interpretation* (Boston: Beacon Press, 1984). Helpful articles are "Missionaries, Apostles, Coworkers: Rom 16 and the Reconstruction of Women's Early Christian History," *Word and World* 6 (1986), 420–33; "Women in the Early Christian Movement" in Carol P. Christ and Judith Plaskow, eds., *Womanspirit Rising: A Feminist Reader in Religion* (San Francisco: Harper & Row, 1979), 84–92; "Word, Spirit, and Power: Women in Early Christian Communities" in Rosemary Radford Ruether and Eleanor McLaughlin, eds., *Women of Spirit: Female Leadership in the Jewish and Christian Traditions* (New York: Simon and Schuster, 1979), 29–70; and "Women in the Pre-Pauline and Pauline Churches," *Union Seminary Quarterly Review* 33 (1978), 153–66. Also helpful are two co-edited *Concilium* volumes: Anne Carr and Elisabeth Schüssler Fiorenza, eds., *The Special Nature of Women? Concilium* (1991); and Mary Collins and Elisabeth Schüssler Fiorenza, eds., *Women: Invisible in Church and Theology, Concilium* (1984). In the latter, see Schüssler Fiorenza, "Breaking the Silence—Becoming Visible," 3–16.

3. Cf. Rita Nakashima Brock, *Journeys by Heart: Christology of Erotic Power* (New York: Crossroad, 1991); Mary Daly, *Beyond God the Father: Toward a Philosophy of Women's Liberation* (Boston: Beacon Press, 1973); Mary McClintock Fulkerson, "Sexism as Original Sin: Developing a Theocentric Discourse," *Journal of the American Academy of Religion* 59:4 (1991), 653–75; Kathleen M. Sands, *Escape from Paradise: Evil and Tragedy in Feminist Theology* (Minneapolis: Fortress Press, 1994); Christine Smith, "Sin and Evil in Feminist Theology," *Theology Today* (1993), 208–19; and Marjorie Hewitt Suchocki, *The Fall to Violence: Original Sin in Relational Theology* (New York: Continuum, 1995). For sin in *mujerista* and womanist theologies, see Ada María Isasi-Díaz, "Defining Our *Proyecto Histórico: Mujerista* Strategies for Liberation," in Charles E. Curran, Margaret A. Farley, and Richard A. McCormick, S.J., eds., *Feminist Ethics and the Catholic Moral Tradition: Readings in Moral Theology 9* (New York: Paulist Press, 1996), 120–35; and Emilie M. Townes, *A Troubling in My Soul: Womanist Perspectives on Evil and Suffering* (Maryknoll, NY: Orbis, 1993). See also Ivone Gebara, *Out of the Depths: Women's Experience of Evil and Salvation*, trans. Ann Patrick Ware (Minneapolis: Fortress Press, 2002); and Ann Gilroy, "Original Sin (1)," 165–67 and Dorothea McEwan, "Original Sin (2)" in An *A to Z of Feminist Theology*, Lisa Isherwood and Dorothea McEwan, eds. (Sheffield: Sheffield Academic Press, 1996), 165–67 and 167–68.

4. Primary texts are available in collections such as Elizabeth A. Clark and Herbert Richardson, *Women and Religion: The Original Sourcebook of Women in Christian Thought* (San Francisco: HarperSanFrancisco, 1977).

5. Identification of the doctrine with the story, however, is not new or surprising. The development of a theology of original sin in the minds of the

early patristic writers occurred in tandem with reflection on Genesis 3. In their arguments for the necessity of Christ's redemption, the Yahwist story of expulsion from the garden became central in patristic theologies of sin. By historicizing a symbolic story, Genesis 3 was given a theological significance not found in the Hebrew scriptures or in postbiblical Jewish interpretation. Cf. Ruether, *Sexism and God-Talk,* 166.

Christian theologians were not the first, however, to interpret Genesis 3 literally. See the texts given in "Jewish Postbiblical Interpretations (200s BCE–200 CE)" in Kristen E. Kvam, Linda S. Schearing, and Valarie H. Ziegler, eds., *Eve and Adam: Jewish, Christian, and Muslim Readings on Genesis and Gender* (Bloomington: Indiana University Press, 1999), 47–76.

6. On 1 Timothy, see Linda M. Maloney, "The Pastoral Epistles," in Elisabeth Schüssler Fiorenza, ed., *Searching the Scriptures: A Feminist Commentary,* vol. 2 (New York: Crossroad, 1994), 361–80. Maloney reflects a consensus among scholars in her judgment that the "pastorals are pseudepigraphical: their author is someone other than Paul desiring to claim Pauline authority for his ideas" (364). In giving Eve alone responsibility for sin, the author of 1 Timothy draws on a marginal tradition in the Hebrew Bible. Only Sirach 25:24 represents this view. Paul acknowledges that Eve was created second and was deceived by the serpent but emphasizes that it was Adam's sin that brought death into the world (370). Cf. 1 Cor 11:8; 15:21–22; and 2 Cor 11:3.

7. We will return to the 1 Timothy text. On early Christian interpretations (50–450 C.E.), see Kvam et al., *Eve and Adam,* 108–55.

8. See Schüssler Fiorenza, *In Memory of Her,* for an account of the patriarchalization of the early Jesus communities and the resubjugation of women (and others) to the structures of the patriarchal household. For an extension from the first century to the present time, see Ruether, *Women and Redemption.* The introduction provides a succinct overview of the historical conflicts and theological positions (1–11).

9. Maloney, "The Pastoral Epistles," 370.

10. Ambrose, "Paradise," cited in Kvam et al., *Eve and Adam,* 138.

11. From Tertullian's treatise, "On the Apparel of Women." Cited in Kvam et al., *Eve and Adam,* 132. Italics are in the text.

12. John Chrysostom, "Homily 17," cited in Kvam et al., *Eve and Adam,* 146.

13. Ruether, "The Future of Feminist Theology," 707. Emphasis added.

14. Walter Wink, *Engaging the Powers* (Minneapolis: Fortress Press, 1992), 81.

15. Patriarchalism refers to a kind of hierarchically structured social system in which the privileges of the minority (elites, ruling political and religious figures, males) are protected. Patriarchy is not simply gender domina-

tion. See Ruether, "Patriarchy," 205–6. Also Schüssler Fiorenza, "Breaking the Silence," 4.

16. Schüssler Fiorenza, *Discipleship of Equals,* 140.

17. Ruether, *Sexism and God-Talk,* 182. On sexism, see esp. 181–88.

18. Ruether, *Women and Redemption,* 8.

19. In the modern context, the assertion that scripture "speaks the word of God" has become problematic. For an examination of the problem and meaning of the assertion in light of a critical hermeneutical theory, see Sandra M. Schneiders, *The Revelatory Text: Interpreting the New Testament as Sacred Scripture* (Collegeville, MN: Liturgical Press, 1999), 26–63.

20. The issue is not whether texts are canonical. The number of selected writings of the New Testament—the canon—is an historical product of the early Christian centuries. Patriarchal texts remain canonical but, as Ruether and Schüssler Fiorenza argue, they must be rejected as revelatory. Texts legitimizing slavery, for example, are no longer considered revelatory. To distinguish between that which is essential for salvation and that which is not is a long-accepted principle of evaluation. The remark quoted is found in *Sexism and God-Talk,* 18–19. Ruether continues, "Theologically speaking, whatever diminishes or denies the full humanity of women must be presumed not to reflect the divine or an authentic relation to the divine, or to reflect the authentic nature of things, or to be the message or work of an authentic redeemer or a community of redemption" (19).

21. Schüssler Fiorenza, *Bread Not Stone,* xiii.

22. Ibid., xii. Emphasis added. The introduction and first chapter of *Bread Not Stone* offer a helpful introduction to feminist literary and historical interpretation of the Bible (ix–22).

23. Schüssler Fiorenza, *Bread Not Stone,* 1. For a more recent account of Schüssler Fiorenza's method, see her *Rhetoric and Ethic: The Politics of Biblical Studies* (Minneapolis: Fortress Press, 1999). On the emergence of nineteenth-century feminist biblical interpretation, see p. 21.

24. Cf. chap. 1 and the discussion of Jewish texts and the lives of Jewish women.

25. Ruether, "Patriarchy," 205. A helpful bibliography of historical studies is found in the footnotes accompanying pp. 39–43 in Wink, *Engaging the Powers.*

26. Walter Wink, *The Powers That Be: Theology for a New Millennium* (New York: Doubleday, 1998), 39. The equation of patriarchy with male domination is inaccurate. *Domination system* is a more descriptive term, suggesting a complex social reality orchestrated by interests, power, and violence. For the features of domination systems, see Wink, *Engaging the Powers,* 65–86.

27. See Ruether, "Patriarchy," 205.

28. Ruether, "Patriarchal Religion," 56.

29. While female subordination is a basic feature of patriarchal societies, the actual lives of women—for example, participation in the public world of politics and religion—were influenced by many factors such as biological family, wealth, and free status. See pp. 359–407, "The Social Roles and Social Situation of Women in the Mediterranean World and in Early Christianity" in Ekkehard W. Stegemann and Wolfgang Stegemann, *The Jesus Movement: A Social History of Its First Century* (Minneapolis: Fortress Press, 1999).

30. Wink, *Engaging the Powers,* 39.

31. Schüssler Fiorenza, *Bread Not Stone,* 73.

32. The relevant text in Thomas is *Summa Theologiae,* Pt. I, q. 92, art. 1–4, "The Production of Women." In art. 1, Thomas notes that it "was necessary for woman to be made, as the Scripture says, as a *helper* to man" and that, in regard to individual nature, "woman is defective and misbegotten...but included in nature's intention as directed to the work of generation" (emphasis in text).The purpose of woman's creation was procreative. Thomas believed female subordination existed prior to the fall. He derived the reason from an anthropology characterized by gender dualism. Male nature is identified with reason: "woman is naturally subject to man, because in man the discretion of reason predominates." Cf. Ruether's discussion of the text in *Sexism and God-Talk,* p. 96. In Kvam et al., *Eve and Adam,* see 169–70 and 225–35.

33. The work of Marilyn Arthur is cited by Elisabeth Schüssler Fiorenza in "Breaking the Silence," 5. A valuable article is Linda M. Maloney, "The Argument for Women's Difference in Classical Philosophy and Early Christianity," *Concilium* (1991), 41–49.

34. For an analysis of economic and social stratification of the first-century Mediterranean world of Jesus, see Stegemann and Stegemann, *The Jesus Movement,* 15–96. Estimates of the percentage of the upper stratum of the overall population in the Roman Empire suggest a "thin upper stratum" between 1 and 5 percent, leaving 95 to 99 percent of the population lower stratum (77).

35. Ruether, *Sexism and God-Talk,* 165.

36. The author of 1 Timothy links salvation with a condition, motherhood: "Yet she will be saved through childbearing...." The text is discussed more explicitly below.

37. In the contemporary world, gender dualism often takes the form of an anthropology of gender complementarity. The complementarity of male and female natures, however, retains patriarchal assumptions. Male nature is defined in relation to active participation in the "public realm" and female nature in relation to procreative roles and the "private realm." For examples of how papal statements reflect these gender assumptions, see Schüssler Fiorenza, *Discipleship of Equals,* 74. Of interest, too, is the essay by Christine E. Gudorf, "Encountering the Other: The Modern Papacy on Women" in

Charles E. Curran, Margaret A. Farley, and Richard A. McCormick, S.J., eds., *Feminist Ethics and the Catholic Moral Tradition: Readings in Moral Theology 9* (New York: Paulist Press, 1996), 66–89. Gudorf notes that a predominant theme in papal teaching is women and motherhood. "This is as true of John Paul II today," she writes, "as it was of Pius XII in the 1940s and 1950s. Women are created to be mothers, either physically, as wives, or spiritually as with women religious. One arresting thought of John Paul's thought is that motherhood is not an element of what it is to be a woman, but rather that motherhood defines womanhood" (70).

Note the "Letter of Pope John Paul II to Women," written in June 1995, prior to and for the Fourth World Conference on Women in Beijing held in September 1995. Pope John Paul begins by saying that he wants to speak directly to every woman and to reflect with her on what it means to be a woman in our time. This dialogue needs to begin with a word of thanks. The pope begins his identification of women in groups with "Thank you, women who are mothers!" He then moves to identify women in their relation to men: wives, daughters, sisters. His final groups are women who work, consecrated women, then every woman. He apologizes for the harm done to women through cultural attitudes, shared by some in the church, and refers to the openness and respect with which Jesus treated women. He appeals for real equality in every area for women. The pope condemns sexual violence against women and holds up as heroic women who proceed with pregnancies due to rape. He expresses admiration for women who have fought for their basic rights. His appeal to Genesis 1:18 notes that the creation of woman is marked by the principle of help: she is to be a helper to man, although help is to be mutual. Woman and man are complementary to one another in their humanness. This complementarity [difference] is ontological. The pope expresses appreciation to women for the help they give to men in their roles as mothers, sisters, and co-workers in the apostolate. Mary is held up as the highest expression of the feminine genius. She accepted her roles as wife and mother, putting herself at the service of others.

38. Cf. Ruether, *Sexism and God-Talk,* 72–92.

39. Ruether, "Patriarchal Religion," 56–57.

40. Ibid., 55–56.

41. *Torah* refers to the first five books of the Hebrew Bible, Genesis through Deuteronomy, also called the Pentateuch. In the post-exilic period (sixth century B.C.E. and later), observance of the Torah increasingly shaped the identity of Israel.

42. While androcentric texts describe a world in which women have virtually no access to the public realm, archeological evidence points to Jewish women as leaders of synagogues and engaging other important roles within first-century Jewish communities. See the discussion in chap. 1. On women in Israel, see Bernadette Brooten, *Women Leaders in the Ancient Synagogue,*

Brown Judaic Studies 36 (Atlanta, GA: Scholars Press, 1982); and Shaye J. D. Cohen, "Women in the Synagogues of Antiquity," *Conservative Judaism* 34 (Nov/Dec 1980), 23–29. A further resource is P. J. Haas, ed., *Recovering the Role of Women: Power and Authority in Rabbinic Jewish Society* (Atlanta: Scholars Press, 1992).

43. Ross Shepard Kraemer, *Her Share of the Blessings: Women's Religions among Pagans, Jews, and Christians in the Greco-Roman World* (New York: Oxford University Press, 1992), 105. Kraemer's comment was made with specific reference to the Mishnah, a second-century Jewish document. Kraemer's description of unequal spheres differentiated by gender can be applied without injury to the Torah. The Torah is the precedent for the Mishnah. The priestly code of Leviticus and Numbers in the Torah makes the cult of the sanctuary an exclusive preserve of males.

44. On New Testament household codes, see Schüssler Fiorenza, *In Memory of Her*, 251–84.

45. Gen 2:21–22; Gen 3:6.

46. The adoption of patriarchal class and gender structures as normative continued in the Christian tradition until challenged by modern emancipatory movements. For an insightful study of Christian justification of slavery and female subordination in the modern world, see James Newton Poling, *Deliver Us from Evil: Resisting Racial and Gender Oppression* (Minneapolis: Fortress Press, 1996).

47. On the claims and resurrection faith of early Christians, see Luke Timothy Johnson, *The Writings of the New Testament: An Interpretation* (Minneapolis: Fortress Press, 1999), 99–150.

48. See Gerd Theissen and Annette Merz, *The Historical Jesus: A Comprehensive Guide* (Minneapolis: Fortress Press, 1998), esp. the summary of the history of research and bibliography, "Jesus as Prophet: Jesus' Eschatology," 240–80. The authors write that the eschatological and saving message of the rule of God is central to Jesus' preaching. It is proclaimed as already come and not-yet. It appears in numerous parables and sayings. The symbol of the rule of God was familiar to his Jewish hearers as a summary of salvation. The authors note, "Although there is now a consensus that the kingdom of God forms the centre of Jesus' preaching, there is a controversy over how to interpret it" (240).

49. Stephen J. Patterson, *The God of Jesus: The Historical Jesus and the Search for Meaning* (Harrisburg, PA: Trinity Press International, 1998). On the implicit contrast of two empires, God's and Rome's, see 55–89. On the geographical and social framework for the life of Jesus, see Theissen and Merz, *The Historical Jesus*, 162–84. For a discussion of the Gospel sources and the ministry of Jesus, see Paula Fredricksen, *Jesus of Nazareth, King of the Jews: A Jewish Life and the Emergence of Christianity* (New York: Alfred A. Knopf, 1999), esp. "Contexts: The Galilee, Judea, and Jesus," 155–234.

50. On the relation of social stratification and poverty in the ancient Mediterranean world, see Stegemann and Stegemann, *The Jesus Movement,* 7–96. See also the detailed account of features of the first-century Roman Empire such as the economics of imperial domination in K. C. Hanson and Douglas E. Oakman, *Palestine in the Time of Jesus* (Minneapolis: Fortress Press, 1998).

51. Wink, *Engaging the Powers,* 112.

52. Central to Schüssler Fiorenza's reconstructive work is *In Memory of Her.* The collaborative works edited by Schüssler Fiorenza, *Searching the Scriptures: A Feminist Introduction,* vols. 1 and 2 (New York: Crossroad, 1993 and 1994), are valuable resources for feminist studies of canonical and non-canonical writings. All citations in this chapter are to vol. 2.

53. Wink, *Engaging the Powers,* 134.

54. Ruether, *Women and Redemption,* 1. On women in the first-century Mediterranean world, see Stegemann and Stegemann, *The Jesus Movement,* 359–88.

55. "Then Jesus' mother and his brothers came; and standing outside they sent to him and called him. A crowd was sitting around him; and they said to him, 'Your mother and your brothers and sisters are outside, asking for you.' And Jesus replied, 'Who are my mother and my brothers?' And looking around him, he said 'Here are my mother and my brothers! Whoever does the will of God is my brother and sister and mother'" (Mark 3:34–35).

56. See Joanna Dewey, "The Gospel of Mark," in Schüssler Fiorenza, *Searching the Scriptures,* 470–509; 478–79. See also Schüssler Fiorena, *In Memory of Her,* 147. In Schüssler Fiorenza's discussion of the prior texts, Mark 10:2–9 and 12:18–27, she notes that the point of the Jesus' exchange with the Sadducees is that "'in the world' of the living God *patriarchal* marriage does not exist either for men or women" (144); the "'house of Israel' is not guaranteed in and through patriarchal marriage structures, but through the promise and faithfulness of Israel's powerful, life-giving God....In God's world women and men no longer relate to each other in terms of patriarchal dominance and dependence, but as persons who live in the presence of the living God" (145). Jesus insists, Schüssler Fiorenza writes, that "God did not create or intend patriarchy but created persons as male and female human beings" (143). See Ruether's discussion of Mark 3:34–35 in *Women and Redemption,* 19.

57. The Gospel writer's inclusion of the historical memory of Jesus' rejection of patriarchy and his acceptance of women as equal members of the family makes 1 Timothy's reappropriation of patriarchal relations as normative even more striking as a deviation from Jesus' own redemptive vision. On family, see Leo G. Perdue, Joseph Blenkinsopp, John J. Collins, and Carol Meyers, eds., *Families in Ancient Israel* (Louisville: Westminster John Knox, 1997).

58. Luke 13:10–17. Wink, *Engaging the Powers,* 129. The next example is from Luke 11:27–28, noted by Wink, 131.

59. Jesus' affirmation of Mary in the story of Martha and Mary (Luke 10:38) gives Mary the prerogative of a male disciple of a teacher. Jesus' exchange with a Gentile woman (Mark 7:24–30) is an occasion for changing his mind. Cf. texts discussed in Schüssler Fiorenza, *In Memory of Her,* 105–59. The reference to inclusive table fellowship with "sinners" (Mark 2:15) can refer to those who violate Torah commands but can also mean pagans, that is, Gentiles (136).

60. The parable of the leaven is found in Luke 13:20–21; Matthew 13:33b; and Thomas 96:1–2. On its original meaning as suggested here, see Patterson, *The God of Jesus,* 135.

61. Sheila Briggs, "Galatians," in Schüssler Fiorenza, ed., *Searching the Scriptures,* vol. 2, 218–36; 218. Further exegetical discussions of the text are found in Hans Dieter Betz, *Galatians,* Hermeneia (Philadelphia: Fortress Press, 1979), 181–201; and Schüssler Fiorenza, *In Memory of Her,* 205–41; and *Rhetoric and Ethic,* 154–73. In Ruether, see *Women and Redemption,* 22–30.

62. The perjorative connotation of "works of the law" originates in the Christian tradition subsequent to Paul. Cf. chap. 1 and discussion of the Galatian conflict. As alternative conditions of Gentile inclusion into Israel, "faith in Christ" and "works of the law" bear gender ramifications.

63. Kraemer, *Her Share of the Blessings,* 105. While androcentric literary texts describe separate and unequal roles for women and invite the historical conclusion that women played a minor role in Jewish religious cult and social life, the texts do not necessarily reflect history as lived. See nn. 39, 40. Of value in the matter of differentiating text from history is Judith Romney Wegner, *Chattel or Person? The Status of Women in the Mishnah* (New York: Oxford University Press, 1992). Also Tal Ilan, *Jewish Women in Greco-Roman Palestine* (Peabody, MA: Hendrickson Publishers, 1996); idem, *Integrating Women into Second Temple History* (Peabody, MA: Hendrickson Publishers, 1999).

64. The invocation of the so-called household codes functioned as a Christian substitute for Torah mandates that create separate and unequal spheres for women and men. But their use belongs to the pseudonymous authors of the deutero-Pauline letters, not to Paul himself. See Maloney, "The Pastoral Epistles." Also Schüssler Fiorenza, *In Memory of Her,* 245–84.

65. Cf. 1 Cor 11:13. "Judge for yourselves: is it proper for a woman to pray to God with her head unveiled?" The mandate at 14:34 (that "women should be silent in the churches. For they are not permitted to speak, but should be subordinate, as the law also says") is judged by scholars to be an editorial insertion in the letter by a later hand.

66. Paul's reference to the "yoke of slavery" (5:1) is unlikely to refer to the Torah because Gentiles had not been under the law. How could they submit *again* to something they had not submitted to yet? If the Gentile Jesus followers were God-fearers, they would have observed some Jewish customs (hardly "a yoke of slavery") but were not responsible for all the commands given to men and those given to women.

Paul's polemical language about law, especially in Romans and Galatians, has been a problem in the tradition. Early patristic writers interpreted his contrast between faith and law as a contrast between a higher religion (faith) and a lower religion (law). Helpful resources for understanding the difference between the polemical anti-Jewish language in the New Testament and later Christian anti-Semitism are Craig A. Evans and Donald A. Hagner, eds., *Anti-Semitism and Early Christianity* (Minneapolis: Fortress Press, 1993); and John T. Pawlikowski, O.S.M., "Christology, Anti-Semitism, and Christian-Jewish Bonding," in Rebecca S. Chopp and Mark Lewis Taylor, eds., *Reconstructing Christian Theology* (Minneapolis: Fortress Press, 1994), 245– 68.

67. Schüssler Fiorenza, *Bread Not Stone,* 75.

68. See Elizabeth A. Castelli, "Romans," in Schüssler Fiorenza, ed., *Searching the Scriptures,* 272–300. On Romans 16, Castelli writes, "The authenticity of this chapter is not questioned by scholars though its placement at the end of Romans is a matter of some debate" (276). Debate on this issue is reviewed by A. J. M. Wedderburn, *The Reasons for Romans* (Minneapolis: Fortress Press, 1991), 18. He concurs with the judgment that the passage belongs to Romans. Castelli refers to the significance Schüssler Fiorenza attributes to this text in reconstructing the participation of women in the early Jesus movement. See Schüssler Fiorenza, "Missionaries, Apostles, Coworkers," 420–33.

69. Cf. Ruether, *Women and Redemption,* 1, 40–41.

70. Ruether, "The Future of Feminist Theology," 707. The history of the use of this text is traced in *Women and Redemption.*

71. Colossians, Ephesians, and 1 Timothy are pseudonymous, written in Paul's name by authors some time after the death of Paul. See the articles by Mary Rose D'Angelo, Sarah J. Tanzer, and Linda M. Maloney in Schüssler Fiorenza, ed., *Searching the Scriptures,* 313–24, 325–48, and 361–80 respectively. In her essay, "Reconstruction of Women's Early Christian History," in Schüssler Fiorenza, ed., *Searching the Scriptures,* vol. 1, 290–310, Karen Jo Torjesen writes that "while women's leadership in early Christian churches had much in common with women's religious leadership in Greek and Roman societies, there was one striking difference—women's leadership in some Christian circles was bitterly contested" (300). She refers to texts edited by Ross Kraemer, *Maenads, Martyrs, Matrons, and Monastics: A Sourcebook on Women's Religions in the Greco-Roman World* (Philadelphia: Fortress Press,

1988) and pursues the reasons for this conflict in the discussion following (302–7).

72. Schüssler Fiorenza, *Bread Not Stone,* 73. See these New Testament and early Christian writings: 1 Pet 2:18–3:7; 1 Tim 2:11–15; 5:3–8; 6:1–2; Titus 2:2–10; 3:1–2; 1 *Clement* 21:6–8; Ignatius to Polykarp 4:1–6:2; Polykarp 4:2–6:1; *Didache* 4:9–11; *Barnabas* 19:5–7. See her analysis of the household code in *Bread Not Stone,* 70–83. On these letters, see Mary Rose D'Angelo, "Colossians," and Sarah J. Tanzer, "Ephesians," in Schüssler Fiorenza, *Searching the Scriptures.* For a comparison of egalitarian and hierarchical texts, see Kvam et al., *Eve and Adam,* 116–19, and "Early Christian Interpretations (50–450 C.E.)," 117–78.

73. See Karen Jo Torjesen's discussion of this development in terms of gender and private/public space in "Reconstruction of Women's Early Christian History," 304–7, "Public Man and Private Woman." She describes this statement of Chrysostom as giving a Christian baptism to the public/private gender ideology of the ancient world. In *The Kind of Women Who Ought to Be Taken as Wives,* Chrysostom writes, "Our life is customarily organized into two spheres: public affairs and private matters, both of which are determined by God. To the woman is assigned the presidency of the household; to man all the business of the state, the marketplace, the administration of justice, government, the military and all other enterprises" (4).

74. Cited in Alvin John Schmidt, *Veiled and Silenced: How Culture Shaped Sexist Theology* (Macon, GA: Mercer University Press, 1990), 43. The original treatises are Irenaeus, *Against Heresies* 3. 22; Origen, *Selecta in Exodus* 17.17; Ambrose, *Paradise,* chaps. 4 and 6; John Chrysostom, *Homilies on Timothy* 9; and Augustine, *The City of God* 15.22. Further examples are cited in Kvam et al., *Eve and Adam*; Origen, *Homilies on Genesis* (133–35); Ambrose, *Paradise* (135–41); John Chrysostom, *Homilies on Genesis* (141–47); Augustine, *The Literal Meaning of Genesis: A Commentary in Twelve Books* (147–55).

75. Kvam et al., *Eve and Adam,* 152. The following quote is from the same context. Emphasis added. Thomas Aquinas followed Augustine's view that female subjugation to male rule is part of the order of creation prior to sin and not a result of the fall. See his *Summa Theologiae,* Pt. I, q. 92, art. 1.

76. Elaine Pagels, *The Origin of Satan* (New York: Vintage Books, 1995). The use of the word *human* is given as an example by Rosemary Ruether in *Sexism and God-Talk,* 162.

77. Phyllis Trible, *God and the Rhetoric of Sexuality* (Philadelphia: Fortress Press, 1978), 76. Chapter 4, "A Love Story Gone Awry," is an analysis of Genesis 2–3 (72–143). The Hebrew word *hā'ādām,* is a play on the word *hā'ādām* (earth) and *adām* (earth creature), one who is to serve the earth (76). Cf. the discussion of Genesis 2–3 and its use in present-day ecclesial docu-

ments in Marie de Merode de Croy, "The Role of Woman in the Old Testament" in Virgil Elizondo and Norbert Greinacher, eds., *Women in a Men's Church, Concilium* (1980), 71–79.

78. Ruether, *Sexism and God-Talk,* 168–69.

79. Ibid., 163.

80. In *Chattel or Person?* Judith Wegner distinguishes between the two: "Personhood means the legal status defined by the complex of an individual's powers, rights, and duties in society. An entity possessing no powers, rights, or duties is not a person but merely an object or chattel" (10). In identifying the perception of woman by the framers of the Mishnah (second century C.E.), Wegner writes that "the conception of woman as an incomplete creature (specifically an imperfect man) was widespread in Greek culture. This Aristotelian view of women's biological nature prevailed throughout the Hellenistic world well before the mishnaic period. The first-century exponent of Hellenistic-Judaic thought, Philo of Alexandria, repeatedly describes the female as physically, intellectually, and morally inferior to the male. Philo's denigration of women seems to have been shaped at least as much by his Hellenistic background as by his interpretation of Jewish Scripture. Indeed, the notion of female incompleteness appears in all Western systems influenced by Greek philosophy" (193).

81. Schüssler Fiorenza, *Discipleship of Equals,* 69.

82. Ibid., 69–71.

83. The "one nature" anthropology in the tradition conceived of full human nature as male. In some sense, women have to negate or transcend their femaleness in order to be included in this nature. Cf. Kari Vogt, "'Becoming Male': One Aspect of an Early Christian Anthropology," in Mary Collins and Elisabeth Schüssler Fiorenza, eds., *Women: Invisible in Church and Theology, Concilium* (1984), 72–83. The more recent "two natures" anthropology of complementarity would appear to be an improvement. However, complementary gender differences turn out to be similar to that found in a patriarchal gender dualism. Men continue to be identified with reason (mind) and the public realm; women are identified with motherhood (childbearing/body) and the private domestic realm. A theological anthropology free of gender bias goes beyond either a one nature or two nature anthropology. Humanness is sexually differentiated but one reality. An example is given in chap. 8. Cf. Ruether, "Women's Difference and Equal Rights in the Church," 11–18. Ruether discusses the patristic/modern reversal as one of contradiction between the church's anthropology and christology.

84. This argument grounds the restriction of ordination to males in the Roman Catholic Church. The eucharistic minister models the maleness of Christ. The identification between the male priest and Christ is an ontological one. The implicit assumption is that female nature is not ontologically the same

human nature as that of male nature. Two central ecclesial documents are the statement on the admission of women to the ministerial priesthood issued by the Sacred Congregation for the Doctrine of the Faith, *Inter Insigniores* (October 15, 1976), and on reserving priestly ordination to men alone issued by Pope John Paul II, *Ordinatio Sacerdotalis* (May 26, 1994).

85. Ruether, *Gaia and God*, 140–41.

86. Ruether, *Sexism and God-Talk*, 181.

87. Ibid., 37. Emphasis added.

88. Ruether, *Gaia and God*, 142.

89. Ibid.

90. Ruether, *Sexism and God-Talk*, 181–82.

91. Schüssler Fiorenza, "Breaking the Silence," 14.

92. Wink, *Engaging the Powers*, 69. For his interpretation of the fall, see pp. 68–73.

93. Ruether, *Sexism and God-Talk*, 163.

94. Ibid., 181.

95. Ibid., 162.

96. Wink, *Engaging the Powers*, 62.

97. Brock, *Journeys by Heart*.

98. Suchocki, *The Fall to Violence*, 13.

CHAPTER 8

1. See Bernard J. F. Lonergan, S.J., *Insight: A Study of Human Understanding* (London: Darton, Longman and Todd, 1957); and *Method in Theology* (New York: Herder and Herder, 1972). Lonergan's essays are found in four volumes: *Collection*, ed. Frederick E. Crowe, S.J. (New York: Herder and Herder, 1967); *A Second Collection*, ed. William F. J. Ryan, S.J., and Bernard J. Tyrrell, S.J. (Philadelphia: Westminster Press, 1974); *Lonergan: A Third Collection*, ed. Frederick E. Crowe, S.J. (New York: Paulist Press, 1985); and *Collected Works of Bernard Lonergan: Philosophical and Theological Papers*, *1958–1964*, ed. Robert C. Croken, Frederick E. Crowe, and Robert M. Doran (Toronto: University of Toronto Press, 1996). A helpful secondary resource is Vernon Gregson, ed., *The Desires of the Human Heart: An Introduction to the Theology of Bernard Lonergan* (New York: Paulist Press, 1988).

2. Lonergan, "Aquinas Today: Tradition and Innovation," *Third Collection*, 52. Emphasis added. In Lonergan's judgment, Thomas understood the experiential referent of the systematic categories but did not make them explicit. The medievals did not have the language to talk about subjectivity, which is a product of modern existential philosophy and psychology. Their

terms and categories were metaphysical and abstract rather than experiential and concrete, derived from an analysis of subjectivity.

3. Lonergan, *Method in Theology,* 239–40. Sensible or empirical operations such as seeing are only one component of genuine knowledge. Knowing is a process constituted by empirical, intelligent, and rational operations of conscious intentionality.

4. Lonergan, "Healing and Creating in History," *Third Collection,* 106.

5. Lonergan, *Method in Theology,* 289. Cf. 107: "This gift we have been describing really is sanctifying grace but differs notionally from it. The notional difference arises from different stages of meaning. To speak of sanctifying grace pertains to the stage of meaning when the world of theory and the world of common sense are distinct but, as yet, have not been explicitly distinguished from and grounded in the world of interiority. To speak of the dynamic state of being in love with God pertains to the stage of meaning when the world of interiority has been made the explicit ground of the worlds of theory and of common sense. It follows that in this stage of meaning the gift of God's love first is described as an experience and only consequently objectified in theoretical categories."

6. Lonergan, *Insight,* 630. David Tracy notes Lonergan's understanding of what the tradition has called the condition of original sin in "Horizon Analysis and Eschatology," *Continuum* 6:2 (1968), 166–79: "The inability to indefinitely sustain development represents Lonergan's definition of original sin" (175–76). This is the formulation of Lonergan's *Insight* period (1957). The understanding—or in Lonergan's terms, transposition—of *peccatum originale originatum* as the *absence of religious conversion* corresponds to *Method in Theology* (1972). In Lonergan's later work, the human problem is sustained unauthenticity. Unauthenticity—not only in individuals but in traditions, social structures, and meaning—reflects humankind's alienation from God.

7. Lonergan, *Method in Theology,* 52. See pp. 237–44 for an extended discussion of intellectual, moral, and religious conversion. About the sequence of conversions, Lonergan notes, "Though religious conversion sublates moral, and moral conversion sublates intellectual, one is not to infer that intellectual comes first and then moral and finally religious. On the contrary, from a causal point of view, one would say that first there is God's gift of his love. Next, the eye of this love reveals values in their splendor, while the strength of this love brings about their realization, and that is moral conversion. Finally, among the values discerned by the eye of love is the value of believing the truths taught by the religious tradition, and in such tradition and belief are the seeds of intellectual conversion" (243).

8. Lonergan, "The Response of the Jesuit as Priest and Apostle in the Modern World," *Second Collection,* 165.

9. Ibid.

10. Lonergan, "The Subject," *Second Collection,* 73.

11. The account here assumes Lonergan's expansion of *Insight* by the insights found in *Method in Theology*.

12. Lonergan, *Method in Theology*, 6–13; also 13–20 and 282–86. Lonergan refers to this basic set of conscious operations as "transcendental method." The operations are common to human intentionality as human. Any type of human knowing—symbolic, ordinary/common sense, theoretical, scientific, scholarly—utilizes the operations. Particular methods constitute particular applications of it. Transcendental method is the ground of method as method.

13. Lonergan, "The Subject," *Second Collection*, 73.

14. Lonergan, *Method in Theology*, 9.

15. Lonergan, "Cognitional Structure," *Collection*, 237.

16. Lonergan, *Method in Theology*, 37. In *Insight*, see chaps. 9 and 10.

17. Lonergan, "Mission and the Spirit," *Third Collection*, 29.

18. Lonergan, *Insight*, 628.

19. On the relation between the individual and social spheres, see Lonergan, *Insight*, 628.

20. Lonergan, *Method in Theology*, 37.

21. Ibid., 47–52.

22. Lonergan, "Theology and Man's Future," *Second Collection*, 145.

23. Lonergan, *Method in Theology*, 107.

24. Ibid., 242.

25. Lonergan, "The Future of Christianity," *Second Collection*, 155.

26. Lonergan, *Method in Theology*, 242–43.

27. Ibid., 351; also 52–55.

28. Rom 7:19.

29. A useful introduction to the relation between an empirical anthropology and theory of history is Lonergan's essay "Healing and Creating in History" in *Third Collection*, 100–12.

30. Lonergan, "Dialectic of Authority," *Third Collection*, 8.

31. Ibid., 9.

32. Cf. Lonergan, *Method in Theology*, 52–55.

33. Lonergan, *Insight*, 218–22.

34. Lonergan, "Healing and Creating in History," *Third Collection*, 105.

35. Lonergan, *Method in Theology*, 53.

36. Lonergan, *Insight*, 666.

37. Lonergan, *Method in Theology*, 55.

38. Lonergan, *Insight*, 630.

39. Lonergan, *Understanding and Being*, 290.

40. Lonergan, *Method in Theology*, 55.

41. Lonergan, *Insight*, 666.

42. The cumulative and historical result of basic sin is social, systemic, structural sin. For an analysis that attends to Lonergan's work, see Mark

O'Keefe, O.S.B., *What Are They Saying about Social Sin?* (New York: Paulist Press, 1990).

43. On the social surd and the reign of sin, see *Insight,* 693.

44. Ibid., 666.

45. Lonergan, *Method in Theology,* 364.

46. *Method in Theology,* 55; emphasis added.

47. Lonergan, "Dialectic of Authority," *Third Collection,* 9.

48. Lonergan, *Method in Theology,* 55.

49. Lonergan, *Insight,* 463–69.

50. A fuller analysis, not taken up here, would include psychic factors and the bias of scotosis.

51. Lonergan, "Dialectic of Authority," *Third Collection,* 9.

52. Deut 10:12–13.

53. Ezek 36:26.

54. Rom 5:5.

55. Gal 5:16–21.

56. Gal 5:16, 22.

57. Cf. Ludwig Ott, *Fundamentals of Catholic Dogma,* James Canon Bastible, ed., Patrick Lynch, trans. (St. Louis, MO: Herder Book Co., 1962), 254–61, on sanctifying grace.

58. Lonergan, *Method in Theology,* 241.

59. Lonergan, "Dialectic of Authority," *Third Collection,* 9–10.

60. Ibid.

61. Lonergan, *Method in Theology,* 291.

62. Ibid., 117–18.

63. Ibid., 55.

64. Ibid., 291.

65. Ibid., 116.

66. Ibid., 116–17.

67. Lonergan, *Insight,* 666.

68. In *Insight,* see Lonergan's explanations of emergent probability on pp. 132 and 171–72. The index notes other relevant page references.

69. The work of Bernard Lonergan reflects a large-scale project to meet the intellectual challenges of modernity. Other theologians come at the reconsideration of a Christian anthropology in different ways. Cf. Rosemary Radford Ruether's appreciative remarks regarding Jürgen Moltmann's anthropology in his writings such as *God in Creation: A Ecological Doctrine of Creation,* trans. Margaret Kohl (London: SCM Press, 1985). Ruether's own essay provides an insightful summary of gender problems in the theological anthropology of the tradition and considerations for a Christian anthropology free not only from gender bias but from the individualism characteristic of modern thinking. Rosemary Radford Ruether, "Christian Anthropology and

Gender: A Tribute to Jürgen Moltmann," in Miroslav Volf, Carmen Krieg, and Thomas Kucharz, eds., *The Future of Theology: Essays in Honor of Jürgen Moltmann* (Grand Rapids, MI: William B. Eerdmans Publishing Co., 1996), 241–52.

70. Walter Wink describes a critical apprehension of the fall this way. The fall did not happen "once upon a time," he writes, but is a "structural aspect of all personal and social existence.... [It] affirms the radicality of evil." Wink, *Engaging the Powers* (Minneapolis: Fortress Press, 1992), 69. Expressed in different ways, the theologians we have discussed—Piet Schoonenberg, Reinhold Niebuhr, Rosemary Ruether, among others—share this as a common theme. The meaning of the fall is *present,* not past. It is a way of capturing in historical existence what Bernard Lonergan calls the social surd, "the actual existence of what should not be," a "false fact." For Lonergan, the surd is the cumulative effect of "basic sin," the individual and collective interference of biases in decisions, actions, and meaning and the justification of bias in ideology. Historical and systemic consequences of basic sin, for example, are the distortions created in the ancient world by patriarchy and embedded in present-day domination systems.

CHAPTER 9

1. Ps 14:2–3; cf. 53.
2. Amos 5:13; 2:6–7.
3. Rom 7:15; 19.
4. Rom 7:20. Emphasis added.
5. Augustine, "On Marriage and Concupiscence," in *Augustine: Anti-Pelagian Writings, Nicene and Post-Nicene Fathers,* vol. 5, ed. Philip Schaff (New York: Christian Literature Society, 1893). Augustine believed that only marital sexual relations open to procreation were moral. Marital sexual intercourse for pleasure was a venial sin. Augustine equated sexual desire with lust, and lust with concupiscence. Consecrated virginity is preferred to marriage.
6. In synthesizing the central meaning of the doctrine of original sin, Karl Rahner writes, "The fundamental conviction of Christianity about redemption and grace is that all men are offered divinizing and forgiving grace but in such a way that *it is given to all only through Christ,* and not simply because they are human beings or members of mankind (if this is thought of without Christ) and it is given to all as forgiving sins" (1152; emphasis added). Rahner does not advert in this context to the implications of this conviction for the salvific meaning and value of non-Christian religions. (His famous term "anonymous Christian" comes from such an attempt.) "Original Sin," in Karl Rahner, S.J., ed., *Encyclopedia of Theology: The Concise Sacramentum Mundi* (New York: Seabury

Press, 1975), 1148–55. In the same volume, Heinz Robert Schlette notes that the 1965 declaration of Vatican II on non-Christian religions represented a "decisive and even unique advance" (1396). In contrast to the church's condemnations and dismissals of the past, in the view of *Nostra Aetate,* he says, other religions "must be counted as social forms which embody religious experience. The true, good and holy is to be met within them (art. 2)." This explicit openness to the salvific import of other religions has not yet been theologically integrated with the classical doctrine of original sin. Heinz Robert Schlette, "Theology of Religions," in Karl Rahner, S.J., ed., *Encyclopedia of Theology: The Concise Sacramentum Mundi* (New York: Seabury Press, 1975), 1396–98. The preliminary integration will take place in the theological consideration of religious pluralism and the distinctiveness of Christ. For an historical survey of the question of salvation and other world religions, see John P. Galvin, "Salvation Outside the Church," in Peter Phan, ed., *The Gift of the Spirit: A Textbook on Ecclesiology in Honor of Patrick Greenfield, O.S.B.* (Collegeville: Liturgical Press, 2000), 249–66.

7. In Rebecca S. Chopp and Mark Lewis Taylor, eds., *Reconstructing Christian Theology* (Minneapolis: Fortress Press, 1994), see John T. Pawlikowski, O.S.M., "Christology, Anti-Semitism, and Christian-Jewish Bonding," 245–68; and Francis Schüssler Fiorenza, "Christian Redemption between Colonialism and Pluralism," 269–302. The early church's exclusivist claims were derived from the New Testament (Acts 4:12; 1 Tim 2:5–6; Luke 12:8–9; John 12:48). In the third century, Origen gave Christian exclusivism its classic ecclesial expression: "There can be no salvation without this church," Origen wrote. Cited in Quasten, *Patrology,* vol. 2, *The Ante-Nicene Literature after Irenaeus* (Utrecht-Antwerp: Spectrum Publishers, 1953), 83.

With regard to colonial conquest, Fiorenza writes, "The holocaust of the Indians demands that Christians examine the degree to which their deepest convictions lead them to impose their beliefs, practices, and values upon others or lead them to resist practices of colonization and oppression. Christian theology must honestly face the problem that its biblical past and theological tradition, as well as its modern practice, entail not only resistance but oppression" (270–71). He continues, "The conviction linking belief in Jesus with salvation and disbelief with condemnation has been at the basis of Christianity's mission to convert all nations. Through the history of Christianity this conviction has also been used to justify the use of force for the sake of salvation" (272).

8. Reinhold Niebuhr, *Man's Nature and His Communities* (New York: Charles Scribner's Sons, 1965), 24. His remark reflects a sentiment expressed by G. K. Chesterton.

INDEX